Covert Action

Covert Action

THE LIMITS OF INTERVENTION IN THE POSTWAR WORLD

Gregory F. Treverton

Basic Books, Inc., Publishers New York

Printed in the United States of America
Designed by Vincent Torre
87 88 89 90 RRD 10 9 8 7 6 5 4 3 2 1

CONTENTS

PREFACE

This book originated more than a decade ago when I went to work for the first Senate Select Committee on Intelligence—usually called the Church Committee after its chairman, Frank Church—formed to investigate intelligence abuses in the aftermath of Watergate. It was for me an exhilarating, frustrating introduction to covert action. Since then I have had the chance to reflect on the issues posed by covert intervention into the politics of foreign nations while an academic and a government official, in both Congress and the executive, as a Senate investigator of covert action and as a White House consumer of intelligence.

It seemed to me then and now that the debate over covert action too often painted it only in black and white: for some Americans, it was a moral evil given what America stands for, while others saw it as a moral imperative given the relentless conflict with the Soviet Union. This book is my attempt to treat a passionate subject with more reflection, to hazard judgments about four decades of American covert action. I look at the past to seek guidance for the future: what has changed and what has not in the circumstances that surround decisions to intervene covertly in foreign nations.

Yet covert action is unpromising terrain for serious analysis, even more so than most of modern foreign policy. It is, after all, meant to be kept secret at the points of both decision and action, as closely guarded as any of government secrets. To be sure, covert actions seldom remain secret; their broad contours and details seep into the public domain.

I draw examples from a number of major American covert actions in the postwar period. For the earlier cases, particularly Guatemala in 1954 and Cuba in 1961, many documents have become available. For Iran in 1953, less documentary evidence is available and many participants have died; what I have drawn from are memoir accounts. In addition, America's more recent encounters with Iran have spawned considerable scholarly interest in this earlier encounter. Still, while the broad outline of the story is clear, details of the processes of authorization and control within the U.S. government are in short supply, and a number of anecdotes must be treated as illustrative, and not necessarily factual in all particulars.

In one case, Chile, I am fortunate. When the Church Committee on Intelligence was formed in 1974, alleged improprieties by intelligence agencies during the Watergate affair were its first agenda item; Chile was its second. In the early 1970s, a number of newspaper articles had begun to detail, and sometimes distort, American covert action in Chile, particularly from 1970 to 1973, both before and during the presidency of Salvador Allende, a self-proclaimed Marxist. The Committee determined, therefore, that it would lay out and discuss what the United States had done in Chile.

We regarded the investigation as a once-in-a-generation clearing of the air. My report, *Covert Action in Chile, 1963–1973,*[1] served as the basis for that hearing; it is the complete story, with the benefit of access to all the relevant CIA and State Department secret cables. This book is, I hope, enriched by my own government service, but I have been careful not to abuse the obligations of that service. Accordingly, I sent a draft to the current Senate Intelligence Committee for review, to make sure I had not inadvertently violated those obligations.

Preface

For the more recent cases, a few documents are available about Angola, and the investigations have provided a wealth of information about Nicaragua and Iran. All of these episodes have been controversial, and there has been investigative journalism aplenty. I have checked and supplemented these investigations with interviews, which I refer to in general terms in the notes.

Nevertheless, I am vulnerable in the lack of some details and to pitfalls of other sorts. What has been told to the public is bound to be colored by the memories, or the stakes, of those who do the telling, whether they are former participants or journalists. It may even be that my assessments are skewed systematically; suppose that the "failures" of covert action are more likely to be revealed than the "successes?" That is possible but unlikely: if success has a thousand authors, that is true even of covert successes, and so a major success would have found its way into the public view. Even documents must, in a world of leaks and investigations, be treated with skepticism, for they may have been written more with an eye to history—or self-protection—than to accuracy.

Yet covert action is a serious, sometimes searing, issue. Moreover, as I delved into the history of covert action, I realized to what extent it mirrored the history of postwar America and its encounter with the world. And so my conclusions, while still speculative, rest on a broader base than a dozen cases, for in those cases are displayed changes in both the United States and the world, changes that form the backdrop for thinking about covert action in the years ahead. Also I was struck by how much my general insights into the politics of decision making helped me understand the Central Intelligence Agency as an organization and the stakes of political leaders who decided whether or not to embark on covert intervention.

For this book, unlike most scholarly enterprises, I have no pecuniary debts to acknowledge, but I do have a number of intellectual ones that I happily recognize. I owe an unusual debt to the CIA officers with whom I worked most closely during the

Church Committee investigations, especially Walter Elder, and Seymour Bolton, the latter recently deceased. For Bolton, old habits of tradecraft had persisted; his favorite idea of a meeting was drinks at two in the morning at a Georgetown tavern. While we argued, I learned, and if I doubted the wisdom of some CIA activities, I never doubted these officers' commitment to serving their country.

I have received comments on earlier drafts, sometimes more than once, from John Bross, Leonard Bushkoff, William Colby, Richard Cottam, Robert Coulam, Stephen Flanagan, Derek Leebaert, Richard E. Neustadt, and Raymond Vernon, as well as from Martin Kessler of Basic Books. My debt to Loch Johnson, Church Committee colleague and friend, will be clear in chapter 7 but is present throughout the book. Martin Linsky discussed the book's themes over and over while we ran, then pored over drafts when stationary. As he has done at other times, Robert Klitgaard went through my draft in great detail, pressing me to sharpen my prose and to ask myself why the causal arrows pointed in one direction rather than the other. Julie Pearl and James Dickinson provided valuable research assistance. To these patient people, and to several others whom I cannot name, I am extremely grateful.

Finally, one person I happily can name—my wife, Glen—is more responsible for this book than she can know.

Those whose minds are already made up no doubt will criticize the book from both sides, either as another blow to America's ability to meet the global Soviet challenge or as an apology for intervention in the politics of foreign nations. Rather than taking solace from these opposite criticisms as an indication that I must be doing something right, I hope the book will help those who are concerned but whose minds are not closed. In any case, I alone am responsible for the judgments that follow. It is for the reader to see if they are convincing.

Covert Action

Introduction

"Secret" operations in a democracy are a paradox, all the more so if those operations intervene in the politics of another country. I first confronted that paradox seriously in the spring of 1975, when I went to Washington to work for the newly formed Senate Select Committee on Intelligence, better known as the Church Committee, after its chairman, Frank Church. It was my first job in Washington. The committee staff moved into quarters and inherited some people from the Senate Watergate committee, allegations of misdeeds by intelligence agencies during the Watergate investigation being one reason the Church Committee had been created. In those circumstances, we had unusual claim to the attentions of our senators. We also had media attention aplenty—heady stuff for one still in his twenties.

I had written my doctoral dissertation on presidential decision making in the realm of foreign policy, and so I assumed, naively, that I would spend most of my time with the committee looking at how intelligence assessments affected foreign policy decisions in the White House. In fact I spent nine-tenths of my time examining covert action. In retrospect it could hardly have been otherwise, for a second central motivation for forming the committee had been a spate of newspaper stories about CIA intervention in Chile before and during the tenure of Chile's president, Salvador Allende, a self-proclaimed Marxist, elected in 1970 and killed in a military coup in 1973. The CIA had secretly funded Allende's opponents, the accounts alleged, or even conspired to overthrow him.

Secret Operations and Open Society

The Church Committee work was the beginning of my fascination with covert action. The secrecy surrounding it was exciting. Yet because the secrecy is paradoxical, secret operations* did not, and do not, remain secret for long. President Gerald Ford admitted the covert American intervention in Chile within two years of Allende's overthrow. A decade later, in 1985–86, when the Reagan administration decided to sell arms to revolutionary Iran, it held the operation in the utmost secrecy. At first, even the CIA was cut out, and the operation was run from the White House by the National Security Council. Later, when a presidential "finding" authorized CIA involvement, the Agency was specifically instructed not to reveal the operation to the congressional intelligence committees, the CIA's overseers, thus breaking the spirit if not the letter of the law.

Even so, the operation remained secret for less than two years. When it became public, the administration was seen to have been trading weapons for American hostages, in direct contradiction to its own stated policy. The verdict of the American people, overwhelmingly negative, earned the administration the gravest crisis of the Reagan presidency.

Covert interventions, by definition initiated in secret, nonetheless eventually become public, usually sooner rather than later. It is a manifestation of the paradox that secret decisions

* "Secret operations" could refer, as I will note, to all of the CIA's clandestine intelligence activities abroad, not just covert action. With a few clearly indicated exceptions, I use "secret operations" narrowly, to refer to "covert action."

produce public results—yet decision makers have presumed otherwise, that the operation could remain secret enough to conceal the hand of the United States. Covertness is, after all, the whole point. Since the process is the very antithesis of open debate and public decision, the question therefore becomes, given the presumption of secrecy, can the American people hold covert actions accountable at all? And, if so, how?

When interventions are meant to be secret, not only may the American people and even the Congress be unaware of them, hence unable to hold them accountable, but so may the responsible officials in the executive branch. In 1975 Senator Church likened the CIA to "a rogue elephant on the rampage."[1] Early covert actions were dealt with in a special way within the executive branch, a way designed to achieve "plausible denial": that is, to enable the U.S. government to argue plausibly that it and, failing that, at least the president, had not been involved. Yet, in the crunch, plausible denial had not protected presidents. What it had done was permit a looseness in the chain of command. Subordinates were in the position of interpreting what the president wanted without asking directly for authorization lest the trail of responsibility lead to the Oval Office itself.

By the 1970s plausible denial had plainly outlived whatever usefulness it ever had, so the Congress acted to put the president directly at the head of the chain of command, requiring that he sign a "finding" that the covert action was necessary to America's security, a finding then submitted in secret to the Congress. In 1986, however, that process was short-circuited and the Congress evaded, with looseness again the result. This time the "rogue elephants" were not in the CIA but on the president's own staff. Aides there had diverted the profits from clandestine arms sales to Iran into Swiss bank accounts for the benefit of the Nicaraguan Contras, to which the CIA was then barred by law from providing weaponry, and apparently did so *without* the president's knowledge, let alone his approval.

Now, as was true a decade ago, the issues are fundamental

ones: Should the United States undertake covert interventions into foreign politics at all? If the answer depends on the case, how should one case be distinguished from another? In those cases when covert action is deemed appropriate, how should it be authorized and controlled? In particular, what role should Congress play?

In 1975 I was frustrated by the committee's tendency to frame the issues narrowly, more as a search for villains than an inquiry into public purposes. In the years afterward, as I observed covert action from more distance both inside and outside government, I came to feel that my frustration ran through the larger public discussion of covert action. Perhaps because it is both secret and emotional, covert action is too seldom the subject of hard thought. It seems to be discussed mostly in polemics, for or against, by assertions either that the world is a nasty place or that secret war is nasty business. Witness the following comments by two distinguished observers who are also former government officials. For Ray S. Cline, a former senior CIA official:

> We are already engaged in a protracted secret war against the Soviet Union. . . . The United States is faced with a situation in which the major world power opposing our system of government is trying to expand its power by using covert methods of warfare. Must the United States respond like a man in a barroom brawl who will fight only according to the Marquis of Queensberry rules?[2]

By contrast, consider George W. Ball, who served the Kennedy and Johnson administrations as undersecretary of state:

> In principle I think we ought to discourage the idea of fighting secret wars or even initiating most covert operations. . . . When the United States violates those principles—when we mine harbors in Nicaragua—we fuzz the difference between ourselves and the Soviet Union. We act out of character, which no great power can do without diminishing itself. When we yield to what is, in my judgment, a childish temptation to fight the Russians on their own terms and in their own gutter, we make a major mistake and throw away one of our great assets.[3]

Both positions are considered ones, but in both cases the premises determine the conclusions. That is not to diminish their arguments, however. The moral issues raised by covert U.S. interventions in the affairs of foreign nations—from Nicaragua to Afghanistan to Angola to Iran—are compelling, and I will return to them in chapter 6. They involve both how we think the world ought to be ordered and how we behave in a world that is not what we would have it be. For that matter, they are not unique to covert action, for they run through many foreign policy choices. They cannot be avoided, for instance, when the United States decides whether it will intervene overtly, with military forces, in or against a sovereign nation. The moral issues attached to covert action are not unique, but they are sharper because of the presumption that the operation itself, not just the decision, can remain unconnected to the United States, thus suggesting that the larger moral questions might be evaded.

It seemed to me ten years ago that the history of U.S. covert action deserved to be assessed, not just praised or damned. It seems so to me even more strongly now in the wake of the Iran-Contra affair. For me, the moral issues are not settled by assertions either that our adversaries do not play by the Marquis of Queensberry rules or that we must whether they do or not. Then and now, it seems foolhardy to reach moral judgments about covert action—or about how it can or cannot be made to fit with the requirements of governance in a democracy—without examining what covert action is, and is not, what it can do and cannot do.

Intentions, Commitments, and Results

To examine covert action—both the operations themselves and how they have changed since World War II, in the American body politic as well as in the nations that have been targets of

U.S. covert intervention—is the central purpose of this book. In the heat of the cold war, CIA operations in Iran and Guatemala in the 1950s seemed great successes. They are so regarded in the lore of intelligence. With a few men and a little money, the new Agency determined the fate of governments. The operations made careers and set the image of the CIA as the leading edge of America's undeclared war against the spread of Soviet power. Quick, cheap, and tolerably secret, they encouraged policy makers to believe other operations elsewhere could be the same.

Yet the questions remain: In what terms were they successes? And if they were successes, what relevance do those events of the 1950s have for the 1980s and beyond?

Those early operations were risky, but they worked, and so the riskiness faded from view, along with other questions about secret operations, such as whether covert interventions could remain tolerably secret. Once begun, even if small, they still created commitments for the United States. Operational realities set deadlines, the political stakes of American leaders changed, and the human stakes represented by those secretly supported by the United States began to acquire force. For instance, once the United States began planning the secret Bay of Pigs invasion of Cuba in 1961, the intervention acquired a life of its own. There seemed no place else to put the CIA-trained rebel force except Cuba.

Moreover, as time passed, many of the targets of U.S. intervention became more formidable. Some learned their own lessons from history, including that of American covert action. They were less likely to commit the errors of Mossadeq in Iran and Arbenz in Guatemala, who assumed that American hostility doomed their cause; far from it, some welcomed that hostility as the rallying point for their movements. They sought to assure themselves the support of armed force by making sure the army was loyal or by supplanting it with their own cadres. If they could, they mobilized their own citizenry. And they could rely on other sources of military weaponry and advice—Cuba, the

Soviet Union, or their allies. They did not wait, as Arbenz had, until it was too late to turn to those alternatives.

In the United States, after Vietnam, Watergate, and the Iran-Contra affair, neither the Congress, nor the media, nor the public is as prepared as in the 1950s to accord presidents easy resort to covert action. When reports of covert action play back to the United States from abroad, or surface in Washington, those reports are less likely to be dismissed. When they are denied, the denials are less likely to be believed. By the end of the 1970s Congress had attached itself, however imperfectly, to decisions about covert operations. It could not prevent a determined president from evading it, but it could put presidents on notice that they did so at their peril.

If the foreign targets of intervention are more formidable, then small operations are not likely to achieve their purposes. As the scale of the intervention grows, the chances of maintaining secrecy diminish. Rarely is it possible to achieve large foreign policy purposes, to wage war on governments or decisively alter their prospects, through secret political actions without the world knowing. Too many people are involved; moreover, many of them, especially the foreign targets of covert action, have powerful incentive to publicize the American hand.

Not only are covert actions unlikely to stay secret, their results are especially likely to differ from policy makers' intentions. That is an issue for public programs of all sorts, at home and abroad, but does it have special force for covert action? Clandestine relationships are by nature hard to control. For example, in Chile before the coup of 1973, U.S. officials drew a fine distinction between covertly supporting opposition groups, which was the U.S. purpose, and aiding a coup, which was not. Yet in the chaos of Santiago that fine distinction could not hold. Thus, the lesson history drew from Allende's overthrow is not that his experiment failed on its own terms but that the CIA overthrew him.

Given all these cautions, why has covert action remained the "middle option," less than war but more than nothing? Why have policy makers been tempted again and again to believe it could stay tolerably secret?

From Covert to Overt

The tidy oversight arrangements that Congress created in the wake of Chile—presidential findings delivered in secret to permanent intelligence committees in each house—worked well enough in the late 1970s, when there was little covert action, but they seemed overwhelmed in the 1980s as covert interventions multiplied. New circumstances raised new questions. In the case of Central America in 1982 and 1984, Congress resorted to broad—and public—prohibitions on covert action, just as it had earlier in the instance of Angola, in 1975. These prohibitions were signs that Congress did not trust its own overseers, that the executive did not heed them, or both.

Covert action had come in from the cold. It had become overt. By the middle of the 1980s, what was striking about major covert action was how little about it was secret; American operations—from Nicaragua to Angola to Cambodia—were openly debated. Nicaragua was the most striking example. It was not just that both the covert action and the broader policy of which it was a part were controversial, and so the controversy surged into public. It was also that the Reagan administration was not much interested in keeping it secret. The White House regarded "covert" action as good policy and good domestic politics, a key element of the Reagan doctrine intended to challenge Marxist-Leninist states around the world.

In a sense, the United States had come full circle. In Nicaragua, the Central Intelligence Agency had become the agent of "overt" covert action. Thus, when the Reagan administration decided to sell arms to Iran and keep the operation secret, it turned inward, to the White House staff. In embroidering that operation to divert money for the Contras, White House aides apparently kept the president ignorant in order to protect him—to allow him "plausible denial" of the sort the CIA long since had abandoned.

Hence, a broader assessment of covert action as an instrument of foreign policy is all the more timely. Secret operations in a democracy remain a paradox, one about which the American people are deeply ambivalent, as captured by the juxtaposition of the Cline and Ball views quoted earlier, or by Henry Kissinger's reported sentence about Chile—"I don't see why the United States should stand by and let Chile go communist merely due to the stupidity of its own people"—paired with that attributed to Henry Stimson, secretary of state in 1929—"Gentlemen do not open each other's mail."[4]

On one hand, meddling secretly in other people's internal politics is distasteful; it is so much at odds with our domestic arrangements and values. On the other hand, however much Americans might like it otherwise, the world frequently *is* a nasty place. If we are to compete, it often seems, we may have to be just as nasty as our adversaries. We measure our response by light of their advantages and assume that they, closed societies, must be better and more ruthless at secret operations than we are.

If covert interventions are hard to accomplish and harder still to keep secret, and if we are ambivalent about them in any case, why not act openly? What would that bias toward openness entail, and how far could it extend? What role, if any, would it leave for covert action? And what would "covert" mean in those circumstances? These questions, like the moral issues, are tempting to pursue, and I shall return to them, too, but speculating about the future surely is idle without first understanding the past.

1

The Political Culture of Covert Action

"Covert action" does not apear in the National Security Act of 1947, which established the Central Intelligence Agency. Nor do "covert operations," "clandestine warfare," or "paramilitary operations." Nor, for that matter, do "espionage" or "clandestine intelligence collection." Rather, the act authorized the CIA to "perform such other functions and duties related to intelligence affecting the national security as the National Security Council may from time to time direct."[1] Slender words those, yet they formed the basis for the CIA's covert involvement in the politics of foreign countries. In the period following World War II, that involvement has meant literally thousands of operations; between 1951 and 1975, for instance, there were some nine hundred major or sensitive projects, plus several thousand smaller ones.[2]

This book is about major league covert actions—ones that were sometimes large in size and always large in purpose, seeking not just to affect foreign politics at the margin but often to overturn governments. These major covert actions cannot, however, be understood or assessed in isolation from the broad sweep of American covert action in the period since World War II. That is so not just because the same organization, the CIA, carries out both big and small covert actions but also because the small interventions—propaganda, for instance—form both the basis (the "infrastructure," in the language of the trade) and the component pieces of the big.

The history of covert action might be loosely grouped into three categories. *Propaganda* can be no more than a little money distributed secretly to a few journalists in country X to get them to write articles favorable to the United States—a "project," in CIA practice, but one that might have a budget of only a few thousand dollars. At the other extreme are covert *paramilitary operations*, secret military aid and training. Most though not all of these are large; the "secret" war in Laos, for instance, was not so much secret as unacknowledged, consuming several million dollars a day as a second front to the war in Vietnam but one managed by the CIA. In between, *political action* attempts to change the balance of political forces in a particular country, most often by secretly providing money to particular groups.

In total numbers, propaganda probably has represented about half of all covert actions in the postwar period, political (and related economic) action a third, and paramilitary operations the remainder, though the last have been the most expensive and often the most controversial.[3] Only at the peak of the Vietnam war did covert action claim more than half the total budget for the Central Intelligence Agency. If the CIA's role in Southeast Asia was small by comparison to that of the military, it was huge by comparison to what the CIA had done before. The Agency came to own, secretly and not so secretly, a string of bases and airlines from Arizona to Thailand.

As the war wound down, so did covert action, a trend abetted by Watergate, the investigations of intelligence, and the surrounding climate of the mid-1970s. The change was pronounced during the Carter administration, but it began with Ford. The CIA's "dummy" companies were sold and many of its clandestine operatives pensioned off. By 1980 covert action accounted for less than 5 percent of the total CIA budget.

With the Soviet invasion of Afghanistan in 1979, the Carter administration got back in the business of covert action. When Ronald Reagan acceded to the presidency, the upward move became a rush; covert actions perhaps tripled in number, to over forty.[4] The increase in expenditures was much steeper, largely because of rapidly growing military assistance to resistance forces in Afghanistan, well over $300 million per year by 1986. CIA budgets remain classified, but by the mid-1980s the total came to perhaps $1.5 billion per year, of which covert action consumed about a third.[5]

Most covert action proposals are initiated by CIA officers in foreign countries, who work undercover and together comprise the CIA "station." Covert actions are also suggested by ambassadors, officials in the State or Defense departments, or advisers in the president's inner circle. For instance, an ambassador may call on the CIA to provide security gear to a friendly local leader—something the State Department could not do. More dramatically, the idea of selling arms, in secret, to revolutionary Iran in 1985–86 was very much a White House initiative, run from the National Security Council.

Propaganda

Propaganda is the bread and butter of covert action. In "normal" times it is done both for its own sake and to sustain the infrastructure for expansion should need arise. Of the thirty-odd covert actions undertaken by the CIA in Chile between 1961 and 1974, propaganda was the principal element of a half dozen. It was an important subsidiary part of many others, when Washington did not see times as "normal." In attempting to influence the 1970 Chilean elections, the CIA managed to generate at least one editorial a day at *El Mercurio,* the major Santiago daily, based on American "guidance."[6]

The overthrow of Arbenz in Guatemala in 1954 looks like a paramilitary operation but was in fact more a propaganda success. The CIA-sponsored rebels' "Voice of Liberation" broadcast in short wave from neighboring countries. It even managed, through a fictitious Mexican entrepreneur, to place announcements of its first broadcast in major Guatemalan newspapers.[7] It created successes for the rebel army where there were no battles. It appealed to Arbenz's soldiers to desert and his airmen to defect. It made use of subtle disinformation, suggesting in one broadcast, for example, that it was *not* true that a particular lake had been poisoned. The result was a spate of rumors that it might have been.

The same was true two decades later, in Angola. The CIA planted articles in the two main newspapers in Kinshasa, Zaire—*Elimo* and *Salongo*—and also in Lusaka, Zambia. The Zambian papers recorded that UNITA, a CIA-sponsored faction in the war, had captured a particular city, taking Soviet advisers captive. Only there was neither a victory nor Soviet advisers—at least not at the time of the articles.[8]

In the most "routine" cases, the CIA simply develops "assets"—that is, journalists—in media organizations who will place or write articles when so asked. A particular CIA station then receives guidance from CIA headquarters in Washington about what sort of propaganda is desired. One covert action project in Chile, for example, supported from one to five assets in *El Mercurio.* Those assets were asked to write articles or editorials favorable to U.S. interests (for example, criticizing the Soviet Union in the wake of the invasion of Czechoslovakia); to suppress news items harmful to the United States (for instance, about the war in Vietnam); or to criticize the Chilean political left.

Propaganda is all the more attractive because CIA officers count on a "multiplier effect": any individual item might be picked up and repeated by other media outlets. During the Angolan war, the CIA copied its propaganda products and sent them to CIA stations in Asia, Europe, and Latin America, to be passed on to other journalist-assets there. Even better, individual pieces printed in one paper sometimes were picked up by wire services or other papers without any CIA involvement. In the process, American papers or wire services might also pick up a piece, thus inadvertently playing it as real for American audiences as well.

Covert propaganda includes "black" propaganda—that is, material falsely purporting to be the product of a particular individual or group. Tailoring their products for unusual circumstances, CIA propagandists in Guatemala, for instance, made use of a technique known as snuggling. A rebel mimicked the voice of the official announcer on the government station, and the rebels broadcast on a frequency just adjacent to that government station. Unwary listeners thought they *were* listening to the government when in fact they were hearing rebel propaganda just accurate enough to be credible but fanciful enough to be helpful.

In some cases the form of propaganda is more direct still. In 1975 the CIA station in Kinshasa provided a mimeograph machine for the FNLA, the other U.S. supported faction in the Angolan war. It produced leaflets and then dropped them over the Angolan capital, Luanda, the next morning. Unaccountably, the enemy faction controlling Radio Luanda read the leaflet verbatim over the air, much to the amusement of CIA officers.

In Santiago, the CIA financed Chilean groups that put up wall posters, passed out political leaflets—some of which were prepared by the station—and engaged in other street activities. Most but not all of these direct propaganda activities formed part of larger efforts to influence Chilean elections. For instance, in the 1970 campaign CIA-financed sign-painting teams had instructions to paint the slogan *su paredón* (your wall) on two thousand walls in Santiago, evoking an image of Communist firing squads. Other posters exploited the violence of the 1968 Soviet invasion of Czechoslovakia, with large pictures of Prague and of tanks in downtown Santiago. Still other posters, resembling those used in the 1964 Chilean presidential election, portrayed Cuban political prisoners before firing squads and warned that an Allende victory would mean the end of religion and family life in Chile.

Political Action

Most CIA covert wars did not begin as paramilitary operations. Rather, they began as secret political operations, then expanded as American purposes and foreign circumstances changed. The 1953 operation in Iran began as an attempt to use influence, tokens of American support, and small amounts of money to convince the wavering shah, in secret, that he was strong enough to dismiss his prime minister, Mohammed Mossadeq. Only when that political operation failed did CIA operatives turn seriously to organizing street mobs and armed force.

Similarly, the CIA's first intervention in the Angolan civil war of 1975 was political, not military: in January 1975 it secretly provided one of the competing Angolan factions, the FNLA, with $300,000, not for arms but for a radio station and newspaper to bolster the FNLA's position in the political jockeying once Angola became independent. And American covert action in Nicaragua in the 1980s began, in the waning days of the Carter administration, with political action—money for Nicaraguan opposition groups and media that Washington believed might not survive under Sandinista rule. Just as any distinction between propaganda and political action is fairly arbitrary, so, too, is the line between political and paramilitary operations.

In Chile, U.S. covert action during the years between 1963 and 1973, primarily political in character, was broad and deep.

In the 1964 Chilean presidential elections, the CIA spent $3 million, or about $1 per Chilean voter. (By contrast, in the 1964 U.S. presidential elections, candidates Johnson and Goldwater together spent about 50 cents per voter!) CIA covert actions in Chile over a decade covered the range of what the CIA has done at other times and in other places.

What did the money buy? In "normal" times, when Chile was not considered a "problem" by Washington, it bought propaganda favorable to the United States in Chilean media and modest support for a range of Chilean political parties, labor unions, and student, worker, women, and peasant groups. When times were not "normal"—when senior officials in Washington perceived special dangers or opportunities in Chile—the CIA undertook special projects, ranging from large-scale support for opposition groups, to attempts to influence elections, to efforts to promote a military coup. In one instance, they even included passing guns to coup-plotters, an example of how the categories of covert actions can blur!

SUPPORT FOR MEDIA

In addition to buying propaganda retail—that is, supporting individual assets and stories—the CIA sometimes buys it wholesale. It subsidizes—or establishes—friendly media outlets that might not exist without American support. This is propaganda writ large, propaganda merging with political action. From 1953 through 1970 in Chile, for example, the CIA subsidized wire services, magazines written for intellectual circles, and a right-wing weekly newspaper (support for which had to be terminated when it was judged to have become so ideological as to turn off responsible Chilean conservatives).

Again, a Chilean example illustrates how wholesale support for media organizations sometimes arises. In 1971 the CIA station in Santiago, which had been passing money to several media assets in *El Mercurio,* the main opposition paper once the Allende government was in place, judged that the paper could not survive in the face of government pressure. Government advertising had been withdrawn from the paper, and it could not count on its supply of newsprint, a government monopoly. Under those circumstances the CIA asked for and received permission from the 40 Committee—the Washington interagency group charged with approving major covert actions at the time—to pass $700,000 to *El Mercurio* in September 1971, and another $965,000 in April 1972. The publisher of the paper certainly knew whence the money came, and others on the paper may have suspected, but they would not have been informed, at least not by the CIA.

SUPPORT FOR LABOR UNIONS

Labor unions have been important CIA targets since the beginning of postwar covert action in Western Europe in the late 1940s. Given the success of Communists in organizing unions and the links between union movements and left-wing parties, the CIA has sought to assist anti-Communist labor organizations of all political shades, ranging from conservative to socialist. In Chile during the period 1964–68, for example, the CIA sought to combat the Communist-dominated Central Única de Trabajadores Chileños by assisting rival democratic labor unions (not very successfully, it turned out, judging from the CIA's own postmortems).

SUPPORT FOR POLITICAL PARTIES

Like labor unions, political parties have been a focus of CIA covert action, for obvious reasons. The CIA most often has supported parties favorable to the United States during elections, in an effort to tip the outcome. Sometimes, however, the CIA has provided more general support when elections were not imminent, reckoning that particular parties might not survive without support or that there was an opportunity to alter the balance of political forces within the country in question.

In Chile during the Allende years, 1971–73, the CIA believed that opposition parties of the center and right might not survive either as opposition forces or as contestants in the next elections. Accordingly, the 40 Committee authorized nearly $4 million, most of which was passed to the Christian Democratic party (PDC), with a smaller amount going to the National party (PN), a conservative grouping more stridently opposed to the Allende government than was the PDC. The CIA also tried to split the ruling Popular Unity coalition by using small amounts of money as inducements to breakaway elements.

The CIA's efforts in Chile during the 1970s had parallels in the 1960s, though on a smaller scale. In 1962 the Special Group (predecessor to the 40 Committee) authorized several hundred thousand dollars to build up the PDC organization in anticipation of the 1964 elections. In 1963 and 1967 the CIA provided smaller amounts to moderate elements within the Radical party (Chilean parties, like the Italian ones to which they are akin in many respects, often bear little political resemblance to their names).

INFLUENCING ELECTIONS

"Election projects" over the years have been as important as any set of covert actions by the CIA. Early Agency successes, most notably in the 1948 Italian elections, when secret CIA money helped the Christian Democrats stave off a severe Communist challenge, set the pattern. In Chile, secret U.S. intervention was a factor in almost every major election in the decade between 1963 and 1973. In several instances U.S. intervention was massive.

The 1964 presidential election in Chile was the most striking example. The CIA spent more than $2.6 million in support of the election of the Christian Democratic candidate, Eduardo Frei, in large part to prevent Salvador Allende's accession to the presidency. More than half the PDC campaign chest was furnished by the CIA. Eduardo Frei was not formally told of the support; whether he was aware of it in some sense is another question.

In addition, the CIA station secretly supported an array of pro-Christian Democratic interest groups and passed money to two other political parties in an attempt to spread the vote.

The CIA assisted the Christian Democrats in running an American-style campaign, complete with polls and voter-registration and get-out-the-vote drives, as well as covert propaganda. In a curious parallel between covert and overt, the CIA station in Santiago was sent additional officers for the project, which was mounted, in secret, with all the paraphernalia of its public counterparts—leaflets, campaign posters, and chalkboards toting up the results in tense back rooms. The secret campaign was managed in Washington by an interagency election committee composed of White House, State Department, and CIA officials.

SUPPORT FOR OTHER INSTITUTIONS AND GROUPS

Depending on the circumstances of a particular country, the CIA may give secret support to a wide variety of groups, public and private, the goal being to shift the balance of that country's politics by countering groups perceived as threatening to American interests and aiding those friendly to the United States. Most of these efforts include a substantial dose of propaganda.

In Chile between 1964 and 1968, for example, the CIA developed contacts in the Chilean Socialist party, on the one hand, and the Chilean cabinet on the other. It also undertook projects intended, in the language of its own documents, to

1. wrest control of the Chilean organization of university students from the Communists
2. support a women's group that was thought influential in Chilean political and intellectual life
3. exploit a civic action front group to counter Communist influence in cultural and intellectual circles
4. assist private-sector trade organizations, primarily for voter-registration and get-out-the-vote drives.

SEEKING TO OVERTHROW GOVERNMENTS

Almost all the major covert interventions I explore in this book sought, either explicitly or as a secondary objective, to change governments. Iran in 1953 and Guatemala in 1954 were short-run "successes"; governments changed. In the 1961 Bay of Pigs invasion of Cuba, the United States failed. The question marks around "successes," however, suggest questions that are my concern in this book: Are the successes more apparent than real? And if real, by what definition, over what time period, and at what cost?

In Angola in 1975 and Nicaragua in the 1980s, the initial American aim apparently was less dramatic. In Angola the CIA sought not to overturn a government in power but to affect the balance of forces to prevent a government from consolidating. In Nicaragua, U.S. purposes were disputed but initially seem to have been broadly similar to those in Angola; U.S. officials apparently believed that harassing the regime would also prevent it from supporting antigovernment guerrillas in neighboring El Salvador.

In both Angola and Nicaragua, U.S. purposes expanded as the conflict wore on. In Angola, the United States at first set limited goals but plainly hoped for more, not just to prevent the consolidation of a government but perhaps to supplant it. It failed in its limited aim and, ignominiously, in its broader one as well. In Nicaragua, too, the line between containing a government and overturning it was a fine one. Over time that line seemed to dissolve even in the minds of policy makers, and the purpose turned to changing the government.

In the 1970 Chilean presidential election, Salvador Allende finished first but no candidate received a majority, so the Chilean Congress had to vote between Allende and the runner-up, a conservative. During the interim between election and congressional vote, on September 15, 1970, the CIA was directed to prevent Allende from taking office, an order given directly to the CIA director, Richard Helms, by President Richard Nixon; the effort was to be kept secret not just from the secretaries of State and Defense but also from the American ambassador in Santiago. Helms's handwritten notes of his meeting with the president convey the urgency of his order: "One in 10 chance perhaps, but save Chile! . . . not concerned risks involved . . . no involvement of Embassy . . . $10,000,000 available, more if necessary . . . make the economy scream."[9]

This more direct "Track II" in Chile emerged because the first track of covert action, designed to sway the Chilean Congress's vote for the presidency, was failing. Under pressure, Nixon and Henry Kissinger took the next step, and it soon became clear to both White House and CIA officials privy to Track II that a military coup was the only way to prevent Allende's accession to power. To that end, the CIA established contact with two loose and overlapping groups of military plotters, knowing that the coup plans of both began with the abduction of the Chilean army's chief of staff, General René Schneider, a staunch constitutionalist opposed to any coup.

The CIA broke contact with one group it judged unpromising and eventually supplied three weapons and tear gas to the other—more, it seems, as tokens of support than because it needed them. This group's plans never came to fruition, and the weapons were subsequently returned, apparently unused. On October 22, however, the group with which the CIA had broken contact a week earlier attempted to kidnap Schneider, who resisted, was shot, and later died.

ASSASSINATIONS OF FOREIGN LEADERS

The killing of Schneider was apparently inadvertent, but in other cases, killing was not inadvertent. In some cases, like Schneider's, the killing happened after the CIA broke contact with or lost the ability to control particular antigovernment groups. In others, the idea of assassination emerged not as an explicit first purpose but rather at the end of a long train of covert intervention. Yet the plots to kill Cuban leader Fidel Castro, of which there were at least eight between 1961 and 1965, were not accidental or inadvertent.[10]

I have not included a detailed discussion of those unhappy events in this book. They have been much written about, perhaps too much; they dominated the deliberations of the Senate select committee on which I served. Indeed, watching my hopes for the committee's broad inquiry into covert action and U.S. foreign policy being squeezed by the time spent on assassinations, I quipped to a colleague, too fliply, that "the only successful CIA assassination plot has been against the Church Committee itself."[11]

Not all of the possible lessons for covert action are inappropriate, but the assassination events do seem to me exceptional, sad, and special reflections of an unusual period. John Stockwell, the CIA operative in Angola who made his disillusionment public, cites his horror on learning that the CIA, contrary to what he had been promised, had been involved in assassinations, especially that of Patrice Lumumba, the Congolese leader who had grown up in a church community that overlapped with that of Stockwell's missionary parents.[12] During 1975–76 I heard similar reactions from other CIA officers as I walked the halls of CIA headquarters in Virginia or rode the shuttle bus from there to Washington.

Whether presidents and their senior aides, especially in the Kennedy administration, ever specifically authorized or even knew about the attempts will remain one of history's unknowables, a frustration to historians and policy analysts alike. Certainly, the CIA officials who managed the assassination attempts felt themselves to be so authorized. They were under enormous pressure to "do something" about Castro. *Nothing* seemed excluded to them. And in those days covert operators did not march back to the White House to ask: "Mr. President, when it says 'remove' Castro, does that mean I can kill him? And can I have it in writing?" *That* issue of authorization, one still with us, is important for this book. The diversion of profits from Iranian arms sales attests to that fact.

Looking back at those assassination attempts now, and putting aside the nature of the act in question, what strikes one is their fecklessness. The agency that overturned governments never came close to killing Castro. While working for the Senate committee, I was preparing some public remarks for then Senator Walter Mondale. In describing the assassination plots, I borrowed Jimmy Breslin's line about the Mafia and described the CIA as "the gang that couldn't shoot straight." Fortunately, the senator's taste was better than mine, and he deleted the phrase from the remarks he made.

Yet part of the reason the attempts were so ineffective, I believe, is that CIA officers never quite had their hearts in them. They did not square with those officers' sense of their profession. If making revolutions, like making omelets, requires breaking some eggs, the same is true of making counterrevolutions. People will be killed, and some of those killings will be intentional. CIA officers accepted that as their profession. But targeting a single individual, a foreign leader, for killing was another matter. It was something for the Mafia, not the Clandestine Service—the CIA's Directorate of Operations—and in that sense it may be no accident that CIA plans to kill Castro relied so heavily on the Mafia.

Paramilitary Operations

Covert military or paramilitary operations often seek to overthrow a government, and thus are a special means of achieving that political end. But the means are special enough to consider separately.

At one extreme, paramilitary operations have been tantamount to full-scale wars—"covert" only in the sense that the United States wanted to be able to deny that it was directly involved. Witness the "secret war" in Laos, an unadmitted war on the cheap, with CIA paramilitary specialists providing the advice and Laotian hill tribesmen doing the fighting. I have not treated Laos in any detail in this book. Like earlier CIA paramilitary campaigns in Korea, Laos was part of an open American war; if the campaigns were meant to be secret, neither the war nor its purposes were.

At the other end of the spectrum, some paramilitary operations have amounted to little more than the clandestine transfer of a few weapons or of small amounts of training—for instance, for "palace guards" to protect friendly heads of state who would prefer not to be widely known as protected by the United States.

Angola and Nicaragua fell somewhere in between. In the instance of Angola during 1975–76, the 40 Committee authorized a total of $32 million for two of the three contending factions, most of it to provide arms. Less than a hundred CIA officers were directly involved in the field. In Nicaragua, the armed groups fighting the Sandinista government, principally the Contras, had some ten thousand men under arms by the mid-1980s. By then they had been allocated an estimated $200 million from the CIA over the five years of their support. As in Angola, the number of CIA officers in Central America was small, and those present were barred from accompanying the Contras into Nicaragua, although as the program expanded the U.S. military also became involved in training.

All these paramilitary operations involved the same elements: money and weaponry for groups and movements the United States was supporting, plus clandestine ways to transfer both, plus CIA officers and others to provide training and advice. The weaponry was "sterile"—that is, not easy to identify as coming from the United States. For that reason, Brigade 2506, which mounted the Bay of Pigs invasion in 1961, was supported by ancient aircraft that plausibly could have been taken from Castro's own air force by defectors; while the Angola forces were aided by the CIA with transferred weapons from or similar to those in the arsenal of neighboring Zaire.

In the early postwar years, weaponry manufactured by the Soviet Union and its allies, prized because it could most easily be denied as supplied by America, was hard to come by. More recently, with more such weaponry circulating in world arms markets and with several former Soviet allies—most notably Egypt—having switched sides, more of it is available for the CIA. When the United States began covert support to the resistance forces in Afghanistan in the early 1980s, the weaponry they received from the CIA was almost all of Soviet manufacture.

To backstop these paramilitary operations, the CIA has developed networks of air carriers, some CIA "fronts," and some contractors to move arms and supplies—if not secretly, then at least as less visibly "American." During the Vietnam war, that network, centered on Air America, amounted to a large air force. After Vietnam, the CIA divested itself of these "proprietaries" but retained contacts with those companies; in many cases, the "new" private managers were the "old" CIA managers, now retired. Nor did even the names change: Southern Air Transport, a CIA company during the Vietnam war, shipped supplies to the CIA-sponsored Contras in Nicaragua two decades later as a "private" company.

Transferring weapons and training both require bases. Nicaraguan dictator Somoza provided bases for CIA-supported operations against both Guatemala in 1954 and Cuba in 1961, and Guatemala, the object of a CIA operation in 1964, became an ally in 1961, serving as Brigade 2506's main training site. By the 1980s, when Nicaragua was the target, Honduras served as the host, however nervously, for the main Contra training bases. Indeed, for one Nicaragua port town, covert war came full circle:

having served as a base for the CIA-sponsored invasion of Guatemala in 1954, it was a target of the CIA-sponsored Contras three decades later.

Covert Action in the World of Intelligence

Covert action is only part of the world of intelligence, albeit one sensitive far beyond its size. That world is one of some derring-do but much more plodding. Few Central Intelligence Agency officers are "spies" in the sense of popular novels. (Indeed, most of those novels are not about spying—that is, espionage—but rather about counterespionage.) The "spying" typically is done by foreigners employed or managed by CIA officers—in the jargon of the trade, foreign "assets" "run" by their CIA "case officers."

The classic task of intelligence comprises two parts: collecting information, and putting it together to see what it means, usually referred to, respectively, as collection and analysis or assessment. Raw information comes from a variety of sources. Foreigners provide it, knowingly (openly, to State Department political officers, or secretly, to their CIA case officers) or unwittingly, when communications are intercepted or when assets report on the doings of their contacts. Information also comes from satellite photographs and from foreign media broadcasts monitored openly.

Collection, especially by satellites and other "national technical means," consumes the bulk of the over $20 billion annual budget of the American intelligence agencies—together referred to, by custom, as the intelligence community. By comparison with technical collection, analysis and even espionage are cheap. The collecting is done by a variety of institutions of the U.S. government: the State Department, the CIA, military attachés, the National Reconnaissance Office, the National Security

Agency, and the Foreign Broadcast Information Service, to name the most prominent.

The task of assessment is largely the province of one half of the CIA—the Directorate of Intelligence—although the Defense Intelligence Agency (DIA) provides analysis of military issues, the State Department has its own small Bureau of Intelligence and Research (INR), and there are still smaller groups of more specialized analysts scattered throughout the government.[13] These analysts work in Washington, not abroad. Their job is to sift through the piles of information from all available sources, secret and not. They get much of their information about foreign governments and their actions in the same way we learn about our own government: they read foreign newspapers and magazines. These analysts are hardly James Bonds. They tell their friends and neighbors openly that they work for the CIA; by temperament they are more professorial than conspiratorial.

The other half of the CIA—the Directorate of Operations (which used to be called, in bureaucratic euphemism, the Directorate of Plans)—is America's secret intelligence service, usually called the Clandestine Service. When abroad, the service's officers work under "cover," usually the "light" and "official" cover provided by other agencies of the U.S. government, but they are in fact CIA operatives.

When they operate under "deep" cover, CIA officers pose as businesspeople or other private individuals unconnected to the U.S. government. Deep cover is difficult to arrange, hard to sustain, and, since it does not confer the protection of formal association with the U.S. government, can be dangerous, so it is almost never used. Even light cover is a nuisance since, if taken seriously, it means doing two jobs—one for cover, one for real. Small wonder that the cover of many CIA officers abroad is so threadbare.

The Clandestine Service has three missions: intelligence gathering, or espionage; counterintelligence; and covert action. Counterintelligence is just what the name implies: protecting

American institutions from penetration by foreign intelligence services. It was once described by James Angleton, long-time head of counterintelligence for the CIA and a legendary character in the Clandestine Service, as a "wilderness of mirrors."[14] In a world of double and triple agents, sorting out for whom a person "really" works, and thus owes loyalty, is no mean feat. Debates have raged for years in Washington about whether particular defectors from the East were legitimate émigrés or Soviet "plants." In one well-known case of the 1960s, a Soviet defector was kept under virtual house arrest for three years while the intelligence agencies argued about him.[15]

Both espionage and covert action involve clandestine relationships between American CIA officers and foreigners, however the purposes of the contacts are different. To gather intelligence, a CIA officer establishes a relationship with a foreign asset in a political party or government institution of interest to the United States. The asset then, in effect, betrays his institution or country by reporting to his CIA officer what is going on there. The asset may be motivated by ideology, money, or other inducements. The relationship is secret to protect the asset, and depending on the country, communication between case officer and asset may be extremely circuitous—using "cutouts," "dead drops," and other elements of intelligence tradecraft à la John le Carré.

But the purpose of such espionage is information, not action. The case officer makes no attempt to induce the asset to act in a particular way, in large measure because to do so would be to increase the risk of revealing the asset's link to the CIA. For covert action, by contrast, action is the point, although the relationship is secret. Case officers give their assets instructions to do something specific, to try to influence the actions of a particular foreign institution in a way the United States deems favorable. They may also supply their assets with information, money, weapons, or training.

The three Clandestine Service functions—espionage, counterintelligence, and covert action—are handled somewhat differently by the CIA in Washington, and typically they are performed by different CIA officers in the field. Yet in practice it is not easy to draw neat boxes around the different functions of the Clandestine Service. Networks of agents for information purposes can be and sometimes are used for covert action. Some conflict between action types and those who conduct espionage is thus built into the Clandestine Service. From the espionage officer's perspective, his calling relies on patience and secrecy. By contrast, major covert action programs seek quick, dramatic results and therefore are likely to become known—"blown"—and thus make espionage more difficult.

Intelligence gathering itself may convey signals to the gatherers. That is an issue as old as intelligence. It arose in stark form in CIA contacts with the Chilean military during the Allende government, ostensibly for collecting intelligence. Those from whom the CIA seeks information seldom are passive purveyors of facts. Their reasons for establishing a connection with the CIA may be merely money, or flattery, or adventure, or escape from their country, or some other tangible gratification. But often those "assets" are political actors with purposes and agendas of their own. They are bound to read their CIA connection as U.S. support for their purposes and to seek in the winks and nods of their case officers signs of that support.

Institutionalizing a Clandestine Service

America came late to the notion of an institutionalized intelligence service. Although Americans have engaged in spying since George Washington's time, it was only World War II and the cold war coming hard on its heels that led to the creation of the Central Intelligence Agency—and the permanent Clandestine Service. Wartime success and postwar threat—these formed the backdrop for the creation of the CIA. The early history of the CIA is that of America's plunge from the euphoria of victory in World War II to the perception of looming Soviet attack on Western Europe. Neither the Agency nor its covert warfare can be separated from that history.

The roots of the CIA and of covert action lie in the World War II Office of Strategic Services (OSS), America's first independent intelligence service.[16] Led by William J. ("Wild Bill") Donovan, a prominent attorney and World War I hero, the OSS provided inspiration, structure, and a cadre of veterans for the CIA. Forty years after war's end, the recently deceased CIA director, William Casey, was an OSS veteran.

Donovan conceived his plan for a single intelligence organization in 1940 and secured President Roosevelt's approval in the summer of 1941. A year later the United States was at war with both Germany and Japan, and the OSS came into being in full form, under the direction of the U.S. military's Joint Chiefs of Staff. OSS officers parachuted into France and Norway to join resistance fighters, fought with Partisans in Italy, and organized Burmese tribes to resist the Japanese. Almost everywhere the OSS worked closely, although not always easily, with British intelligence, which had served as the model for the OSS.

The OSS emerged from the war successful and heroic. In Burma, three hundred OSS officers mobilized a force of tribesmen thirty times that size. In preparation for the invasion of Normandy, the OSS parachuted in "Jedburgh" teams to meet up with local resistance units. By the time of the invasion, five hundred Free French and 375 American officers were already inside occupied France.[17]

The OSS set the pattern for American intelligence. Its organization served as the model for the CIA. It also prefigured the CIA in the ragged edges of its cooperation with other pieces of the Washington governmental machine. On the intelligence side, its Research and Analysis Branch never became a consistent channel to Roosevelt, who relied on a shifting set of aides and informal conversations. The military, wary of its unconventional offspring, tried to limit OSS operations and was reluctant to share information with it. General Douglas MacArthur succeeded in excluding the OSS from China and the Pacific Theater. The FBI retained its responsibility for domestic intelligence activities and, to boot, kept its jurisdiction over intelligence in Latin America, including clandestine operations.

The rush to demobilize at war's end did not spare the OSS: despite its luster, and over Donovan's objections, President Harry Truman disbanded it on October 1, 1945, dispersing its components to separate departments of government. Yet little over a half dozen years later, by 1952, those constituent parts had been reassembled into the CIA, which was by then engaged in clandestine intelligence collection, the production of intelligence assessments—and covert action.

Surprisingly, covert operations did not at first figure prominently in the postwar American debate over how to organize the government to confront the perception of an imminent Soviet threat. The first priority was improving the war's often sorry record of cooperation among the military services. The second was related—how to avert another "Pearl Harbor," a problem defined as fragmented military intelligence that could neither sort out warning indicators from surrounding "noise" nor make its assessments compelling to officials at the top of government.

Through a series of internal studies, it became clear that neither the military services nor the State Department were prepared to yield their roles in intelligence assessment to a centralized agency. Accordingly, in January 1946 Truman adopted the recommendations of the Eberstadt Report, a study directed by Ferdinand Eberstadt, an influential investment banker. Truman created the Central Intelligence Group (CIG), headed by the first director of central intelligence (DCI), Admiral Sidney Souers. The various departments, however, retained their intelligence offices, and the CIG's budget and staff were drawn from them. The CIG was the creature of the departments, its role limited to coordinating and disseminating intelligence but with no real clout over those it was meant to coordinate.

Over the next several years, successive DCIs concentrated on establishing the CIG as an independent producer of finished intelligence assessments, but in August 1946 the CIG did get into the business of espionage. The postwar dismantling of the OSS had sent a remnant capability for clandestine collection, the Strategic Services Unit (SSU), to the War Department as a temporary measure, one intended at the time to phase out the unit, not save it. For the CIG, however, the acquisition of the SSU, with its seven field stations in North Africa and the Near East, betokened a major change in mission. The SSU became part of the CIG's newly created Office of Special Operations (OSO), responsible for both espionage and counterintelligence. The OSO had eight hundred officers by the end of 1946.

The National Security Act of 1947 ratified the changes in governmental structure that had been debated since war's end: it created a separate air force, amalgamated that service plus the army, the navy, under a secretary of defense, created the military Joint Chiefs of Staff, and established the National Security Council (NSC). Military arrangements, not intelligence, were the focus of attention for both the executive and Congress, and other than renaming the CIG the Central Intelligence Agency, the act left its functions unchanged.

A string of apparent Soviet successes, however, brought covert action into the limelight: in March 1946 Moscow had refused to withdraw its troops from the Iranian region of Azerbaijan; two months later, civil war broke out in Greece; and by 1947 Communist governments had taken power in Poland, Hungary, and Romania.

The first line of American response to the onset of the cold war was overt: the surge of assistance to Europe through the Truman Doctrine and the Marshall Plan. But the second line was renewed interest in what was then called covert "psychological warfare"—what we would now call propaganda, a way to respond to the Soviet Union that was less than war but more than nothing. By the autumn of 1947 senior officials seemed agreed on the need for such a dimension in U.S. policy, but they had not yet decided exactly how it should be used or where, organizationally, the capability should reside.

In November, Truman approved a recommendation from the newly constituted Defense Department that all propaganda, both overt and covert, be assigned to the State Department. Secretary of State George Marshall, the "silent hero" of World War II, however, would have none of it. He argued vehemently that covert operations, if revealed, would discredit both the department and U.S. foreign policy. In December the National Security Council took up the issue at its very first meeting, and the next day, December 14, Truman signed NSC directive 4/A, charging the CIA with covert psychological operations.

Then, as later, the choice of the CIA not only spared other departments the risks of covert operations, it also was convenient. A third of the CIA's officers were OSS veterans; the Agency had a network of overseas facilities in place, and it already used unvouchered funds for its espionage, so the CIA required no fresh congressional appropriation for covert operations. Within a week of NSC 4/A, the CIA set up a Special Procedures Group (SPG) in the OSO; by the next year, the SPG was broadcasting into the East, secretly printing propaganda in West Germany, and dropping propaganda by balloon into Eastern Europe.

The rush of the cold war pushed policy makers to consider how to make this "extra dimension" of foreign policy even stronger. In February 1948 a Communist coup succeeded in Czechoslovakia, while Communist agitation grew in France and Italy. By March the government whipped itself into near hysteria when the American high commissioner in Germany, General Lucius Clay, cabled his warning that war with Russia "may come with dramatic suddenness."[18] In this atmosphere, in June the NSC approved NSC 10/2, a plan that had originated with

George Kennan, then director of the State Department's Policy Planning Staff and the author of the famous "Mr. X" cable outlining the policy of containment of the Soviet Union.

NSC 10/2 was the turning point for covert action, expanding it from propaganda to direct intervention. In the words of the document, covert action comprised

> propaganda, economic warfare; preventive direct action, including sabotage, anti-sabotage, demolition and evacuation measures; subversion against hostile states, including assistance to underground resistance movements, guerrillas and refugee liberation groups, and support of indigenous anti-communist elements.[19]

NSC 10/2 also codified the notion of "plausible denial": Operations were to be "so planned and executed that any U.S. Government responsibility for them is not evident to unauthorized persons and that if uncovered the U.S. Government can plausibly disclaim any responsibility for them."

These activities, unlike propaganda, were at the time regarded as direct extensions of the military missions of the Defense Department and the political role of the State Department, and so a special organizational arrangement was constructed to match that conception. The Office of Policy Coordination (OPC) was created within the CIA, replacing the Special Procedures Group. The CIA gave the OPC "rations and billets";[20] the OPC was in the CIA but not of it, for the OPC's director was appointed by the secretary of state, and it took policy guidance from State and Defense, bypassing the DCI. For the first time, a president had designated a process for approving and managing covert actions.

Its creators, especially Kennan, intended the OPC to be small, and on hand should events require. In Kennan's words: "We had thought that this would be a facility which could be used when and if an occasion arose when it might be needed. There might be years when we wouldn't have to do anything like this."[21] Suffice it to say that it did not turn out that way. Each time the cold war turned colder, the OPC was available; moreover, its services to its two masters, State and Defense, required different capabilities, and that, too, provided arguments for becoming bigger and more permanent in structure. By 1952, when it was merged with the OSO, the CIA's espionage branch, the OPC had achieved both a scale of operations and an organizational independence far beyond Kennan's conception.

Giving Pride of Place to Covert Action

The OPC's first head, Frank Wisner, made the most of its broad mandate, moving the office away from the close identification with State that had been the original conception for it. Appointed assistant director for policy coordination (ADPC) in September 1948, Wisner, then thirty-nine, was a man of immense energy who collected ideas from everywhere and was impatient with organization and eager for action. A Mississippian who had graduated third in his class from the University of Virginia Law School, he had served the OSS in Germany. After a brief stint practicing law, he returned to Washington to serve as assistant secretary of state for occupied areas before being tapped as ADPC.

The OPC's organization by "project," still the CIA practice, suited Wisner's temperament. It meant that he could set officers to work in a number of directions, sometimes assigning several groups the same mission, then devote his energies to particular projects as he saw fit. In theory, the OPC's four functional staffs (political, psychological, economic, and paramilitary) were to generate project outlines for the office's six geographic divisions, and the latter in turn would provide detailed instructions to overseas stations. In fact, however, the staffs, divisions, and stations soon became competitors for the running of projects, rather than joint participants. Then, as later, running projects, not monitoring them, was the way to make a reputation.

For the past three decades, the targets of American covert action most often have been the less developed nations, or as Senator Frank Church put it in summing up his committee's investigation, "small, weak countries."[22] That was not the case in the early postwar years, when the cold war looked as though it might soon become hot and as Western Europe teetered in the balance. By July 1948 Soviet harassment of Western traffic into Berlin had become a blockade; the United States, Britain, and France countered with the Berlin airlift. The cold war was on.

In Europe, America's first task was holding the line against the Communists in Western Europe. The Italian election in 1948 had been much of the motivation behind creating the OPC. The CIA's stunning success there in cobbling together its first major postwar election project was followed by others. The CIA provided money for anti-Communist intellectuals who organized the Congress of Cultural Freedom in Paris, and it funded *Encounter* magazine.

These early successes set the pattern for twenty years. One element was supporting parties of the center and democratic left, a second was developing assets in the media. The third was organizing anti-Communist unions, a major covert activity until the mid-1960s. The OPC began by inheriting the fledgling labor activities of the Economic Cooperation Administration (ECA), the Marshall Plan administrator. By 1952 some forty-odd covert action programs were under way in "one central European country alone."[23] The OPC's operations in Germany employed twelve hundred people by 1952.[24]

If the West's worst fears were confirmed and the Red Army did sweep into Western Europe, the CIA sought to develop "stay-behind" or "retardation" networks to organize uprisings against the Soviet occupiers. If the Soviet Union did not attack, then the task became sowing unrest in "denied areas" behind the iron curtain. Another OPC inheritance was the propaganda operations of the Special Procedures Group, which by 1950 had expanded into Radio Free Europe (RFE). The first president of RFE's nominal parent organization was Allen Dulles, wartime spymaster for the OSS in Switzerland, consultant to successive DCIs, and later himself DCI.

Wisner's OPC also mounted operations into "denied areas." For these purposes it became deeply involved with refugee organizations. The United States also received another inheritance, this one a curiosity of war's end and sometimes embarrassing to the United States. The head of the German general staff's intelligence on the Soviet Union, Reinhard Gehlen, contrived to have himself captured by the Americans and then offered his services. The CIA inherited him and his network from the U.S. army in 1949. The Gehlen group was useful (and later became the nucleus of the Federal Republic's intelligence service), but Gehlen had been more fastidious about his associates' expertise than their intelligence tradecraft or political backgrounds: some were former Nazis, and the group was penetrated by Soviet agents.

The OPC resumed the wartime pattern of cooperation with the British Secret Intelligence Service (SIS). The two parachuted teams into the Baltic states and to the Soviet Union itself, and they supported a paramilitary operation code-named VALUABLE to oust Albania's Communist leadership. As the 1950s wore on, however, these covert thrusts dwindled. In the case of VALUABLE, the Albanian émigrés were splintered; nor were the OPC and the SIS always of one mind about which groups to support. Soviet control gradually stamped out partisans operating in "denied areas."

In reflecting on these ventures eastward, John Bross, then CIA division chief for Central and Eastern Europe, thought them not fruitless, but a reflection of the pressure of the times: the World War II image of resistance forces led to hopes for "resistance groups in Eastern Europe, prepared to carry out paramilitary operations against the hated . . . Soviets . . . [an] assumption . . .

stimulated by fabricators who carried on a lucrative trade with the press and government with tall tales of pitched battles between armed dissidents and security forces in Czechoslovakia and Poland." Given the pressure to find such groups, the "OPC had little alternative to try or lose its franchise." A better "understanding of conditions behind the curtain and what security controls were really like . . . was immensely important" in dampening the enthusiasm of an "Eisenhower administration [that] came into office on a . . . platform of overthrowing the communist governments by revolutionary means."[25]

Once the dark days of 1950 passed, the center of the battle against communism moved, as official Washington saw the world, first to Asia and then to the "small, weak"—and vulnerable—countries. The covert war in Europe, successful in the West, wound down to propaganda and intelligence gathering in the East.

Events in Europe put the OPC into the business of covert political action, but it was Asia—with the onset of the Korean war in the summer of 1950—that got the office into paramilitary operations in a big way. MacArthur again tried his best to constrain the CIA's role in "his" theater, but with much less success than in World War II. OPC budgets and personnel skyrocketed. In 1949 it spent $4.7 million; by 1952, $82 million. In 1949 it had 302 employees and 7 field stations; by 1952 it had 2,812 plus 3,142 overseas contract personnel and maintained 47 stations.[26] During the Truman administration, the OPC's State and Defense overseers—the "10/2 Group," as it came to be known—authorized 81 covert actions.[27]

The OPC's position in the CIA had been an anomaly from the start, and as it mushroomed, successive DCIs chafed at their lack of authority over it. Within a week of taking office as DCI in 1950, General Walter Bedell ("Beetle") Smith asked that State and Defense guidance to OPC be channeled through him, not go directly to Wisner. Given Smith's stature—he had been Eisenhower's wartime chief of staff and had served as ambassador to the Soviet Union after the war—State and Defense quickly agreed.

Another part of that anomaly—the existence of two clandestine services, the OPC and the OSO, in one agency—was a still harder problem. Covert action and espionage, while different, do overlap. Yet instead of supporting each other, the OPC and the OSO ran separate operations from the same overseas station and often competed for foreign agents. In one celebrated case in Bangkok in 1952, the competition turned to outright hostility as the OSO sought to lure away a senior Thai official who had close links to the OPC.

Differences in style and background compounded the tension between the two services. Barred from poaching in the OSO, Wisner turned to OSSers and Ivy League college graduates just returning from the war—men labeled the "bold Easterners" by a friend of Wisner, journalist Stewart Alsop.[28] Given Wisner's disdain for tidy management, the competition for projects was chaotic enough inside the OPC. Worse, many OSO officers, older OSS veterans, regarded the quiet, patient practice of espionage as the essence of professional intelligence. For them, the OPC's new recruits were green and its high-risk operations a threat to the OSO's ability to do its job. Moreover, they resented the OPC's generous budgets and the rapid promotions they made possible. By June 1952 the OPC was larger in people and budget than the OSO.

By 1951 it was plain to all concerned that some merger of the OPC and the OSO was imperative, although they disagreed on the form that merger should take. In January 1951 Smith created the post of deputy director for plans (DDP), filling it with Allen Dulles. This first integration was, however, more cosmetic than real: Dulles was responsible for both the OPC and the OSO, but the two directors still ran their offices. The OSO leaders, fearing that they would be engulfed by the OPC, argued for an integration of OPC functions under OSO control.

The process of real integration began with the Western Hemisphere division in June 1952, and in August the OSO and the OPC became the Directorate of Plans. Wisner was named DDP (Dulles moved up to become deputy DCI), and to allay OSO concerns, Richard Helms from the OSO became Wisner's number two, chief of operations. Although the merger was completed on paper, the clash of operating styles persisted for years.

The merger confirmed the fears of the OSO: it represented the ascendancy of covert operations over espionage. Given Wisner's background, it was natural for him to give pride of place to covert action. Officers soon recognized that professional rewards and career advances came faster through running big covert action projects than through silent cultivation of espionage agents. As one veteran of the period put it: "Collection is the hardest thing of all; it's much easier to place an article in a local newspaper."[29]

America had institutionalized an intelligence service of a special kind, one in which clandestine operations dominated intelligence assessment and covert action had pride of place over espionage, developments begun with the secret wars in Europe and completed with the Korean war. By 1952 the Clandestine Service accounted for 74 percent of the CIA budget and three fifths of its personnel.[30] Future presidents inherited a powerful tool but also an institution with a strong bias toward covert action. Worse, given the special place of covert action and the secrecy surrounding it, the CIA those presidents heard was something of a fiction. What they were most likely to hear was not the view of the analysts or spymasters but rather that of the covert operators, those with the most direct stake in covert action.

In November 1952 Dwight D. Eisenhower was elected president; his campaign had called for a more active response to the Soviet Union than the passive containment of the Truman administration. John Foster Dulles became secretary of state, and in February 1953 his brother Allen Dulles was named DCI. Campaign pronouncements and personalities suggested that covert operators would be a key weapon in the new administration's war against the global threat of communism.

Located in the center of Washington, in a set of makeshift buildings of World War II vintage, the new agency had attracted some of the nation's ablest young men (there were then no women among them, although later there were)—lawyers, academics, and investment bankers. They had talent, many had experience from either the OSS or the covert campaigns of the early postwar years or both, and most brought with them a web of social and professional connections that enabled them to move easily in official Washington.

2

Setting the Mold: Early Successes

On August 21, 1953, after a week of turmoil in the streets of Teheran, the Iranian prime minister, Mohammed Mossadeq, surrendered to General Fazlollah Zahedi. Three days later the shah, who had fled Iran the previous week with his queen, returned to the capital. At his palace a few days later he offered a toast to Kermit ("Kim") Roosevelt, as close to a James Bond as appears in this book, the chief of the CIA's Near East and Africa division and the man who had improvised Mossadeq's downfall: "I owe my throne to God, my people, my army—and you!"[1]

On June 16, 1954, Guatemalan Colonel Carlos Castillo Armas crossed the border into his country from Honduras with a few hundred men trained and armed by the CIA. Pilots under CIA contract flew air cover. The president of Guatemala, Jacobo Arbenz Guzmán, was deserted by his air force and his army, which refused his order to arm workers and peasants. The U.S. ambassador in Guatemala, John Peurifoy, hastily arranged a transfer of power to the chief of the armed forces, Colonel Enrique Díaz. In a moment of tragicomedy, Díaz immediately pledged to continue the struggle against Castillo Armas, America's designated successor. Peurifoy secured Díaz's resignation, and after complicated negotiations between the armed forces and Castillo Armas, the latter emerged as president.[2]

It is striking that, in the mid-1980s as in the mid-1950s, the targets of American covert action were Iran and Central America. Yet the parallel may mislead as much as it instructs, for if the more recent episodes testify to how hard covert action is, the earlier seemed to show how easy it was. Iran and Guatemala, coming within a few years of the CIA's successes in Western Europe, made the Agency's reputation and set the pattern for covert action in the years ahead. Small, cheap, fast, and tolerably secret, they encouraged Washingtonians to think other covert actions could be likewise. When the next administration confronted revolution in Cuba, its covert response was the same as in Guatemala. So were the CIA officers who carried it out.

Actually, short-run success obscured several underlying cautions. In both Iran and Guatemala, the operations had nearly failed and were only rescued by upping the ante. As the operations, especially the one in Guatemala, grew, so did American stakes, and so did the difficulty of hiding the U.S. role.

Iran took six months from first order to end, and its cost was perhaps a million dollars, certainly not more than a few.[3] Roosevelt and his band of Americans numbered only a handful, yet they were able to pull the strings of Iranian politics. Guatemala was bigger and took longer, so the hand of the United States was harder to hide. It became a paramilitary operation, albeit a small one, involving some twenty to thirty CIA officers plus a few military men on loan. Yet in dollars it cost only five or six times as much as Iran, and when the end came for Arbenz, it seemed swift and easy.

The Context of Covert Intervention

The Iran and Guatemala operations emerged in a climate of anti-communism whose force is easy to understate in retrospect. Between the elation of victory in 1945 and the dark fears of the cold war lay less than a half dozen years, years that had been disillusioning and frustrating for Americans. The language is evocative of the times: an "iron curtain" had fallen in Europe, and China had been "lost" to the "Soviet bloc." With the Korean war, a new consensus about the Soviet Union had spread among policy makers, Congress, the press, and the public. Moscow would expand its influence and its empire, through subversion if possible but through military force if need be. It was imperative for both the United States and the "free world" that this Soviet expansion be contained. It was a life-or-death struggle.

From that perspective, the Eisenhower administration criticized it predecessor as too passive and too fixed on Europe in fighting the spread of Soviet influence. The struggle was urgent and global. For Eisenhower's secretary of state, John Foster Dulles, the son of a Presbyterian minister and himself a prominent churchman, the struggle was literally theological, Christianity versus communism, two hostile worldviews between which there could be no compromise. Eisenhower's diary entries reflect both his views and his sense of how broadly shared they were by the American political establishment: "The free world is under threat by the monolithic mass of Communist Imperialism," and so the United States "must wake up to prepare a position of strength . . . those who were then asleep [during the wartime alliance with Moscow] now are professional patriots and Russian haters."[4]

Under these circumstances, it was natural to turn to the CIA, especially when after January 1953 the director of central intelligence (DCI) was Allen Dulles, the secretary of state's brother.

Setting the Mold: Early Successes

Allen Dulles's wartime experience with the OSS had left him fascinated with the operational details of clandestine operations, including covert action, and relatively uninterested in the analytic side of intelligence. As a former foreign service officer, Wall Street lawyer, and manager of spies during the war, Dulles had a wealth of contacts, and he used them with enthusiasm on behalf of the new agency. He met with the press, gave speeches, and was a regular figure on the Washington social circuit. He had Eisenhower's confidence. With his brother as secretary of state, the personal connection between the two was more important than the institutional relations between State and CIA.

It is important to remember that the prevailing image of the CIA at the time was not just activist and anti-Communist, but also liberal. The United States not only would save the world from communism, it would also show the developing nations the way to peace and prosperity. NSC-141, written at the very end of the Truman administration, joined these objectives in a single sentence: "In Latin America we seek first and foremost an orderly political and economic development which will make the Latin American nations resistant to the internal growth of communism and to Soviet political warfare."[5] This was the image of America's role that the American political establishment held, and it was reflected in the CIA, the best the United States had to offer.

Moreover, in 1953 just as the Iran operation was coming to a head, Dulles took a dramatic stand against Senator Joseph McCarthy and his Communist witch hunt. The State Department and even the military services had deferred to McCarthy, or sought to appease him, but Dulles denied McCarthy's charges publicly, fought off Senate subpoenas, and demanded that the senator make available to him any evidence of Communist influence in the CIA.

Within a month, McCarthy backed down. Virtually alone of the government's foreign affairs agencies, the CIA stared McCarthy down. In doing so it gained luster as a place where independence and creativity were encouraged, not stifled. The McCarthy episode also made a success in Iran all the more important, for success would demonstrate a better way to roll back communism than searching for it in the CIA. It would ensure that the senator's mouth remained closed.

In the near panic of the early cold war, Washington officials were bound to see events in both Iran and Guatemala through the prism of anticommunism. When instability per se anywhere in the world seemed to offer fertile ground for Soviet meddling, it is no surprise that reformers and revolutionaries looked the same, or that trying to differentiate between the two seemed idle.

That perspective is most striking in the instance of Guatemala. In 1944 a student revolt brought down the regime of General Jorge Ubico, a traditional *caudillo* strong man. His successor, Juan José Arévalo, set in train a number of social changes in Guatemala.[6] To many observers these were the signs of a democracy in the making, in a region where democracy had scarcely been the practice. To others, however, the same events looked like a dangerous drift toward communism.

In the elections of 1950, Arévalo was succeeded by Arbenz, his minister of defense and a professional army officer. It was Arbenz who aroused Washington's concern over communism. Arbenz denied that he was a Communist, and the party itself in 1954 was tiny—about four thousand members in a country of three million—though it did have some force in the fledgling labor movement. Two years before, it had changed its name to the Guatemalan Labor party (PGT), in significant part because the word "Communist" was too unpopular.

However, those on the lookout for Communists in Arbenz's entourage could find them. His campaign manager, José Manuel Fortuny, was founder of the Guatemalan Communist party and editor of its newspaper, while the secretary-general of the country's General Confederation of Workers (CGTG) was a self-proclaimed Communist who took the CGTG into the Communist International labor organization, the World Federation of Labor, in 1951. Arbenz accepted Fortuny and the Communists as part of his ruling coalition, but they were minor partners. Party members played a significant role in the land reform agency but were excluded from the Ministry of Foreign Affairs, the national police, and most other domestic agencies. The party had only four of fifty-two deputies in the 1953–54 Guatemalan congress, and Arbenz never appointed a Communist to his cabinet.[7]

In 1953 neither Eisenhower nor John Foster Dulles knew much about Latin America. But they knew enough to be concerned, especially about Guatemala. Eisenhower sent his brother Milton to the region. Both Milton Eisenhower's report and a memorandum attached to it when it was presented to the Cabinet treated Guatemala almost as a lost cause. The report said: "One nation has succumbed to Communist infiltration." The memorandum argued, "The most important question facing the Cabinet is to make up its mind that Latin America is important to the United States . . . timely action was desirable to prevent Communism from spreading seriously beyond Guatemala."[8]

Nationalists and Communist "Tools": Iran

In Iran the danger seemed even more critical. A New York *Times* editorial in February 1953 testified to the depth of American concern over Iran: with Eisenhower's election, "the day of sleep-walking is over . . . the policy of vigilance replacing the Pollyanna diplomacy is evident."[9] The American perspective on Iran was dominated by geography: That country shared a long border with the Soviet Union; it could be seen as the gateway to the Persian Gulf. Since the middle of the nineteenth century, Britain and Russia had contested for predominance in Iran, and Britain had been decisive in placing the shah's father, Reza Shah, on the throne in 1921.

The first crisis of the cold war had ensued in early 1946 when the Soviets refused to withdraw their troops from wartime positions in the Iranian region of Azerbaijan. They had left by year's end, after a sharp exchange between Washington and Moscow, but U.S. officials took it for granted that Moscow hankered after Persian Gulf ports. In 1947 the Truman administration had acted to refurbish its links to Iran that ran back to the Persian Gulf Command of World War II. Washington established the U.S. Army Mission Headquarters (ARMISH) in Teheran, to rebuild the Iranian army and gendarmerie.

British dominance, especially in Iran's oil industry, also made Britain a natural target of nationalist sentiment. From the time the British admiralty converted from coal to oil in 1913, Iranian oil had been important to Britain and Britain had sustained a virtual monopoly over that oil. During World War I, Britain first frustrated Teheran's attempt to control Iranian territory, including the oil province of Khuzistan, then reneged on its commitment to pay the Teheran government 16 percent of the oil profits because that government could not control marauding tribesmen![10]

In 1932 Reza Shah canceled the British concessions, but the company, Anglo-Iranian Oil Company (AIOC), in which the British government held a majority interest, eventually came to a new agreement. This one, for sixty years, was more favorable to Iran, but still AIOC seemed to Iranians imperious, especially in its reluctance to train Iranian technicians.

By 1950 the issue was not whether nationalist attitudes would dominate Iran—the only nonnationalists were the ethnic and tribal minorities who feared a strong central government—but how that nationalism would be defined. The older generation, conditioned to British manipulation of their politics, was inclined to see that dominance as a fact of life, but this was not true of the younger generation who had seen Britain lose control of India and Palestine and was watching the British position teeter in Egypt.

When anti-British nationalism broke through, however, the

politician it brought to power was Mohammed Mossadeq, a somewhat unlikely seventy-year-old wealthy landowner. The chain of events that made him prime minister ran back to 1947, when Iran again sought to renegotiate the oil agreement. For Iran the issue was eliminating Britain's ability to manipulate Iranian politics through the oil industry; as a result, calls for nationalization, not prominent early in the negotiations, became stronger and stronger. Britain and the AIOC, however, regarded the negotiations as bargaining as usual; never subtle either in manipulating or interpreting Iranian politics, AIOC was more concerned about dollar profits and the precedent of a new deal with Iran.

Apparently, AIOC finally did relent and agree to many of the Iranian demands short of nationalization.[11] But it was too late. Before the prime minister, who had been forced to hold off pressure for nationalization, could present the new, more generous terms to Iran's parliament, he was assassinated. Within days, a nationalization bill was rushed through. And within three weeks Mossadeq was prime minister at the head of a government of the National Front, a loose grouping bound together by a commitment to nationalize the oil industry. He prepared to carry out that commitment.

The Truman administration was at first inclined to support Mossadeq, and the major American media also were sympathetic to him—*Time* magazine named him its "Man of the Year" for 1952. In fact, Iran's Communist party, the Tudeh, constantly sought to identify Mossadeq with the United States and American policy with that of Britain. Reflecting on a 1951 meeting, then Secretary of State Dean Acheson later wrote that Mossadeq was not a revolutionary but rather "essentially a rich, reactionary, feudal-minded Persian inspired by a fanatical hatred of the British and a desire to expel them and all their works from the country regardless of cost."[12]

Yet as time went on and Mossadeq's situation became more desperate, in Washington's eyes he came to look much as Arbenz was to look later: if not a Communist, at least their tool. Although the Tudeh had been outlawed in 1949, it operated more and more openly through its front organizations. Unwilling and perhaps unable to repress the feudal right, Mossadeq felt himself unable to move strongly against the Tudeh. In July 1952 he accepted its support, reluctantly, while still refusing to join with it in a popular front government.

That step was enough to confirm the worst fears of the Americans. Suspecting that Mossadeq was a Communist, Washington easily found signs that seemed to confirm its suspicions. When Mossadeq rigged an election in May 1953—never mind that all Iranian elections were rigged to some degree—that looked to Eisenhower like a clear Communist tactic.

Private Interest and Public Policy

In both Iran and Guatemala, Washington policy making mixed private interests with strategic concerns to a much greater extent than was true of later covert action. In Iran, the private interests were British, those of Anglo-Iranian. Not that Americans, either oil men or officials, had any fondness for the company, for they did not. They regarded it with a cordial hatred, seeing it as a colonial holdover, anti-American as well as anti-Iranian. Yet the more the United States turned in opposition to Mossadeq, the more it looked to Iranians as the ally of the British if not of AIOC.

Shortly after the nationalization decree, President Truman signed National Security Council decision NSC 107/2, "making clear both our recognition of the rights of sovereign states to control their natural resources and the importance we attach to international contractual relationship."[13] Accordingly, the United States pressed for resumed negotiations. The U.S. ambassador at the time, Henry Grady, regarded Iranian fears of British manipulation as exaggerated but also recognized that those fears, not economics, were at the center of the negotiations.[14]

AIOC, however, barely moved beyond its last offer before nationalization. Instead, in July 1951 it closed its refinery at Abadan, which Iran took over in September. Only the acrimony increased: since Iran was unable to run the Abadan refinery at full capacity without British technicians, no one was making any money from Iranian oil. Iran thus skated on the brink of financial collapse, or such was the conventional wisdom in Washington, reinforced by London.

In the autumn of 1952, the CIA's British "cousins," the Secret Intelligence Service (SIS) first invited Roosevelt to London to discuss a joint action to overthrow Mossadeq, a plan code-named AJAX. Exactly what role AIOC played in stimulating AJAX remains unclear, but Roosevelt did meet with representatives of the company. For AIOC the ultimate result was mixed: although saved from total nationalization, in a 1954 agreement it lost its monopoly at both the operating and purchasing ends—the former to the National Iranian Oil Company and the latter to a partnership of western companies in which AIOC counted for 40 percent.[15]

United Fruit's position in Guatemala was even more dominant than that of Anglo-Iranian in Iran. A 1936 deal negotiated with Guatemalan strong man Ubico made United Fruit (whose negotiator was a young international lawyer with Sullivan and Cromwell named John Foster Dulles) far and away the largest landowner in Guatemala. With a clutch of tax concessions and a near monopoly on transportation, United Fruit—*la frutera,* to Guatemalans—all but controlled the country's international commerce.[16]

In these circumstances the beginning of the end for Arbenz was his proudest moment—the Agrarian Reform Law of 1952. Under it, uncultivated portions of large plantations were expropriated and United Fruit lost about two-thirds of the 575,000 acres it owned in Guatemala. Arbenz offered over $600,000 for the largest chunk, precisely the value United Fruit had declared for tax purposes; in April 1954 the State Department issued a formal complaint, demanding over $15 million in compensation for that estate, arguing that international law superseded domestic legislation and required "just" compensation.

United Fruit was no ordinary company in its relations with Washington, so that the web of private stakes and public interests in this case is exceptionally difficult to disentangle. The history of financial connections between the company and the men in government provides plenty of fodder for the conspiracy theories so popular with analysts on both the far left and the far right.

Theories aside, United Fruit did get back its land and privileged position after Arbenz was overthrown. Nor was the company bashful in telling its connections that he should be overthrown. It hired as its lobbyist Thomas Corcoran, "Tommy the Cork," a close confidant of Franklin Roosevelt and a man with connections all over Washington, prominent among whom was "Beetle" Smith, DCI and later Eisenhower's undersecretary of state, whom Corcoran insisted he later got appointed to United Fruit's board of directors.[17]

Triggering Intervention

In both Iran and Guatemala, the triggers to American intervention were actions that seemed to confirm the worst fears of both senior officials in Washington and Americans in general. In Guatemala, the trigger was specific: Guatemala's turning to the Soviet Union for military assistance. In Iran, the trigger was less specific, more a pattern of actions that persuaded Washington that Mossadeq was becoming a tool of the Communists. In both cases, however, the triggering events were just that: last straws, not the motivations for launching covert action. By then, plans for intervention were well underway. What they awaited was a signal of final approval from the president.

After 1948 the United States had refused to sell weaponry to Guatemala, the official reason being that Guatemala had declined to sign the 1947 Rio Treaty on inter-American security until its dispute with Honduras over the territory of Belize was settled. After Arbenz's election, the United States used its influence to stop arms deals with Mexico, Cuba, Argentina, and Switzerland.[18] Faced with neighbors hostile to his government, Arbenz turned to the Soviet Union in March 1953. Moscow quickly responded that it would arrange for a shipment of Czech arms. It was, however, more than a year later, on March 13, 1954, that the Swedish ship *Alfhem* arrived in Guatemala with small arms, artillery, and ammunition.

From 1951 to 1953, Iran's Mossadeq had continually appealed to the United States for aid, and he did receive some, but the amounts—some $20 million per year—were small by comparison with Iran's economic woes.[19] In the spring of 1952, Mossadeq began negotiating with the Soviet Union for the sale of some Iranian oil and to talk about the necessity of Iran remaining neutral in the cold war. These actions no doubt were, in Mossadeq's eyes, negotiating ploys for the benefit of Britain—and the United States—but they were enough to set off alarm bells in Washington.

By the end of 1952, Mossadeq's political base was visibly splintering. He had come to power on the passion of the oil issue, so his initial support was strong but inarticulate and ill organized. With the landowning right temporarily in eclipse, his immediate problem was the army, over which the shah retained primary control. In July 1952 Mossadeq took the war portfolio for himself and demanded the right to rule by decree for six months. The Majlis, Iran's parliament, however, influenced by the shah and a perception that Britain and the United States opposed Mossadeq, voted him out of office. When Mossadeq did relinquish his portfolio, rioting broke out, led by the National Front but including the Tudeh. Mossadeq's resignation was rescinded, and his ally, Ayatollah Abd al-Qasem Kashani, became president of the Majlis.[20]

The rioting was distinctly anti-American in tone; the United States was accused of being niggardly in aid and pro-British in sentiment. Even if the violence was ostensibly pro-Mossadeq, it was unsettling for him, evidence of the tiger he might have to ride, like it or not. In October 1952 he felt strong enough to dissolve Parliament entirely. Yet he suffered a series of defections from his National Front, the most serious of which was Kashani's in January 1953. Kashani brought to the front support from lower middle-class, more religious Iranians, which translated into the ability to create and control street mobs. Political outcomes were not necessarily determined in the streets, but the streets were critical as the symbols of political momentum.

Mossadeq was becoming more dependent on the Tudeh for control of the streets. Loy Henderson, who had replaced Grady as the U.S. ambassador in late 1951, believed Mossadeq was naive about communism even as Mossadeq resisted Tudeh overtures. State Department reports in 1952 saw the shift of the Tudeh from opposition to collaboration through the lens of Czechoslovakia—the first step to entering government and thence to Communist takeover.[21] In early 1953, Henderson's embassy rendered in cable-ese its own pithy summary of Mossadeq's shrinking political base: he had "thrown out British; emasculated Majlis; eliminated Senate; forced all well known politicians out of public life; deposed all prominent civilian and military leaders; sent various members royal family into exile."[22]

Even before Eisenhower took office, Mossadeq, hat in hand, had appealed directly to him for economic assistance in a letter. When he received a noncommittal reply, he tried again, in a letter dated May 28, 1953.[23] The letter asked for Washington's help in lifting the British boycott of Iranian oil and for economic assistance; behind the request was an implicit threat that the alternative was communism, a threat made vivid by the Tudeh's "Yankee-Go-Home" campaign, a campaign almost certainly undertaken with Mossadeq's acquiescence and certainly so seen in American eyes.

Given the relationships between the Dulleses and the doctrine of "plausible denial," it is impossible to pinpoint the specific authorization of either the Iranian or the Guatemalan operations. A few quick conversations between the brothers substituted for a long process of interagency review.[24] Planning for intervention in Iran proceeded throughout the spring of 1953 as the newly installed Eisenhower administration became convinced that Mossadeq represented a Communist threat. SIS officials met with their CIA counterparts in Washington in February, and Allen Dulles became an adherent of the plan.[25]

The critical review took place in late June, probably on June 22.[26] Roosevelt reported on his recent visits to Iran.[27] The indirect Soviet threat represented by Mossadeq and the Tudeh was "indeed genuine, dangerous and imminent," but the Iranian people and army would back the shah in a showdown. In response to questions from Allen Dulles, Roosevelt stressed that the plan would be cheap and would not, he believed, fail. If it did, "Iran would fall to the Russians, and the effect on the rest of the Middle East could be disastrous." But, he added, "these are the same consequences we face if we do nothing."

Foster Dulles polled the other senior officials—including Henderson, Defense Secretary Charles Wilson, and several other State Department officials—most of whom reluctantly agreed. AJAX was on its way, although in keeping with his practice during wartime, Eisenhower apparently reserved the right to call it off. On the twenty-ninth the president responded to Mossadeq's letter: the United States would neither increase aid nor buy Iranian oil.[28]

The coup against Arbenz took longer to develop, its roots going back to the final days of the Truman administration. Early planning was limited to an extremely small circle, and so the sequence of events is hazy, but the following approximates what happened.[29] United Fruit officials, including Corcoran, had been pressing Washington for action. In the summer of 1952, Nicaraguan dictator Anastasio Somoza visited Washington and met with a group of State Department officials, including the assistant secretary for inter-American affairs, Edward Miller. Somoza boasted that if Washington gave him enough weapons, "I'll clean up Guatemala for you in no time." Miller did not take the boasting seriously, but Somoza also met with Truman.

Apparently, Truman was sufficiently interested to take further soundings and to pass these reports on to "Beetle" Smith, then DCI, bypassing State. The CIA then arranged for some arms, labeled agricultural machinery, to be loaded aboard a United Fruit freighter. Miller, however, caught wind of the plan and appealed to David Bruce, the undersecretary of state. Bruce alerted his boss, Acheson, who hastily persuaded Truman to call off the plan.[30] The United Fruit freighter was redirected to the Panama Canal Zone, where the weapons probably were unloaded.

This account seems strange even by the standards of covert action, and so may not accurately reflect what happened. Smith himself may have had doubts about the chances of success in 1952, or Guatemala's neighbors other than Nicaragua may have gotten cold feet about an armed conflict on their borders.

Given the temper of the incoming Eisenhower administration, new plans resurfaced almost immediately. The Central American states continued to construct an anti-Arbenz coalition, and United Fruit continued to press its case on Washington. The role of Adolf A. Berle stands as an example of the emerging consensus about Guatemala. Berle, one of FDR's New Deal brain trusters, had been involved in policy making toward Latin America for years; he had good contacts all over the hemisphere and was an adviser to Adlai Stevenson's presidential campaign. In March 1953, after meeting with Latin American leaders, Berle presented a sixteen-page memorandum on Guatemala to Eisenhower's International Information Activities Committee, directed by C. D. Jackson, a man then on leave from Time Incorporated whose experience in psychological warfare ran back to World War II.

Berle's memo focused on the "precise problem of how to clear out the Communists."[31] It rejected direct intervention and warned against organizing regional states to use force because that would only identify the United States with Nicaragua, that "symbol of corruption," yet the most logical leader of a regional coalition. Berle suggested political measures, including "a good deal of quiet work" in the Guatemalan army. He also mentioned in passing the possibility of "American support of a Guatemalan group which would do its own work," an alternative Berle felt he did not have "adequate information to include or exclude."

Arbenz's predecessor, Arévalo, had been the object of twenty-five coup attempts in six years, and Arbenz's fate was similar. In one attempt, in March 1953, rebels seized Salamá, a provincial capital near Guatemala City, the national capital, and held it for seventeen hours before troops loyal to the government retook the city and captured the rebels. At the rebels' ensuing trial, United Fruit was found to have contributed some $50,000 to the plotters.

It was in that same month, March 1953, that Arbenz turned to the Soviet Union for assistance. That spring and summer, as United Fruit properties were expropriated, official Washington moved toward a decision to topple Arbenz. By all accounts, Allen Dulles was the driving force in securing approval of the plan, now code-named PBSUCCESS—"PB" was CIA code for Guatemala, just as "IA" signified Angola. As Richard Bissell, who ran the Bay of Pigs operation seven years later as the CIA's deputy director for plans (DDP), recalled: Dulles "was closer to the Guatemala operation than he was to the Bay of Pigs. . . . The Guatemalan operation was authorized at a higher level at the very beginning, like the Bay of Pigs."[32]

In the late summer or early fall of 1953, the planning was

reviewed by a group composed of Allen Dulles, Smith, then moved to undersecretary of state, Wilson, the secretary of defense, and Jackson, Eisenhower's adviser on psychological warfare.[33] No doubt the timing was no coincidence, for this was when AJAX was having its initial success.[34] Those senior officials who a few months earlier had harbored quiet qualms about AJAX's risks and chances would have found it harder to oppose SUCCESS.

With this group prepared to go forward, Dulles took the plan to the president, estimating that there was a 40 percent chance of success. Again, Eisenhower apparently gave his tentative approval but made clear that he had not given the green light to actual operations. That go-ahead did not come until the *Alfhem* arrived in Guatemala.

Building PBSUCCESS

Washington also changed ambassadors to Guatemala in August 1953, at least a sign that pressure on Arbenz was accelerating. Rudolf Schoenfeld, a soft-spoken man who had remained on friendly terms with Arbenz, was recalled. His replacement was John Peurifoy, an appointment by the previous Democratic administration and then serving as U.S. ambassador to Greece. His appointment was applauded by the New York *Times* as a "change in the asserted passivity with which the United States has watched the growth of Communist influence."[35]

By no account was he a man of intellect or subtlety—the columnist Drew Pearson wrote that he "did not seem to have much imagination."[36] What he did have was flair and a reputation for zealously fighting Communists in Greece. He may also have been attractive to the Eisenhower administration as a way to put more distance between a Republican president and PBSUCCESS in case the operation went awry.[37]

Ike's "tentative" approval set the CIA in motion. Dulles put

Frank Wisner, the DDP, in command of the operation. Wisner, in turn, chose Colonel Albert Haney to head the special task force in charge of the operation. Haney, who reported directly to Wisner, had recent experience not in Latin America but in Asia, as the CIA's station chief in South Korea, where he built guerrilla networks inside hostile territory. Haney's deputy for political action—that is, propaganda—was E. Howard Hunt, later prominent in the Bay of Pigs and later still in the Watergate break-in.

By November 1953 Haney had received Dulles's permission to establish the task force with its own chain of command outside Washington—the first time the CIA had done so and the beginning of a pattern for later covert actions. PBSUCCESS had become the Agency's primary business. It was installed at the Opa-Locka Marine Air Base outside Miami. The project's leaders in Washington—Wisner, Bissell, Tracy Barnes—met several times a week with Dulles, daily in Bissell's office.[38]

Colonel J. C. King, the division chief, was in effect sidestepped by the task force. When responsibility for covert operations in Latin America passed from the FBI to the CIA, King had transferred with it. He was regarded as more attached to espionage and counterintelligence than action, hence not the man for PBSUCCESS.

The plan stressed psychological warfare more than direct military action. It was sleight-of-hand. The key to Arbenz's survival, like Mossadeq's, was the loyalty of the army, which became the first propaganda target. A June CIA memorandum to the president described the effort well, if not elegantly, even though the memorandum was written by the acting head of current intelligence, a man who probably was unaware of the role of his CIA "colleagues":

> The action of Colonel Castillo Armas is not in any sense a conventional military operation. . . . The entire effort is . . . more dependent upon psychological impact rather than actual military strength . . . to

> create and maintain for a short time the *impression* of very substantial military strength.[39]

A force of some three hundred mercenaries and Guatemalan dissidents would divide, half to engage in sabotage and the other half to pose as the " 'spearhead' of a fictitious invasion force."[40]

If Arbenz were to be forced out, the United States needed a successor, and the CIA had begun choosing one the previous summer. Castillo Armas emerged as the candidate. He and Ydígoras Fuentes—a former general and official under Ubico who had run a poor second to Arbenz in the 1950 elections—had formed an alliance in March 1952. Castillo Armas was to take command of the counterrevolutionary forces and become provisional president; Ydígoras Fuentes would stay out of the armed conflict and thus retain a "civilian" image suitable to a presidential candidate in the ensuing elections.

However, the State Department regarded Ydígoras Fuentes as too reactionary to be popular, with too much the visage of a Spanish noble to be credible. In Hunt's words: "You don't rally a country made up of *mestizos* with a Spanish don."[41]

United Fruit had its own candidate, but he, sick with throat cancer, deferred to Castillo Armas, and Nicaragua's Somoza also seconded the nomination. Castillo Armas was also attractive to the United States for some combination, depending on the account, of his charisma and dark good looks, his military status—which added plausibility to the invasion as a military operation undertaken by dissident Guatemalan forces—and his willingness to agree with American aims, including those of United Fruit.[42]

In October 1953, Castillo Armas was brought secretly to Florida to meet with King, and two months later, on December 23, he announced his new "National Liberation Movement" in Honduras. The CIA had agreed to provide him with $3 million and to help him build small paramilitary units. For its part,

United Fruit offered to smuggle arms on his behalf into Guatemala through its port facilities.

The aim of PBSUCCESS was to frighten Arbenz into stepping down, not actually to overthrow him by force. Yet both the logic of the plan and its size began to worry Haney's superiors. Even Haney admitted that the U.S. marines might have to be sent if all else failed. For their part, Wisner and King remained concerned that the size of the operation would make it impossible to keep the American role secret. There were a hundred security people alone at Opa-Locka.

Moreover, the CIA's first efforts to subvert officers loyal to Arbenz came to naught; Opa-Locka concluded that too many officers either were loyal or were cautious careerists as yet unwilling to risk an open break with Arbenz. The scale of SUCCESS increased. The CIA had created a dummy arms company, the International Armament Corporation (InterArmco), to serve as a conduit for arms to the rebels in Nicaragua and Honduras, by then called the liberation army. Most of these arms were distributed through France's Field, a little-used airfield in the Panama Canal Zone. The CIA also planned to plant Soviet made weapons in Guatemala just before the invasion, to giv credence to the charge that the Soviets were trying to establis a foothold there.[43]

In addition to InterArmco, the CIA used a variety of ot dummy organizations to send planes to the rebels. In Decem 1953, for example, Dulles persuaded a friend, an American b nessman, to create a charitable foundation that would, in sell war surplus fighters to CIA front companies in the C bean. National Guard units in the American South lo planes to the CIA, which then "rented" them to Nicarag one dollar each.[44] The liberation "air force" of a dozen p however makeshift, was still enough to frighten Guatem

The origin of these planes could not be kept secret sinc had never appeared in Central American air forces. Mo

Haney had to recruit American pilots to fly them. King sent one of his deputies, who also was a relative of Dulles, to visit Opa-Locka in early 1954. He is reported to have told Haney: "What Teddy Roosevelt did in Panama will pale by comparison to what you're planning to do in Guatemala."[46] Dulles, however, apparently took his own trip to Florida and came away satisfied with the progress of PBSUCCESS.

On the propaganda front, Hunt and his colleagues worked in Opa-Locka recording a series of "terror broadcasts" about the future of Guatemala under Arbenz, preparing pamphlets on the same theme for distribution there and training Guatemalan exiles in the use of radio propaganda.[47] What the CIA did covertly, the U.S. Information Agency (USIA) did more openly. It furnished a flood of pamphlets, recordings, and newspaper articles, all aimed at demonstrating Arbenz to be a Communist.[48]

All these operations required facilities, and by February 1954, with Somoza's agreement, the CIA was building bases for training in weapons, demolition, and sabotage in Nicaragua (one site was on a Somoza plantation, El Tamarindo), an airstrip at Puerto Cabezas on Nicaragua's Atlantic coast, and a number of hidden radio stations in Nicaragua and other neighboring countries.

In late January the predictable happened: the plot leaked to the public. A Castillo Armas courier betrayed the cause and delivered the liberation's plans to Arbenz. On January 29 Guatemalan papers published correspondence among Castillo Armas, Ydígoras, and Somoza that revealed almost everything: the role of Somoza and the camps in Nicaragua; the help from a number of countries, including the "government of the North"; even the invasion routes![49]

Yet, surprisingly, the episode was only a minor hitch in the CIA's plans. State denied the charges of U.S. involvement as "ridiculous and untrue," adding, "It is the policy of the United States not to intervene in the internal affairs of other nations."[50] And most of the American media were more concerned about Communists than about the proprieties of American action.

Time magazine, in a typical response, shrugged off the revelations as "fanciful . . . less of a plot than a scenario . . . masterminded in Moscow and designed to divert the attention from Guatemala as the Western Hemisphere's Red problem child."[51] The CIA continued almost as if nothing had happened. PBSUCCESS rolled on.

"Success"

In both Iran and Guatemala, events moved rapidly once Washington decided to pull the trigger, an indication of just how vulnerable both Iran and Guatemala were to covert interventions by the United States (and how tempting it was for the CIA and Washington policy makers to see them, in hindsight, as successes easily replicated elsewhere).

After Mossadeq had opened negotiations with the Soviets and Eisenhower had given the go-ahead, while still reserving the right to call off the plan, Roosevelt entered Iran, in mid-July 1953. Roosevelt, an OSS veteran and grandson of Teddy Roosevelt, operated out of second-floor offices in the small, drab U.S. embassy. He began with only four other CIA men in Teheran and, more important, a handful of Iranian agents that had been run by the British SIS.

Roosevelt's first problem was convincing a young shah to act against Mossadeq. In Washington Roosevelt had assured the Dulleses that the shah was ready to take decisive action. In fact, as Henderson knew and Roosevelt soon learned, the thirty-four-year-old shah was wavering. To buck him up, Roosevelt devised a plan worthy of any spy novel, a plan that captures the spirit of the enterprise even if it has been embellished some in the recollections of participants.

On August 1 Roosevelt was driven to the shah's palace, lying on the floor of the car covered by a blanket so as not to be recognized. To prove he represented Eisenhower and Churchill—to demonstrate his *bona fides,* in the language of the trade—he quickly told the shah to watch for two signals. One would be a phrase in a speech Eisenhower was to give in San Francisco; the other would be the word "exactly" inserted into the BBC's announcement of midnight the next night. Roosevelt had arranged these two signals using the British communication network on Cyprus.[52]

The initial plan was a small, direct operation more in the style of the British SIS than the CIA's pattern later in Guatemala: the shah would fly to a remote town on the Caspian Sea, leaving behind two decrees, one dismissing Mossadeq, the other naming Fazlollah Zahedi his successor. Two Iranian businessmen, the main SIS agents, were given some $100,000 in small Iranian notes to build a supporting mob from athletic club thugs and the poor of south Teheran.[53]

Meanwhile, Mossadeq, no longer reluctant, resorted to decree powers as the turmoil increased. He also resorted to visibly rigging the referendum on dissolving the Majlis, held August 3–15—the rigging that looked to Eisenhower like a "Communist" tactic. Voting was open, not secret, with Tudeh toughs getting out the vote; in Teheran the total was 101,396 for, 67 against. Playing his own Communist card, Mossadeq also thanked Moscow for improving relations and proposed a bilateral commission to settle outstanding differences. A New York *Times* editorial paralleled official Washington's gloomy prognosis: Mossadeq was "trying to eliminate the last citadel of opposition to his ambition by crushing the final vestiges of parliamentary government. . . . Iran [would] pass under a dictatorship which the communists support as a precursor of their own tyranny."[54]

Through intermediaries, Roosevelt finally convinced the shah to sign a decree dismissing Mossadeq and naming General Fazlollah Zahedi prime minister. The shah left for the relative safety of his palace on the Caspian Sea, leaving his signed decrees behind. The plan in motion, Roosevelt retired to a friend's house to await success.

The plan, however, had gone awry. The Imperial Palace Guard colonel who was to deliver the decrees and arrest Mossadeq was betrayed and was himself arrested by Mossadeq supporters. When the Americans heard Teheran Radio at 7 A.M. on August 16, instead of success they heard that "foreign elements," had attempted a coup, that the colonel had been arrested, and that Mossadeq thus had been compelled to take all power in his hands. (In fact, Mossadeq did have some legal ground since the constitution was unclear whether the shah had the power to dismiss the prime minister by royal decree.)

Tudeh mobs hit the street. The shah had fled to Baghdad on August 15, and then on to Rome, where Allen Dulles also arrived, from Zurich, in order to use embassy communications to find out what was afoot. Mossadeq ordered the Iranian chief of staff, General Tazhi Riahi, a Mossadeq loyalist, to arrest the plotters. Riahi's police searched in vain for Zahedi, who was in hiding at a rural family estate.

Ambassador Henderson, who had been, diplomatically, "on vacation" in Beirut—only two other diplomats at the embassy even knew of AJAX—returned in haste to a grim embassy. The mood was just as bleak in Washington; Smith ordered the CIA operatives home. Henderson, however, called on Mossadeq to threaten U.S. withdrawal of all its citizens from Iran—thus making Mossadeq appear incapable of governing—if Tudeh rioting did not stop. Mossadeq was in a bind: if he did not take action, the United States would turn to open hostility; but if he agreed, he ran the risk of losing control of the streets. He picked up the phone, in Henderson's presence, and ordered his chief of police to break up the gangs on the street.[55] The police and troops went gleefully to work. As the New York *Times* correspondent on the scene put it, they "swung into action . . . against rioting Tudeh partisans and Nationalist extremists. The troops appeared to be in a frenzy."[56]

The next morning, with "Yankee Go Home" chants being replaced by "Long Live the Shah," the tide turned. Roosevelt's Iranian SIS agents persuaded Kashani to send his people into the street—ironic in retrospect, since Kashani's people were the parents of what became, a generation later, the core of the Ayatollah Khomeini's support. The pro-shah mob was complete with giant zurkhaneh weight-lifters recruited from Teheran athletic clubs. One observer called it "probably the best advertised street fight in Middle Eastern history. . . . [It had the] appearance of casting, costuming, and issuing instructions to film a biblical epic's mob scene rather than preparing the overthrow of a government."[57]

This strange assemblage grew as it converged on Mossadeq's house. Zahedi's supporters carried him from hiding to a waiting tank for a ride through the center of Teheran. The Zahedi forces prevailed in two hours of fighting after Riahi's men ran out of ammunition; a hundred were estimated to have died and three hundred wounded in the fighting. Mossadeq slipped through the fighting but surrendered the next day, the twenty-first. Three days after the coup, the shah returned to Teheran to drink his toast to Roosevelt. Henderson assured the new regime of continued aid and of a $45 million emergency grant.

"Liberation" in Guatemala

The final overthrow of Arbenz in Guatemala was less zany, although it, too, had its tragicomic moment when the the colonel who had come to power as a result of the coup misread his lines and pledged to contine the war against the United States' designated-successor, Castillo Armas. Rather, Arbenz's end seemed almost inexorable. By the spring of 1954, in the context of visible U.S. hostility toward Arbenz, PBSUCCESS was a big program grinding on, ranging from paramilitary preparations to propaganda.

Throughout 1953 and until the invasion, the State Department was openly critical of Arbenz, accusing him of "unjust and discriminatory" actions and sending him a stream of terse formal complaints. The tenth Inter-American Conference of foreign ministers, held in Caracas in March 1954, was dominated by U.S. pressure to pass a resolution condemning "international communism." The resolution passed, but the conference was less than a resounding success for U.S. diplomacy: considerable arm twisting had been necessary, and Mexico and Argentina still abstained from the final vote (Guatemala, alone, voted "no").

On December 16, 1953, Peurifoy accepted an invitation to dinner with Arbenz, the only time the two men met during the ambassador's tenure. Their dinner turned into a heated conversation that lasted six hours. Afterward, Peurifoy sent Washington a cable that Eisenhower later credited as decisive in his decision to give the final go-ahead for PBSUCCESS: "Normal approaches probably will not work in Guatemala. The candle is burning slowly and surely, and it is only a matter of time before the large American interests will be forced out completely."[58]

Three months later, on March 13, the *Alfhem* arrived in Guatemala, and two days later the CIA confirmed the ship's cargo was weaponry. The next day the American NSC met. Allen Dulles argued that Arbenz's arsenal now posed a threat to his neighbors, and even to the Canal Zone. The NSC officially approved more aid to Castillo Armas, and Dulles set the invasion date for mid-June—before, officials hoped, the new weapons could be distributed. Indeed, the immediate issue was whether it might not already be too late. Foster Dulles fretted that the weapons might have "knocked the props out" from the project. His brother assured him that was not the case, although he doubted that "we can pull it off next month." Checking its premise about Guatemala's army, the CIA concluded that

"Arbenz would not be backed by his army in the event of an anti-communist revolution."[59]

Publicly, Eisenhower said at a press conference on the nineteenth that the weapons shipment could lead to the establishment of a "Communist dictatorship . . . on this continent." Over the next few days Secretary Dulles repeated this message to reporters, documenting it with State Department estimates of Guatemala's military capacity; he asserted that "a government in which Communist influence is very strong has come into a position to dominate militarily the Central American area."[60]

On June 18, 1954, the rebel radio station operating in Honduras and Nicaragua, "Voice of Liberation," announced that Castillo Armas and his troops had invaded. That was true, but only technically. Several trucks, with Castillo Armas in front in a battered station wagon, crossed the border unopposed and bivouacked six miles inside the border.[61] The army was a ragtag assemblage of a hundred and fifty recruits; its "invasion" was mostly smoke and mirrors.

The rebel air force, its pilots recruited by the CIA, flew missions in cumbersome World War II-vintage fighter-bombers. Since weight was at a premium, pilots substituted hand grenades and homemade bombs made of dynamite sticks—anything that would make a loud noise and a lot of smoke—for heavier real bombs.[62] Targets were chosen for the same effect; for instance, one homemade bomb dropped from a small plane on an oil tank created a fire that could be seen for miles away.

Guatemalans had the impression they were living in London during the blitz. They began referring to the rebel air force's planes as *sulfatos*—Spanish for "laxative"—because of their debilitating effect. Meanwhile, the Voice of Liberation did all it could to feed rumors of the rebels' strength. It invented troops and battles. A typical broadcast said: "At our command post here in the jungle we are unable to confirm or deny the report that Castillo Armas has an army of five thousand men."[63] Of course there was no report—and scarcely any army.

The great concern of CIA officers at Opa-Locka was that their charade would be revealed if Arbenz put his own air force into the air. Overflights would reveal how small the rebel army actually was; moreover, its own air force was vulnerable in the air, and the army itself could have been destroyed by a few well-placed bombs. On June 20 Haney phoned Dulles to tell him that the rebels could keep no more than four of their planes operating.

Accordingly, CIA propaganda sought to feed Arbenz's mistrust of his military, especially his air force. Voice of Liberation broadcast accounts of brave Soviet fliers taking their planes with them as they defected to the West. One Guatemalan pilot was persuaded to follow their example and desert Arbenz. The Voice of Liberation then persuaded him to tape an appeal to his fellow airmen.

The results were almost too good to be true. In David Phillips's words: "From that moment the Guatemalan air force was grounded. Arbenz, fearing his pilots would defect with their planes, did not permit the flight of a single military aircraft for the duration of the conflict."[64]

Yet despite all the propaganda, the "war" was a stalemate, and both the CIA officers and their Guatemalan colleagues feared that the bluff would be exposed. Moreover, the Arbenz government had insisted on pressing its complaints in the U.N. Security Council. It was time for one final stratagem.

In Washington, Eisenhower met with the Dulleses and Henry Holland, the assistant secretary of state, to consider Somoza's offer to transfer two fighter-bombers to the rebels, but only if Washington would replace them. Holland opposed the transfer, arguing that the action, if it became known, would be interpreted by Latin Americans as "intervention in Guatemala's internal affairs."[65] The president asked Allen Dulles what Castillo Armas's chances were without the planes: "about zero." And with them: "about 20 percent." Eisenhower assented; the United States committed itself one more step.

CIA officers met with their rebel counterparts. Their plan was a final attempt at intimidating Arbenz. For all the broadcasts and talk of *sulfatos,* Guatemala City itself had not been bombed. On Friday, June 25, the most venturesome of the rebel pilots dropped a single bomb in the parade ground of the largest military encampment in the city. No one was hurt, but the theatrics were exactly as intended: the huge bang was followed by an ominous plume of black smoke. Guatemalans began fleeing the capital.

Two days later, the Voice of Liberation announced that two columns of rebel soldiers were converging on the capital. That was followed by simulated messages to rebel commanders: "To Commander X, to Commander X. Sorry, we cannot provide the five hundred additional soldiers you want. No more than three hundred are available; they will be joining you at noon tomorrow."[66] In fact, Castillo Armas was still just inside the border, there was no invasion, there were hardly three soldiers available, let alone three hundred, and the roads near the capital were clogged with fleeing civilians, not advancing rebel soldiers.

The ruse worked on a tired, dispirited Arbenz. He made *his* fateful error, ordering army officers to distribute arms to peasants and workers. The officers refused, instead demanding that Arbenz resign or come to terms with Castillo Armas. Arbenz knew he could not continue without the support of his commanders. He met with the chief of armed forces, Colonel Carlos Enrique Díaz, and said he would turn the government over to him provided there were no negotiations with Castillo Armas. Díaz readily agreed, for he had supported the revolution and opposed the invasion as much as Arbenz. At 9 P.M. on June 27, Arbenz announced his resignation and the agreement in a nationwide radio broadcast. He then drove to the Mexican embassy to seek asylum; some six hundred of his supporters did likewise at other embassies. The largest battle of the "war" cost but seventeen lives.

PBSUCCESS was a success, although not without one more

last-minute hitch before Castillo Armas became part of the ruling junta. On July 7 the junta selected him provisional president, with elections scheduled for early October. Castillo Armas's National Committee for Defense Against Communism banned all political parties and screened all the candidates. Castillo Armas was the only officially sanctioned candidate. Leaving nothing to chance, the ballot was not secret, with government officials staffing the polling places. Of 486,000 votes cast, all but 400 were for Castillo Armas.

Command, Control, and Congress

At the time of Iran and Guatemala, "plausible denial" governed the process of deciding on covert action in the executive branch. It had seemed imperative that the hand of Washington not be revealed during the CIA's intervention in the 1948 Italian elections, and the principle became dogma: covert action should be undertaken so as to enable Washington to argue plausibly that the United States was not involved; and if the U.S. role became impossible to hide, at least the president should be spared direct implication in the program.[67]

Neither the Guatemalan nor the Iranian operation remained a complete mystery, certainly not in their targets, but the fig leaf of plausible denial could be maintained. When Kim Roosevelt returned from Iran, President Eisenhower was careful not to meet with him, and the president publicly proclaimed ignorance of the whole affair for the next two decades.[68] Allen Dulles was not above a little discreet publicity for his Agency, and the CIA fed a romantic account of AJAX to the *Saturday Evening Post.*[69] That was widely read in Teheran, but as the best book on Iran, written by Richard Cottam, noted in 1966, "In the United States it passed almost unnoticed."[70]

PBSUCCESS was also one of the administration's best kept

secrets, despite lavish praise for the coup makers. Secretary of State Dulles and James Hagerty, Eisenhower's press secretary, advised the president to react moderately to the coup in public lest the U.S. hand be revealed. At his first press conference afterward, however, Eisenhower said it would be "just deceitful" of him to hide his satisfaction. When accepting the credentials of the new Guatemalan ambassador—a man who had held the same job under Ubico—the president waxed eloquent: "The people of Guatemala, in a magnificent effort, have liberated themselves from the shackles of international Communist direction."[71]

The president, however, kept at arms' length from the Guatemalan operation; his memoirs admit only that the United States loaned two planes to Castillo Armas.[72] Moreover, Washington took pains to cover its tracks. The State Department published its own review of the Arbenz period; the title indicates its conclusions: *Penetration of the Political Institutions of Guatemala by the International Communist Movement.* In 1957 State commissioned a second study, *A Case Study of Communist Penetration: Guatemala,* to clear up any loose ends left by the first. The 1954 study, for instance, labeled Arbenz's movement "short of the full strength of militant Communism." The second referred to it as "alien despotism."[73]

Yet as plausible denial protected the administration, by its nature it made for informality—and looseness—in the internal review, a looseness that is plain to see in the cases of Iran and Guatemala. In both instances, the record of authorization is murky not just because time has passed and participants died. The Eisenhower administration was, after all, a tidy one that prized clear organization; it also existed before duplicating machines made officials reluctant to commit secrets to paper and scrambler phones made it easy to do business without paper. Rather, the informality reflected the combination of plausible denial and the unique position of the Dulles brothers. Nods and oblique conversations sufficed; there was no need for interagency meetings and no desire to expand the circle of those who knew about a sensitive operation.

Eisenhower himself worried about that looseness in the wake of SUCCESS. On June 27, a CIA officer with the rebel air force had authorized the sinking of a *British* merchant ship, the *Springfjord,* apparently feared by Somoza to be carrying gasoline to be used in a counterattack against Nicaragua.[74] (In fact, it was carrying cotton.) Whatever the intimidating effect of the sinking on Arbenz, it had a chilling impact on Eisenhower's summit with British Prime Minister Winston Churchill and Foreign Secretary Anthony Eden, then going on in Washington in an effort to mend Anglo-American differences over Southeast Asia.

The CIA officer was cashiered, and Bissell later admitted in an interview that the sinking "went beyond the established limits of policy."[75] (It also cost the CIA more than a million dollars to reimburse the British shipping company.) Eisenhower, however, sought to tighten the executive's control over covert action while still preserving some shred of plausible denial. In March, NSC 5412/1 had established a relatively low-level group to be "the normal channel for giving policy approval for [covert action] . . . as well as for securing coordination of support therefor."[76]

After the *Springfjord* incident, Eisenhower commissioned a fresh review, headed by World War II hero Air Force General James Doolittle, which led to a new directive on covert action, NSC 5412/2, approved in December, and a revamped, more senior review group. The group, which came to be called the 5412 Group, comprised direct designees of the secretaries of state and defense, plus the president's special assistant. The president would retain some deniability by not being a member of the panel but would be able to stay close to its operations through his own assistant.[77]

What was true of the CIA and the executive branch was true in spades of Congress: its review of covert action was informal in the extreme—a "buddy system." Before 1956 there were no formal subcommittees of Congress dealing with the CIA. Instead, ad hoc groups of senior members of Congress reviewed the Agency's budgets, appropriated money, and received a yearly review of CIA activities. DCIs kept these members informed of major covert actions projects. The process, however, was pure courtesy; it involved no formal congressional review or authorization.

The buddy system was reinforced by Dulles's own status and personality, and by the longevity in office of key members of Congress. Dulles was careful to keep those members informed, and they developed absolute trust in him. As chairman of the House Armed Services Committee, Carl Vinson, Democrat from Georgia, presided over CIA matters from 1949 to 1965, with the exception of the two years between 1953 and 1955, when the Republicans controlled the House. Over the same period, Clarence Cannon was chairman of both the House Appropriations Committee and its Defense subcommittee that oversaw CIA appropriations. In the Senate, Richard Russell of Georgia took over the chairmanship of the Armed Service Committee in 1955, after holding it briefly before, and retained it until 1968.

When Dulles met with a group of congressmen, the conversation was fairly perfunctory; as one senator candidly put it, "The most sensitive discussions were reserved for one-to-one sessions between Dulles and individual Committee chairmen."[78]

It is not just that the executive and the CIA did not want to tell Congress much; Congress also accepted the primacy of secrecy and did not want to know that much. With the cold war at its height, members of Congress shared the feeling that the United States had to act. They were prepared to give the president considerable discretion in conducting clandestine operations, including covert action. Had members of Congress known about the Iranian or Guatemalan operations, the broad majority would have supported them. The buddy system worked because there was broad consent to it in Congress. In the instance of Guatemala, Congress as a whole showed little public interest in finding out what American actions were afoot until the *Alfhem* arrived. Even then the names of the committees that planned to hold hearings suggest the tenor of congressional concern: they were the House Select Committee on Communist Aggression and the Senate Subcommittee on Internal Security.

Drawing the Balance Sheet

In neither Iran nor Guatemala was the triggering incident—governments turning toward the Soviet Union for assistance—the real cause of U.S. intervention. In both there was a pattern of open American hostility to the governments in power, hostility that was real, based on the feeling that events in Iran and Guatemala posed the threat of Communist advance. The plans for covert intervention were parts of that pattern of hostility, albeit dramatic parts. It thus seems fair to conclude that the intervention would have happened in any case, touched off by some other specific action that Washington took as confirmation of its worst fears.

Consider Guatemala. At the time, and for years afterward, it looked to the American people that a sudden action by Arbenz was the main reason for the invasion. Yet that was not so. PBSUCCESS was well in train before Arbenz turned to Moscow for arms. Even once he did, Washington had a year of warning that the arms shipment was in the offing. In early April 1953 a memo from Wisner, the CIA DDP, asked King, Western Hemisphere division chief, for "hard evidence" about "the rumor of some weeks ago" that "arms from Czechoslavakia were being clandestinely introduced into Guatemala."[79]

Given what it knew, had the arms shipment itself been the principal concern, the United States might have issued a sharp warning in advance to try to forestall it. Or it might have tried to stop it; that would have been an act of open hostility, but it might have been justified on the high ground of keeping foreign arms out of the Western Hemisphere. In fact, James Haggarty, Eisenhower's press secretary, implied in his diary at the time that it was an accident that the ship slipped through: "Someone pulled a fast one and we were watching the wrong ship."[80]

Yet the conclusion of the then foreign minister of Guatemala seems closer to the mark in assessing the overall pattern of U.S. policy. Even if the ship did slip through, the United States did not much mind. It had an "incident" that would justify an invasion.[81]

Any judgment today about the immediate consequences of AJAX or PBSUCCESS is bedeviled by the passage of time. It is difficult to evoke the climate of the early 1950s and so to understand the context of American decisions or the mind set of the decision makers. In retrospect, neither Mossadeq nor Arbenz looks like a "Communist," nor does the government of either look Communist-controlled. As one historian of the period put it about Guatemala: "The groups which controlled Guatemala under Arbenz had interests and policies established independently of the Communists which the Communists supported. . . . President Arbenz found Communist support useful. As he grew weaker, he needed that support even more."[82]

That, however, is hindsight. It was not how either Iran or Guatemala looked to Amerian policy makers in the early 1950s. We cannot know how the governments of either Arbenz or Mossadeq would have turned out without U.S. intervention, just as we cannot know whether the Sandinistas in Nicaragua, who looked to many Americans more benign in 1979 than they seemed in later years, evolved as they did because of or independent from U.S. hostility.

In the 1950s Eisenhower was convinced, in his words to an interviewer, that if "old Mossy was not a Communist himself, then he was either a fool or a stooge for the Communists."[83] The shadow of recent cold war history shaped Eisenhower's image of Mossadeq: he looked like Czechoslovakia's Beneš, a man whom the Communists would help to power, then destroy.[84] By the same token, official Washington's view of Arbenz was close to the one voiced by Peurifoy, the U.S. ambassador, in the cable to Washington that Eisenhower later felt had been so decisive: if Arbenz "is not a Communist, he will do until one comes along."[85]

U.S. policy toward both Iran and Guatemala was widely associated with the imperialist defense of narrow economic interests. In the context of the 1950s, however, it is fairest to conclude that U.S. officials acted because they believed strategic—not commercial—interests were at stake. If in buying a British operation for Iran, American officials also had, to some extent, bought British purposes as well, still the nationalization of Anglo-Iranian was for those officials less an evil in itself than one in a pattern of actions confirming Mossadeq to be a tool of the Communists. By the same token, Arbenz's move against Western economic interests set off strategic alarm bells.

At a press conference in 1954 Dulles defended the administration against the charge that it was doing United Fruit's bidding: "If the United Fruit matter were settled, if they gave a gold piece for every banana, the problem would remain just as it is today as far as the presence of Communist infiltration in Guatemala is concerned. That is the problem, not United Fruit."[86]

It seems fairest to take Dulles at his word. What United Fruit's access to senior officials bought was their attention. Once attentive, the minds of those officials were dominated by security considerations as they—rightly or wrongly—construed them. Given the "fall of China," the Communist coups in Czechoslavakia and elsewhere in Eastern Europe, the Korean war and the Communist insurgencies in Indochina, the view of Communist aggression held by Eisenhower and Dulles was shared by nearly every member of Congress. It was also shared by the press. Moreover, there was the tempting precedent of success in Iran.[87] Still, having chosen to act, the United States, like it or not, could not avoid becoming identified with the interests of its partners.

Lessons Learned and Obscured

In the early 1950s, both Iran and Guatemala were eminently vulnerable to manipulation by an outside power, particularly the United States. Most of the time the citizens, and even the leaders, of many countries are prone to believe that their fate is being decided by forces beyond their control. That tendency may be pronounced in the third world, where history provides some support for it, and it seems stronger in the Middle East than elsewhere. In 1951 a visitor reading the Iranian press would have learned that every single politician was a British agent.[88] A quarter century later a wavering shah sought to read the tea leaves of Washington's actions for signs of abandonment by the United States, which he implicitly assumed would be decisive for him.[89]

Iranians had a long history of manipulation from afar; for most of the century before 1950 it had been the British pulling the strings. After that, as it became clear that Britain could no longer sustain its imperial burdens in the Middle East, they passed to the United States, for good or ill. Central Americans, too, long had taken for granted that the United States would play a major role in determining their fate. By 1950 Washington still retained enormous influence in Guatemala; its ambassadors were virtual proconsuls.

In this context, Mossadeq's relations with Washington, like those of Arbenz, had a pleading quality to them—very different, to say the least, from the attitude of the Iranians who took power in 1979 after the fall of the shah. In the 1950s it came as no surprise that Iran could not run its oil refineries without British technicians; that only seemed the natural order of things. Similarly, the threat to withdraw Americans from Iran and thereby demonstrate to the world that Mossadeq could not govern was a serious one for Mossadeq. From the perspective of the 1980s it seems almost quaint. When the end came for Mossadeq in

1953, there was an air of resignation about it that was also very different from both the will and ability of revolutionary leaders in later decades to defend themselves and their regimes.

Guatemala in 1954 was also deeply penetrated by outside influences, and thus vulnerable. In retrospect, United Fruit's dominance seems like a gross caricature of the "banana republic." When the company decided to help the plotters by smuggling in weapons for them, there was nothing the Arbenz government could do to stop it. The government had control over neither its borders nor its transportation network. Arbenz came too late to the realization that subsequent revolutionaries took as a matter of course: it was imperative that the revolution assure itself of loyal armed forces, either by exercising political control over the preexisting army or by dissolving it in favor of groups of armed citizen militia. By the time Arbenz sought to distribute arms to peasants and workers, it was too late.

In those years, moreover, World War II was recent memory, and the United States retained much of its luster as the guardian of democracy. In the eastern Mediterranean, the United States had come to the aid of Greek democrats fighting Communists in that nation's civil war, and it had negotiated Soviet troops out of northern Iran. To many Iranians, it was not just that the imperial burden had shifted from Britain to the United States; the "empire" augured to be different as well. The anti-Americanism at the end of the Mossadeq period obscured the earlier pro-Americanism. In Iran, America had been carefully, sometimes frustratingly, noninterventionist, but when it had declared its preference, it had been on the side of the nationalists.

In Central America, America's image was not as interventionist as it had been earlier and became later. Although sending the marines was a living memory for many Central Americans, the marines were no longer *the* embodiment of U.S. influence. The interventionism of U.S. policy had been tempered by the Roosevelt administration's "Good Neighbor" policy and the ensuing wartime cooperation among the states of the Americas. If, in the eyes of Central Americans, the United States had emerged from the war not quite as the guardian of democracy, still its actions had not only the weight of proximity and past influence; they had some moral force as well.

In both Iran and Guatemala, contending political forces were in close balance, which might have tipped against Mossadeq and Arbenz even had the CIA not intervened. When the CIA did intervene, relatively small operations were enough, or so it appeared. Yet if both cases might have tipped without the CIA, in both the intervention might have failed. Roosevelt's amateurish first plot did fail; Dulles was ready to roll up the operation and bring the troops home. And the CIA officers who ran PBSUCCESS were under no illusions: if their deceptions failed and Arbenz were able to get his military into combat, the invaders would be overwhelmed.

Success was purchased at the price of enlarging the intervention. U.S. purposes did not change, but the operational requirements of achieving them did. Once the United States was committed, in secret and in a small way, its stakes changed, and the CIA took the next step. The effort to intimidate Arbenz became a paramilitary campaign, if a small one. In the process, plausible denial became thinner and thinner.

What is beyond question is that at the time both AJAX and SUCCESS were regarded as stunning successes. How close both operations came to failure fell from view. Roosevelt returned to Washington to a hero's welcome, albeit a confidential one. When he reported to the Dulleses and Defense Secretary Wilson, he described his audience as "alarmingly enthusiastic. John Foster Dulles was leaning back in his chair. . . . His eyes were gleaming; he seemed to be purring like a giant cat."[90] (In 1955 Roosevelt was spirited into the White House to receive the National Security Medal from Eisenhower.)

Even more than Iran, the Guatemala operation was regarded not just as a great success but as one that could be repeated elsewhere as the need arose. AJAX was impressive but slightly quirky; Roosevelt's performance seemed virtuoso, but it was an improvisation, relying on British agents and making little use of propaganda or deception operations. By contrast, PBSUCCESS was an institutional triumph for the CIA. It consolidated the ascendancy of covert action over espionage, and of operations over intelligence in the CIA. It also burnished the image of the new agency.

And it made careers for a post-OSS generation of CIA officers. For instance, the man who aided Hunt with propaganda operations in Opa-Locka was David Atlee Phillips, who two decades later headed the CIA operations that sought to prevent Salvador Allende from taking power in Chile. More immediately, almost the entire cast of the Guatemalan operation moved on to planning for the Bay of Pigs seven years later—Dulles, Bissell, Hunt, Phillips, Barnes, and King from the CIA; Berle; and their colleagues from State.

In later years, as in planning for the Bay of Pigs, what sprung to the minds of CIA officers, and of the political leaders who were above them, was "the Guatemalan scenario."[91] That image conjured up not only the relative ease of PBSUCCESS but also its basic elements. Bissell's original plan for the Bay of Pigs spoke of a "powerful propaganda offensive" designed to make Castro, like Arbenz, lose his nerve.[92] Propaganda, plus efforts to build up opposition forces and subvert loyalists, plus planning to support paramilitary intervention if need be: this became the recipe for covert action.

3

The Momentum of Action: Small Operations and Large Commitments

"How could I have been so stupid, to let them go ahead?"[1] The words were John Kennedy's in April 1961, only a half dozen years after the operations in Iran and Guatemala. The subject was the CIA's Bay of Pigs invasion of Cuba. When the invasion force of Cuban exiles hit the beach in the early dawn hours of April 17, events validated Kennedy's words. Everything went wrong.

Late that night, the president, still in white tie from an earlier congressional reception, met with his advisers for three tense hours. He rejected proposal after proposal for direct American action on behalf of the invasion force. It simply seemed too risky. The Soviet Union might retaliate by moving against West Berlin. That, in turn, might set off a chain of events that could lead to World War III. Earlier that day the president had received a note from Soviet leader Nikita Khrushchev. It was polite but threatening:

> We will extend to the Cuban people and its Government all the necessary aid for the repulse of the armed attack on Cuba. . . . We are sincerely interested in the relaxation of international tension, but if others go in for its aggravation, then we will answer them in full measure.[2]

So the president held firm, well aware that his inaction meant death or capture for the 1,400 Cubans of the invasion force, Brigade 2506, so labeled for the number of a recruit who had died in a training accident. Watching Kennedy walk around the White House grounds in the middle of that night, alone and still in formal dress, one of his aides said to another: "He must be the loneliest man in the world tonight."[3]

Iran and Guatemala had seemed so easy that they obscured the risks of covert action. After all, Allen Dulles had first estimated the chances of success in Guatemala at 40 percent, later revising his estimate down to 20 percent, and he was an advocate of the operation. That implied that the chances of succeeding at two such operations in a row were less than one in five—*if* the two opponents were the likes of Jacobo Arbenz in Guatemala.

It turned out, however, that Fidel Castro was no Arbenz and revolutionary Cuba was no Guatemala—as Kennedy, to his great dismay, discovered. He also learned other lessons that had been obscured by success in Iran and Guatemala. Once covert interventions begin, no matter how hesitantly or provisionally, they can be hard to stop. Operational realities intrude, with deadlines attached. New stakes are created, changing the balance of risks and rewards as perceived by political leaders and shifting the structure of the debate: the burden of proof switches from those who would propose covert action to those who would oppose it.

Roots of the Bay of Pigs

Fidel Castro came to power in Cuba in 1959.[4] It was a stunning setback for the United States, a Communist success but "ninety miles away," a realization of the worst fears that had motivated PBSUCCESS in Guatemala. In the last year of the Eisenhower administration, the CIA had developed the first plan to try to unseat Castro using a small—under thirty—force of Cuban exiles. The idea was simple, the analogy to the 1954 coup in Guatemala apparent: the exiles were to join the anti-Castro underground and precipitate a "typical Latin political upheaval."[5] This first plan, however, discussed within the CIA in January 1960, bore scant resemblance to the operation that eventually emerged.

Cuba was becoming a more formidable target. Castro was moving steadily closer to the Soviet Union, with more and more Soviet arms at the disposal of his revolution. Moreover, as time went by, the extent of disarray in the anti-Castro underground on the island became clearer. When Eisenhower, unaware of the first CIA proposal, asked Allen Dulles for an anti-Castro plan, what he got was far more ambitious than the January idea. This new plan called for the formation of a Cuban government-in-exile; "a paramilitary force outside of Cuba for future guerrilla action" was to be accompanied by organization inside Cuba and by a "powerful propaganda offensive."[6]

Richard Bissell, who had succeeded his former boss, Frank Wisner, as the CIA's deputy director for plans (DDP) in the summer of 1958, when it became clear that Wisner had worked himself into a physical and mental breakdown, believed the paramilitary force could be ready in six to eight months. On March 17, the president gave his tentative approval to the project. In June the CIA succeeded in getting the five main exile groups (out of a hundred-odd anti-Castro groups in Miami) to unite. Guatemala's president, Miguel Ydígoras Fuentes—the same

Ydígoras who had directly benefited from CIA covert action in Guatemala—was persuaded to let the CIA establish training camps on his territory, and in July the first Cuban exiles arrived, recruited in Florida and Central America by the CIA.

To Eisenhower, however, progress seemed slow, and he sometimes seemed almost bored by the project, perhaps in part due to his lame-duck status. Only in August did he approve a budget for the project, $13 million. At the same time he also approved the use of Defense Department personnel provided no Americans actually take part in combat. At one point the president expressed his frustration to Dulles and Bissell: "Boys, if you don't intend to go through with this, let's stop talking about it."[7]

After all, Arbenz had been unseated with a force of several hundred exiles, and that image of the operation remained in the minds of both CIA officers and their political superiors. Step by step, however, CIA planning for Cuba was beginning to reflect a different reality: Fidel Castro was an adversary of quite a different order from Arbenz. The original CIA plans had called for quietly infiltrating guerrillas into Cuba, with a small invasion to "detonate a guerrilla resistance." By the time the November presidential elections approached, however, Bissell had concluded that "there was no true organized underground in Cuba," hence no way to infiltrate in enough people and supplies for a serious resistance. Accordingly, Bissell decided, "If there was to be any chance of success, we would have to place main reliance on the landing force, and only minor reliance on any resistance force." He instructed the CIA project officer in Guatemala to limit guerrilla training to only sixty of the more than four hundred recruits; the remainder were to receive instruction in conventional military tactics.[8]

Even under the Eisenhower administration's revised 5412 Group procedures, the change in plans was an "internal" CIA matter. The latest in a series of changes, it seemed to the CIA managers tactical and thus minor; Bissell did not bother Eisenhower with it.[9] It was not a small change for the United States. It meant the training in Guatemala would have to be bigger and noisier, and the invasion itself would be major. All these changes meant that the U.S. role would be harder to hide, any cover stories about the Cuban exiles organizing or invading on their own more and more threadbare. It also meant that the American stake in the project's outcome had grown.

By December 1960, when it briefed its plans to the Special Group—the name of the 5412 Group had been changed—the CIA was counting on a sudden attack by 600–750 exiles, in tandem with air strikes by CIA-trained pilots to eliminate Cuba's air force. Massive propaganda, plus more bombing, would increase the disarray in the Castro regime, and the invading force would only need to hold their own until anti-Castro resistance and defections from Castro's militia sealed Castro's fate.[10]

These secret discussions, however, were overshadowed by the very public fact of John Kennedy's narrow victory over Vice President Richard Nixon for president of the United States. The new team's first three months in office were, in the words of presidential aide Arthur Schlesinger, Jr., "a thrust of action and purpose" by a new generation taking charge after a "decade of inaction"—thirty-nine proposals for legislation, ten meetings with foreign leaders, nine press conferences, and proposals ranging from the Peace Corps to the Alliance for Progress. One symbol of the new spirit was Kennedy's determination to dismantle the "ponderous system of boards, staffs, and interdepartmental committees" that had grown up to manage national security policy in the previous administration. Instead, the new president wanted something more flexible and informal.[11]

Sources of Momentum

Overthrowing Castro fit well with the activism and anticommunism of the new administration. Yet the special circumstance of transition also lent the invasion plan a life of its own: critical planning particulars fell in the cracks between administrations. Kennedy first heard of the revised CIA plan on November 18, ten days after his election, and he received a full briefing from Dulles and Bissell on the twenty-ninth. Kennedy, however, had his hands full preparing a smooth transition; moreover, presidential power was not yet his, and so he made only approving noises about what he considered a contingency plan.[12]

For its part, the Eisenhower administration did sever diplomatic relations with Cuba in its last days of office, but it deferred any decision about covert action to the new administration. In effect, the attitudes of both administrations left the CIA largely on its own, and in January the agency selected the Cuban city of Trinidad as the most promising landing site. By then the exile brigade numbered 800–900.

Senior officials of the new administration were not just new; they were also unfamiliar with the governmental machines they headed. An incident early in the administration is revealing. The military Joint Chiefs of Staff (JCS), unaware of the CIA plan, had begun their own contingency planning. Their conclusion, on which Kennedy was briefed by Brigadier General David W. Gray two days after inauguration, was stark: unseating Castro would require direct American backing. A week later, however, the president and his top aides heard a much more optimistic account from Dulles and Bissell. After considerable discussion, Kennedy approved only the Agency's preparatory activities and asked the JCS to review the Trinidad invasion plan.[13]

The JCS report, submitted to the president on February 3, listed a number of qualifications—for instance, that the "ultimate success" of the invasion "depended upon political factors"—but its bottom line sounded promising: "Despite the shortcomings . . . timely execution of this plan has a fair chance of ultimate success and, even if it does not achieve immediately the full results desired, could contribute to the eventual overthrow of the Castro regime."[14] Gray's working document for the JCS had used more pessimistic language, but in the final JCS draft that language was muted through a combination of customary caution, a sense of professional mission, and interagency comity. Acting in their familiar role as briefing officers, the JCS did not believe they had been asked for a clear opinion; moreover, the operation in question was the CIA's, not theirs, so they were as gentle with a sister service as they would expect in return.

The final JCS report was thus written in a kind of code. Gray later argued that it was meant to sound reserved: "We thought other people would think that 'a fair chance' would mean 'not too good.' "[15] That is not how it was read by senior officials of the incoming administration, unaware of the JCS's reasons for restraint and for the most part unused to dealing with the uniformed military. It is never easy for outsiders, especially a new administration, to fathom closed professional services, such as those in the military or intelligence.

To those newcomers, the report read like cautious support, suggesting that overt American participation might not be necessary after all. Kennedy gave his go-ahead to the Trinidad plan but cautioned Bissell, who was now a subordinate but was also a longtime social friend: "Dick, remember I reserve the right to cancel this right to the end."[16]

By the same token, senior officials lacked access to other "independent" sources of advice on the CIA plan *and* were ignorant of that lack. Even after the guerrilla plan was shelved in favor of a large invasion, success still was premised on the invasion as a trigger for widespread internal opposition to Castro.

Kennedy and his colleagues continued to hear reassuring assessments on that score from Dulles and Bissell.

What they did not know was the institutional history and the "compartmentation" of the CIA. When Kennedy listened to Dulles, what he thought he heard was *the* CIA view. What he in fact heard was primarily the view of those closest to planning the covert action—precisely those with the greatest stake in it. He did not hear the skepticism of the CIA's intelligence analysts about the extent of anti-Castro sentiment in Cuba, for those analysts did not even know of Trinidad planning.

Kennedy's special assistant for national security affairs, McGeorge Bundy, then in the administration fresh from a Harvard deanship, later recalled that he had "listened with a beginner's credulity to the arguments of the eager and dedicated operators who promoted what became the Bay of Pigs, and I did not know enough to ask the other side of the CIA—the estimators—for their judgment."[17]

Senior Agency managers—Dulles, Wisner, and Bissell—took it as an article of faith that special operations called for special procedures, not bureaucratic routine. Moreover, the watchword was security, and so the "compartmentation"—as it was known in the trade—of particular projects sharply limited the number of officials in the CIA who even knew about them. This compartmentation extended to the Clandestine Service itself. That a given covert action even existed might be known only to the DDP and the officers comprising the relevant task force.

In the instance of Cuba, compartmentation plus personal rivalries compounding the lingering ill will of the OPC–OSO merger in the Clandestine Service meant that even Richard Helms—Bissell's rival and now his deputy, and the nation's top espionage officer—was left out. Bissell, the architect of the U-2 program, was the Agency's, and Dulles's, young man on the way up; he had been promoted over Helms, who stayed in the deputy slot he had held since 1952.

This compartmentation sharply limited the internal review of covert actions. The CIA officers in charge of espionage in a given country might be ignorant that a covert action was in the planning, hence they could not render a judgment on the project's assumptions. The walls of compartmentation were even higher in separating the Clandestine Service, the DDP, from the CIA's intelligence analysts in the Directorate of Intelligence (usually referred to, like the DDP, after its deputy director, as DDI). On a day-to-day basis, the DDP's emphasis on protecting "sources and methods" meant that DDI officers, like other analysts in the government, received reports from foreign "assets" that described those assets only in the most general way.

Nor was there much of the informal contact between DDP and DDI officers that might have added background to particular reports. That remained the case even after the two halves of the CIA moved to the new headquarters in Langley, Virginia, in the early 1960s. In their routine business, DDI analysts tended to discount DDP's products. The DDI and his analysts seldom knew a covert action was afoot, and so they, too, could not assess it in light of their broader judgments of foreign politics.

Other sources of momentum derived from operational realities. By early March, with the new administration less than two months in office, the CIA reported that the exiles' morale had peaked, and Guatemala's president, chafing at the delay in moving the exiles out, asked for a guarantee that they would be gone by the end of April. The Guatemalan rainy season was approaching and with it an end to training. Finally, the CIA reported that within several months Castro would receive Soviet-built jets, thus rendering any small invasion suicidal. "After June 1," Schlesinger recalled the prevailing view, "it would take the United States Marines and Air Force to overthrow Castro. If a purely Cuban invasion were ever to take place, it had to take place in the next few weeks."[18]

Under this pressure, there seemed only one place to put

the exiles—Cuba. Dulles put it bluntly at a March 11 Cabinet meeting:

> Don't forget that we have a disposal problem. If we have to take these men out of Guatemala, we will have to transfer them to the United States, and we can't have them wandering around the country telling everyone what they have been doing.[19]

To Kennedy, the problem seemed even worse: "If we decided now to call the whole thing off," he told an aide, "I don't know if we could go down there and take the guns away from them."[20]

The commitment of those CIA officers closest to the invasion planning reinforced the pressure of these operational realities. Well before March, by mid-January, the plan was an open secret, but that scarcely deflected it, just as the leak had not derailed PBSUCCESS in 1954. Both *Time* and the New York *Times* printed details of CIA support and of the exiles' training camps in Guatemala and Nicaragua.[21] In late February the Joint Chiefs of Staff sent representatives for a firsthand look at the training camps. As a result of all the leaks, the inspection team reckoned the odds of an invasion catching Castro by surprise as 85 to 15 *against*. Lacking surprise, the team reported, the invasion was vulnerable in the extreme since a single Cuban plane with a .50 caliber machine gun could sink most of the brigade's ships.[22]

Still, the official JCS report, though hedged, was easy to read as optimistic: "The plan could be expected to achieve initial success. Ultimate success will depend on the extent to which the initial assault serves as a catalyst for further action on the part of the anti-Castro elements throughout Cuba."[23] The chiefs were not alone, for almost all those Washington officials who knew about the Trinidad plan convinced themselves that it could be portrayed as an independent Cuban action—an act, as Bissell later put it, of "self-delusion" that played a large part in the resulting debacle.[24]

By then, those CIA officers in charge of the operation were so committed to it that unpleasant realities simply had no impact. For them—and for their political superiors—images of success in Iran and Guatemala, then only a few years in the past, affected attitudes toward the current operation. Neither Iran nor Guatemala had been a total secret, but in both cases it had been possible to keep the United States role tolerably hidden. Why shouldn't it happen again, despite the unfortunate leaks?

Experts and Politicians

Several of the president's advisers were disturbed about the plan when they learned of it in the first months of 1961. But in the circumstances they were in no position to derail the operation. At the beginning of February, for instance, Arthur Schlesinger wrote a memo to the president arguing that the invasion plan should be abandoned because of the damage it would do to America's image abroad.[25] Two months later, after a meeting on the plan that seemed decisive, Schlesinger came early to his office to write a memo spelling out his objections in more detail for the president.

Yet Schlesinger was a White House junior, fresh from academia, with the vague title "special assistant." On the subject of covert action, he was a newcomer and an interloper, unlikely to carry the day against the CIA and the Joint Chiefs of Staff. To pursue his objections further would, it seemed to him, earn him a "name as a nuisance."[26] So he lapsed then into worried silence. His arguments about the "intangibles—the moral position of the United States, the reputation of the President . . . [and] 'world public opinion' "—looked nice on paper, especially to a future historian looking back on them.[27] But they were not about to tip the balance against the argument that the Trinidad plan, smoothly run, could rid the hemisphere of a Soviet client.

It was not just that members of the new political team lacked the stature or expertise to confront the experts. In the political circumstances of the time, the arguments of those newcomers were bound to seem "soft," too passive to persuade. A more substantial opponent of the plan than Schlesinger met the same fate. Senator J. William Fulbright, chairman of the Senate Foreign Relations Committee, reading the newspaper leaks of the plan, handed the president a long memorandum on March 30. The invasion was illegal and immoral, he wrote, and the American role could not be kept secret. Finally, if the initial assault failed, the United States would be under pressure to "respond with progressive assistance as necessary to insure success." In sum, he wrote, "the Castro regime is a thorn in the flesh; but it is not a dagger in the heart."[28]

Kennedy invited Fulbright to present his arguments to a planning meeting a few nights later, on April 4. His presentation was, according to Schlesinger, "a brave, old-fashioned American speech . . . [that] left everyone in the room, except me and perhaps the President, wholly unmoved."[29] No discussion ensued. Instead, the president began to poll his senior advisers in a way that left several participants uncomfortable, feeling the whole affair was a show for Fulbright's benefit. Like the men who had been polled by Foster Dulles about AJAX in the spring of 1953, it seemed neither the time nor the place to voice any misgivings they harbored.

From time to time the president himself seemed skeptical. He several times postponed the final invasion date. Yet given the rosy assessments of Dulles and Bissell, the political momentum behind the plan was almost irresistible for Kennedy as for other senior officials. After all, the administration had come into office full of activism, arguing—much as the Eisenhower administration had eight years earlier—that the previous administration had been too passive in defense of the free world. When Kennedy seemed doubtful, Dulles would ask him if he was going to be "any less anti-communist than Eisenhower."[30]

Moreover, there was the force of Dulles himself, reappointed DCI by Kennedy as a symbol of bipartisanship in foreign policy.

He was, as Kennedy later put it, "a legendary figure and it's hard to operate with legendary figures."[31] Dulles was not above using his stature, or the precedent of earlier success, on Kennedy, at one point telling him: "I stood right here at Ike's desk and told him I was certain our Guatemalan operation would succeed, and, Mr. President, the prospects for this plan are even better than they were for that one."[32] Notice that for the tactical purpose of persuading a president, 40 percent or even less had become "certain" success.

In this atmosphere, on March 15, Kennedy gave a tentative go-ahead for the invasion. In the previous months, Secretary of State Dean Rusk had kept to himself any doubts he had about the wisdom of an invasion, perhaps fearing being labeled cautious or inactive in comparison with the CIA in the vigorous new administration; he had turned a deaf ear to the passionate opposition of his undersecretary, Chester Bowles. However, in the days just before March 15, Rusk had argued and the president had agreed that the planned landing site, the Cuban city of Trinidad, was "too spectacular . . . too much like a World War II invasion."[33]

The CIA searched frantically for a new, "quieter" site. It found one, the Bay of Pigs. One crucial implication of the change, however, was lost in the momentum of the invasion planning: the original plan had been touted as foolproof—the exile force could simply melt into the mountains. But the nearest mountains to the Bay of Pigs were eighty miles away, across a swamp!

Carrying out the Debacle

The rest of the Bay of Pigs story can be quickly told. The U.N. General Assembly was scheduled to debate Cuban allegations of U.S. aggression in mid-April, and so Kennedy ordered that Adlai Stevenson, the U.S. ambassador to the United Nations, be briefed on the invasion plan. Stevenson was aghast. He insisted at a minimum that there be no American participation.[34] Kennedy agreed and ordered the exile leaders to be so informed. When told, it was their turn to be aghast, for they apparently had assumed all along that U.S. forces would be behind them if need be.

On April 14 Kennedy okayed the initial air strike. This part of the plan had been controversial from the start. The CIA wanted a single massive strike to coincide with the exile landing, but Rusk again broke his inscrutable silence to argue for holding hold off any strike until it plausibly could come from the exiles themselves once ashore. The eventual compromise left no one satisfied. A first strike, smaller than planned, launched from Nicaragua, where the rebel force's pilots were training, would destroy the bulk of Castro's planes; a Cuban pretending to be a defector from the Cuban air force would land in Miami and claim credit for the strike. Then, a second strike two days later would coincide with the landing.

The first strike, launched from Nicaragua, came off as planned, but the cover story began to come apart within hours. Moreover, a U-2 overflight of Cuba showed that in fact only five of Cuba's twenty-nine planes had been damaged. Stevenson, ignorant of the truth, had repeated the cover story before the U.N. Now, he was furious at having been misled.[35] He and Rusk prevailed on Kennedy to defer the second strike until the exiles actually were ashore. When they heard news of the delay, those at CIA headquarters were stunned: the invasion force would be vulnerable on the beach. The game was over.

As it turned out, they were right. Everything went badly. The first landing party ran into a Cuban patrol. The beach was brightly illuminated by vapor lights, not dark. And at dawn, five Cuban jets struck the force, which apparently did not know that the second strike had been canceled. Cuban tanks arrived far more quickly than anyone had thought possible. Perhaps most devastatingly, there was no uprising inside Cuba. If any Cubans on the island knew of the invasion, they "were working in Castro's office," as Kennedy later put it.[36] Cuban police rounded up suspected dissidents with surprising efficiency, herding 200,000 into theaters and auditoriums in Havana alone.

The men of Brigade 2506 fought well, but, outnumbered 20,000 to 1,400, their cause was hopeless. Under pressure, Kennedy still refused to authorize direct American help. He finally agreed that four unmarked U.S. jets would fly cover for another B-26 bomber attack. When the exile pilots, tired and dispirited, refused to fly, Dulles on his own authorized their American trainers to fly the mission themselves. In yet another mix-up, the cover arrived an hour too late. The Americans had no more success than the Cubans in maneuvering the old B-26s—which had been selected because Cuba had such planes, hence the American hand could plausibly be denied—through Cuban defenses. They lost four planes and four American pilots.

The brigade was routed and most of it captured, though Kennedy did authorize considerable American help in trying to rescue the force. To Schlesinger it seemed that "Kennedy was prepared to run more risks to take the men off the beaches than to put them there."[37] In the invasion 114 exiles died, and 1,189 fell into Castro's hands—later returned for $53 million in food and drugs, raised privately at the behest of Robert Kennedy. The president eased Dulles out as DCI, but he took pains to accept his own responsibility at a press conference: "There's an old saying that victory has a hundred fathers and defeat is an orphan. . . . I'm the responsible officer of the government that is quite obvious."[38]

Commitments, Past and Present

In the case of Cuba, once the United States had embarked on covert intervention, the momentum—which had been present in AJAX and SUCCESS as well—became hard and costly to turn off. In Chile, once the United States had intervened, secretly, it became easier and more tempting to do so again. The infrastructure for intervention—networks of assets along with secure routes for getting money and instructions to them—were in place. More important, the fact of past commitment changed the structure of the present debate. The burden of proof shifted to those who would oppose the covert intervention: it worked once, so why not try again?

On July 19, 1975, while working for the Church Committee, I traveled to Briarcliff Manor, New York, accompanied by an amiable sherpa, J. J. Hitchcock, a retired CIA official then on contract to the State Department as a liaison to the committee. My mission was simple but painful.[39] I was to make sure that Edward Korry, the U.S. ambassador to Chile in 1970, had in fact been unaware of Track II, so-called, the effort to touch off a military coup in Chile to prevent Salvador Allende from being seated as president.

I was pretty sure what I would find. President Nixon's instructions to Richard Helms, then DCI, on September 15, 1970, had been explicit: no one in either the State or Defense departments was to know of Track II. But I also knew from my telephone conversations with Korry that he was an intense man, and I had some hints about how deeply bruised he had been by his recent experience testifying before another Senate committee chaired by Frank Church, that one looking into the role of International Telephone and Telegraph and its connections to the CIA before the 1970 Chilean elections. So I expected that I, a freshly minted Ph.D. on my first job in Washington, would have to tell Korry, a man who had served his country with devotion and often with passion, that he had been deceived by his own government on the explicit orders of the president of the United States he had represented in Santiago.

My expectations were on the mark. It was clear that he had not known of Track II. Groping, I turned to Hitchcock for reassurance: "Don't you think we can tell him?" Asking Korry for secrecy, I then laid out Track II for him. His suspicions that the CIA had been up to something behind his back gushed out; once confirmed, past intimations magnified as he recalled them.

Yet the Track II episode turned out to be a minor part of our conversation. For five hours Korry's reflections, passionate and sometimes contradictory, spewed out; I managed to interrupt to ask perhaps a dozen questions. A central issue was the 1970 covert action that Korry *did* know about—the "spoiling operation" designed to prevent Allende from winning the 1970 elections.

Korry had arrived in Chile as ambassador in October 1967. Two years later the U.S. government began to shape its approach to the 1970 elections. At a 303 Committee, successor to the Special Group, meeting as early as April 15, 1969, Helms had warned Henry Kissinger, then assistant to the president for national security affairs and chairman of the committee, that the CIA needed to start early if it was to repeat its successful performance in the 1964 Chilean elections, but Kissinger deferred the issue for the time being.[40] (The committee name changes were a halfhearted attempt to maintain some confidentiality; 303 apparently was the number of a State Department office in which the committee met; it later became known as the 40 Committee after the number of a National Security Council directive reauthorizing the group.)

In Santiago, Korry found himself at cross purposes with his CIA station chief, Henry Heckscher, a man who had served the CIA since the beginning in 1947, a veteran of Guatemala and Laos. Korry was instinctively opposed to intervening covertly in the 1970 elections. But he recalled one climactic argument with Heckscher (neither of us identified Heckscher by name in our conversation). To Korry's objections, the CIA man countered: Do you want to be responsible for electing a Communist as president of Chile?

I was taken aback by the premises of the question: not only how to decide if Allende was a "Communist," but in what legitimate sense was the United States, much less Korry, "responsible"? The question, however, struck a deep chord in Korry. His attitude toward communism had been shaped by his experience as a journalist in Eastern Europe after the war, and he had been recruited to diplomacy by the Kennedy administration, on the lookout for liberal anti-Communists. He thought about it and decided that, yes, Allende was a Communist who would destroy democracy in Chile, albeit by democratic means.

"Responsibility" also had a specific force for Korry. Kennedy, he said, had encouraged public and private American money to flow to Chile under the Alliance for Progress. Korry regarded himself as a "fiduciary" for that investment. He could not simply walk away from that responsibility by remaining aloof while Allende took the Chilean presidency.[41]

However, the sense of responsibility that other senior officials shared with Korry derived less from any idiosyncratic notion of a fiduciary responsibility than from the fact of past interventions in Chile. Given that past, a hands-off policy in 1970 seemed tantamount to indifference to the fate of democracy in Chile; it could even be regarded as pro-Allende. That was the argument Heckscher used on Korry.[42] Later, once Korry had made the argument his own, he used it on Washington. In June 1970, when senior State Department officials were reluctant to increase funding to the anti-Allende project, Korry cabled: "If Allende were to gain power, how would the U.S. respond to those who asked what actions it had taken to prevent it?"[43]

By the time Korry had decided that Allende was indeed a "Communist," the Chilean presidential election had turned into a three-man affair. President Eduardo Frei, a Christian Democrat, was barred by the constitution from succeeding himself, and his party was represented by Radomiro Tomic. There was little love lost between Frei and Tomic, a man well to the left of Frei who was unhappy about having to run on the president's record; Tomic at one point made overtures to the Marxist left. On the right, the National party, buoyed by its good showing in the 1969 congressional elections, nominated seventy-four-year-old ex-president Jorge Alessandri.

Salvador Allende was once again the candidate of the left, this time organized into a Popular Unity coalition that included both Marxist and non-Marxist parties. Allende's platform called for nationalization of the copper mines and other major sectors of the economy, accelerated agrarian reform, wage increases, and improved relations with Socialist and Communist countries.

In December 1969 Korry and Heckscher reached a compromise and forwarded a joint proposal: the CIA would be authorized to undertake propaganda and other activities to prevent Allende's victory in the election, but it would not get the green light to pass money to either of Allende's opponents. The proposal was withdrawn for the time being, however, because the 303 Committee was split. The State Department, represented by Undersecretary U. Alexis Johnson, continued to express qualms about whether the United States should become involved at all. For its part, the CIA believed that Alessandri, then the best bet to stop Allende, needed both money and active help in managing his campaign.

On March 25, 1970, the 303 Committee, now renamed the 40 Committee, did approve an initial $135,000 for the "spoiling operations" recommended along the lines of the joint embassy–CIA proposal. On June 18 Korry submitted a two-part proposal: first, an increase in funding for the spoiling operations; second, $500,000 for a contingency plan to influence the outcome of the Chilean congress's vote between the top two finishers, a vote stipulated by that nation's constitution in the event no candidate received a majority of the ballots.

Again, the State Department was reluctant, its reluctance eliciting Korry's rhetorical question about responsibility. State agreed to the increase in funding for the spoiling operations but spoke against the contingency plan, and a decision on the latter was deferred pending the results of the September 4 elections.

The 40 Committee met again on August 7, but did not discuss support to either of Allende's opponents. On September 4 American officials' fears were confirmed: Allende won a plurality, although not a majority, with 36.3 percent; Alessandri was second with 34.9 percent, and Tomic trailed with 27.8 percent.

From "Spoiling Operations" to "Track II"

Having failed through covert action to prevent Allende's first-place finish, Washington decided to take the next step and try to prevent his seating by the Chilean congress. When it became apparent that Frei, the outgoing president, would not connive in that effort and that the congress could not be budged without him, yet a third covert approach—Track II, so-called—ensued. Track II was not inevitable; it resulted from a decision whose specifics owed much to President Nixon's personal involvement. Yet, in the face of official hostility to Allende, and of past covert attempts to prevent him acceding to the presidency, deciding to foment a military coup against him was more than thinkable. As in Iran, when confronted with a choice between rolling the operation up and committing the United States one level deeper, Washington chose the latter.

Four days after the election, on September 8, the 40 Committee met in Washington. The meeting concluded by requesting the embassy to prepare a "cold-blooded assessment" of the "pros and cons" of a "military coup organized with U.S. assistance."[44] Korry responded on September 12 with a pessimistic assessment, one shared by the CIA station in Santiago: "Our own military people [are] unanimous in rejecting possibility of meaningful military intervention. . . . What we are saying . . . is that opportunities for further USG [U.S. government] action with the Chilean military are nonexistent."[45] At the center of both embassy and station pessimism was the figure of the Chilean commander-in-chief, General René Schneider, a staunch constitutionalist known to be opposed to any coup.

The 40 Committee met again, on September 14, to discuss several variants of so-called Frei gambits, all of which sought an interim government that would then hold new elections in which the popular Frei would be eligible to run. One of these was, in the words of a CIA postmortem, a "Rube Goldberg" scheme "which would see Alessandri elected by the Congress on October 24th, resigning thereafter to leave Frei constitutionally free to run in a second election for the presidency."[46] Another variant, also labeled with inventive locution the "constitutional coup," sought to achieve the same end by having Frei voluntarily yield power to an interim military regime, again followed by fresh elections.

Korry was asked to approach Frei about the schemes, and the 40 Committee authorized $250,000 for "covert support of projects Frei or his trusted team deem important."[47] The money was never spent, for the only proposal for using it that arose—bribing Chilean congressmen to vote against Allende—was quickly perceived by both the embassy and the station to be unworkable.

The next day, September 15, Helms met with Nixon and received his marching orders for what came to be called Track II by those White House and CIA officers who knew of it. Track I—the Frei gambits—and Track II were operationally distinct; the CIA established a separate task force for the latter. Only a few of the DDP officers who normally dealt with Chile, and in Santiago only the station chief and his deputy, were aware of Track II.

Yet the two tracks were less distinct in substance. Track II explicitly sought a military coup; Track I was prepared to countenance and even support a coup, provided Frei was willing to take the lead. To goad Frei or the military into action, the 40 Committee had asked, on September 14, for a continuation of the earlier CIA "scare campaign" designed to touch off a financial panic or political instability in Chile. Indeed, by the time Allende took office several CIA propaganda assets had become so visible that they had to leave Chile.

The United States also attempted to make its propaganda come true by orchestrating economic pressure on Chile—cutting off all official credits, pressing multinational firms to curtail investments in Chile, and approaching other nations to urge them to do likewise. Helms's notes from the September 15 Track II meeting included the notation, "Make the economy scream," and economic leverage was the topic of another White House meeting on September 18. To manage this economic squeeze, another interagency working group, composed of the CIA's Western Hemisphere division chief and representatives from State, the NSC, and Treasury, operated in parallel to the 40 Committee.

Although Korry was unaware of Track II, his cabled situation report to Kissinger and Assistant Secretary of State Charles Meyer, on September 21, reflects the tone of the economic campaign, in Korry's vivid prose rather than bureaucratic jargon:

> Frei should know that not a nut or bolt will be allowed to reach Chile under Allende. Once Allende comes to power we shall do all within our power to condemn Chile and the Chileans to utmost deprivation and poverty, a policy designed for a long time to come to accelerate the hard features of a Communist society in Chile. Hence, for Frei to believe that there will be much of an alternative to utter misery . . . would be strictly illusory.[48]

By September 29 the 40 Committee had concluded that only economic pressure would induce the Chilean military to act.

In the month between mid-September and mid-October, the two tracks moved together, although the operational separation was continued. The September 14 40 Committee instructions had authorized Korry and other "appropriate members of the Embassy Mission" to intensify their contacts with Chilean officers to see if they would support the Frei gambits, and

Korry's September 21 situation report had argued that in order to make the gambit work, "if necessary, General Schneider would have to be neutralized, by displacement if necessary"—apparently a reference to a coup.[49]

As the prospects for either Frei gambit grew bleaker and bleaker, and as official Americans in both Santiago and Washington became correspondingly more desperate, those contacts with the military expanded. On September 23 the station in Santiago reported that there were "strong reasons for thinking neither Frei nor Schneider will act."[50] When Frei made no attempt to dissuade his own party convention on October 3–4 from reaching a compromise with Allende, any hopes for Frei gambits ended. American covert attentions turned to the Chilean military in general and, given Schneider's unwillingness to move against Frei, to lower officers in particular. The same September 23 CIA cable—a cable along Track II—said that "overtures to lower echelon officers (e.g. Valenzuela [General Camilo Valenzuela, commander of the Santiago garrison]) can of course be made. This involves promoting Army split."

Along Track I, Korry was authorized, successively, to tell his military contacts: that if Allende were seated, no further U.S. military assistance would be forthcoming; that assistance and military sales were being held in abeyance pending the results of the October 24 vote, this in response to Korry's own request; and on October 7, that

> if a successful effort is made to block Allende from taking office, we would reconsider the cuts we have thus far been forced to make in Chilean MAP [military assistance] and otherwise increase our presently programmed MAP for the Chilean Armed Forces. . . . If any steps the military should take should result in civil disorder, we would also be prepared promptly to deliver support and material that might be immediately required.[51]

Track II's origins in President Nixon's direct order were unusual—no plausible denial there! Yet Track II was the logical culmination of this sequence. As CIA Track II instructions to the station put it as early as September 21: "Purpose of exercise is to prevent Allende assumption of power. Paramilitary legerdemain [Frei gambit] has been discarded. Military solution is objective."[52] When the election spoiling operations failed, that set the stage for the attempt to interrupt Chile's constitutional process under the facade of legitimacy provided by Frei.

When that too failed, top U.S. government officials decided to take the next step: promoting a military coup not with the connivance of Frei and his commander-in-chief but against them as well as Allende. The CIA officials involved in Track II perceived the mandate for these steps as coming from the top. Thomas Karamessines, DDP at the time, said that Kissinger "left no doubt in my mind that he was under the heaviest of pressure to get this accomplished, and he in turn was placing us under the heaviest of pressures to get it accomplished."[53]

Acquiring Stakes in the Contras

That CIA officers acquire stakes in their projects and those they support; that covert actions expand in response to changing foreign circumstances; and that, perhaps most important, once committed in a small, even secret, way, leaders are more likely to enlarge their stakes than to withdraw—these sources of momentum are familiar to students of large organizations and of human psychology. What is distinctive about covert action is the presumption of secrecy; the stakes are created and expanded in secret, with the expectation—or, more often, the hope—that they will remain so.

Lest the sources of momentum represented in the Cuban and Chilean cases seem period-piece exceptions, consider a more recent episode: covert American support during the 1980s to rebels opposing the Sandinista regime in Nicaragua, known as the

Contras. My treatment of it is necessarily sketchier; we lack access to most documents, especially in the early years of the operation, and can draw on the benefits of neither hindsight nor memoirs. Yet this covert action has been more open and controversial than any other, and so leaks have abounded. The basic outlines of the story are clear enough.

In July 1979 the forty-year rule of the Somoza family in Nicaragua—the family that had been so helpful to the United States and the CIA in 1954 and 1961—came to an end, replaced by a broad front dominated by the leftist Sandinista National Liberation Front (FSLN), named for Augusto César Sandino, a general whose soldiers fought a guerrilla war against U.S. troops occupying Nicaragua in the 1920s and who was killed by the elder Somoza after Sandino began negotiations with him. As in the aftermath of Castro's takeover of Cuba two decades earlier, the government initially had the support of a range of moderate-to-reformist Nicaraguans united in their opposition to Somoza. Also as in Cuba, the opposition to the Sandinista regime comprised a disparate collection of groups—from social democrats to elements of Somoza's hated National Guard, which organized in Honduras after Somoza's downfall as the 15th of September Legion.

Again as in Cuba, the opposition became more disparate still as the Sandinistas moved toward a one-party government and former supporters switched to opposition. One of these was Alfonso Robelo, an original member of the nine-person Sandinista directorate. In May 1982 Sandinista hero Eden Pastora, "Comandante Zero" in his *nom de guerre,* broke with the Sandinistas and set up his own small force in Costa Rica, explicitly refusing to have anything to do with the ex-Somoza Contras in Honduras.

Nicaragua paralleled Cuba, or Guatemala or Iran, in another way: the United States was clearer about what it opposed—dictatorial rule by the Sandinistas under Cuban (and so Soviet) tutelage—than what or whom it favored. When it came to power in 1981, the Reagan administration inherited a small program of covert support to political moderates and private-sector forces inside Nicaragua and seen by Washington as under threat from the Sandinista regime—a smaller version of the kind of support the CIA had provided to opposition groups in Chile during the period 1971–73 and based on the same rationale.[54] The Carter administration, which had at the eleventh hour joined in the anti-Somoza effort by cutting off aid to him, had steered clear of any covert aid to the ex-National Guard elements.

In August the new administration opened informal negotiations with the Sandinistas, focusing on ending Sandinista support to the guerrillas fighting the U.S.-supported government of neighboring El Salvador. Washington held out a carrot, suggesting that if Nicaragua agreed, the United States might then "vigorously enforce" U.S. neutrality laws against anti-Sandinista Nicaraguans training in the United States. In late October, however, these talks broke off in a web of misunderstandings.[55] Most U.S. aid to the Sandinistas had ended the previous March, and the remainder was terminated in September.

Planning within the CIA had proceeded apace and in November came before the Reagan administration's National Security Planning Group—the latest in the series of NSC groups charged with approving major covert action. The CIA apparently offered a set of proposals for the "support and conduct of political and paramilitary operations against the Cuban presence and Cuban-Sandinista support structure in Nicaragua and elsewhere in Central America" in CIA jargon. Part of the program would "build popular support in Central America for an opposition front that would be nationalistic, anti-Cuban and anti-Somoza"—in effect a continuation of the Carter policy, with a price tag of some $3 million.[56]

The second called for funding a 500-man force on the Honduran border, formed of Nicaraguans and Cubans not associated with Somoza, to "collect intelligence and engage in paramilitary and political operations in Nicaragua and elsewhere," estimated to cost $19 million. The force would sabotage Nicaraguan bridges and power plants in an effort to divert attention and disrupt the economy, slowing the flow of Nicaraguan arms to rebels battling the U.S.-supported government of El Salvador. These operations might also be supplemented by CIA "unilateral paramilitary actions—possibly using U.S. personnel—against special Cuban targets."

Finally, the CIA proposal emphasized that support for paramilitary action "should not be confined to that funding level or to the 500-man force described"—a reference to the possibility of supporting a larger force built around ex-Guardsmen. CIA planners, however, recognized that a Guard-dominated force would have little appeal inside Nicaragua.

On November 23, President Reagan approved National Security Council Decision Directive 17, authorizing increased assistance to the internal opposition and to one or both armed groups, though the composition and control of those groups was to depend on discussions with Argentina and other countries of the region.[57] (Argentina was a surprising participant in a Central American conflict. A military government, it had slightly eccentric reasons of its own for being involved: several of the Montonero guerrillas on which it had been waging the "dirty war" in Argentina surfaced in Central America. However, it almost certainly received encouragement from Washington, and later cooperated with the United States, cooperation that ended when the United States sided with Britain in the Falklands/Malvinas war of 1982.)

Apparently, when the congressional intelligence committees were first informed of the 1981 program, they did not object but did insist that no money go toward the overthrow of the Sandinista government. The administration and the committees continued to debate the issue of objectives, a debate fed by controversy over Contra activities. Congress wrote the ban against involvement in overthrowing the Nicaraguan government into the secret CIA appropriation in September 1982 and enacted it publicly at year's end.[58]

In the autumn of 1983 the Contras began an ambitious attack on Nicaragua from both north and south, coupled with attacks on ports to isolate the country. In October a major oil storage facility at the Pacific port of Corinto was hit, a serious blow to Nicaragua's hard-pressed economy, and a week later the Atlantic port of Puerto Cabezas was hit. In early 1984 it was revealed that the CIA had supplemented efforts with its own operations to mine several Nicaraguan harbors. A dozen ships from six nations were damaged in the attacks. Moreover, it turned out that although most of the commandos involved in the speedboat raids on ports the previous fall had been Contras, CIA officers had commanded the mother ship and contract agents piloted it.

The episode spilled into a public row between the executive and Congress; several members of the president's own party alleged that the CIA had failed to brief them on the operations, in effect using the Contra connection as a cover for its own unilateral operations. DCI William Casey responded by pointing to the 1981 decision and to a revised presidential finding submitted to the congressional intelligence committees in September 1983.[59]

Initially the Contras did not enjoy a good press in the United States. They usually were represented in Congress, and on American TV, by hefty men in dark sunglasses, looking uncomfortable in suits and uttering monosyllabic assents to arguments made on their behalf by their American supporters. Their shortcomings were apparent to all. They seemed both savage and feckless on the battlefield, more adept at excess or sabotage than combat. Contra battalions sometimes stayed in the field for up to five months at a stretch and so were extremely difficult to control. In early 1983, for instance, one battalion went on a rampage in villages on the Honduran–Nicaraguan border, resulting in the court martial and execution of two soldiers—a blow to the Contras' image and morale.

It was also plain that the CIA struggled mightily to forge some unity among the varied anti-Sandinista forces—and that it was becoming more and more deeply involved in the process. The CIA first pressed the groups to join in the Nicaraguan Democratic Front (FDN), then created a civilian leadership—with offices in Miami—to try to counter the impression that the Contras were dominated by their military commanders, former Guardsmen.[60] The CIA was reported to have cut off aid to Pastora in April 1984 because he would not join in a common front with the FDN.[61]

In the fall the two houses of Congress were once more at loggerheads. The Republican-controlled Senate was prepared to continue funding the Contra program, whereas the Democratic-controlled House voted to terminate it. In conference, the two houses compromised, limiting Contra aid to $24 million. In the spring of 1984, after the mining of the harbors, the House Intelligence Committee turned even more sharply against continuing aid, while the Senate committee was divided. This time in conference the Senate was forced toward the House position, and in October Congress cut off any more money until the end of February 1985, with any fresh funding after that date only if the administration reported its compliance with a series of strict conditions. The CIA duly withdrew its advisers.

The Debate Shifts

Despite the controversy, extending covert support to the Contras created a self-sustaining momentum. As in earlier instances, the political stakes of American leaders changed and, with it, the structure of the debate. Public opinion polls in the United States suggested a deep ambivalence about Nicaragua that was also reflected in the U.S. Congress. Like their representatives, most Americans agreed that the Sandinista government was both internally repressive and a threat to the hemisphere. At the same time, there was no evidence that Americans were prepared to pay the price of ridding themselves of the Sandinistas if that price was sending U.S. GIs. Quite the contrary.[62]

Despite its losses in Congress, the Reagan administration was succeeding in framing the debate on its own ground. Americans' deep ambivalence left "covert" support standing as a "middle option," cheap in money and American blood, hard for members of Congress, even Democrats, to vote against lest they be branded "soft on communism" by a popular president. The Reagan administration played on that ambivalence by hinting that the alternative to covert action was military intervention. As Langhorne Motley, the assistant secretary of state for inter-American affairs put it in 1985, "The contra program" was created to respond to "two do-not-wants" on the part of the American public: "a second Cuba . . . a second Marxist-Leninist state . . . and . . . a second Vietnam, U.S. combat troops bogged down without a clear purpose." His successor, Elliott Abrams, put the choice even more starkly a year later: without aid to the Contras, it would be either "American military force . . . or . . . surrender."[63]

Yet, as in Cuba, part of the stake was human as well. The United States had acquired a stake in the future of the Contras, who, though still badly split, had come by 1985 to be represented by Arturo Cruz and Alfonso Robelo, both one-time officials in the early Sandinista government. To decide to "abandon" them was of a different order, politically, from the choice about whether to support them in the first place. In the words of David Phillips, the CIA veteran of Guatemala, the Bay of Pigs, and Chile: "Whatever . . . the merits of the various 'freedom fighters,' we should recognize that once our country makes a commitment to them, it is unfair, and perhaps immoral, to turn our backs."[64]

In early 1985, President Reagan again asked for aid to the Contras after the cut-off ended in February, this time for $14 million. The House of Representatives voted down the aid after a sharp debate. When, however, Sandinista leader Daniel Ortega unwisely journeyed to Moscow just after the vote, those Democrats who had voted against covert aid looked soft and foolish. They responded by enacting economic sanctions, largely symbolic, against Nicaragua. In August 1985 Congress compromised on $27 million in so-called nonmilitary aid to the Contras, not to be administered by the CIA and with the Agency barred from direct contact with the Contras or assistance in their training.

The debate resumed again early the next year when the president again asked for military aid to the Contras, this time $100 million. The administration campaign for the aid—by now Nicaragua had become the most public "covert" action in history—was intense: in a speech to the nation Reagan evoked the specter of Latin Americans by the "millions . . . fleeing north into the cities of the southern United States," said that the "Nicaraguan Communists" had been active in countries, like Brazil, that were surprised to learn the news, and argued that aid to the "freedom fighters" was necessary to "prevent a Communist take-over of Central America."[65]

In these circumstances, the House dramatically turned around, voting for aid in June, 222–209, after having rejected it in March and April. When the Senate followed suit, Congress approved in October 1986 the president's $100 million package—divided 70–30 between weaponry and nonmilitary supplies and including training conducted by U.S. military personnel. No longer even nominally covert, the appropriation was public, attached to the military construction budget. The legislation lifted the 1984 restrictions on CIA involvement, except that no agency officer was allowed inside Nicaragua or within twenty miles of the border. The program was to be coordinated by the assistant secretary of state for inter-American affairs.

While conceding the president his way, majorities in Congress sought at the same time to keep some pressure on him by requiring periodic reports on human rights and on the progress of Central American peace negotiations.

These human loyalties, like other sources of momentum, are not overriding. The United States has abandoned groups it supported covertly; sometimes it has done so abruptly, even callously. In 1958, when CIA operations in Indonesia against Achmed Sukarno failed miserably, though in secret, the United States abandoned a group of dissident Sumatran colonels it had been supporting.[66] In 1972 the shah of Iran asked President Nixon for CIA support to Kurdish mountain people fighting the shah's enemy, Iraq. Three years later, however, the shah settled his differences with Iraq and had no further use for the Kurds. The DCI at the time, William Colby, writes that CIA cable traffic "suddenly was jammed with requests to help the refugee and exiled Kurds instead of shipping arms and military supplies to them clandestinely."[67]

Two other CIA-supported groups were casualties of the American exit from the war in Vietnam. When, in 1968, President Johnson halted American air strikes on North Vietnam, resupply drops to Montagnard tribesmen operating behind North Vietnamese lines also stopped. Some of them perished; others were captured. Similarly, the Meo tribesmen who fought the "secret war" in Laos with CIA assistance numbered about thirty thousand at the peak of the war; at war's end, however, in 1975, only a "pitiful remnant" of ten thousand escaped to Thailand.[68]

Yet all these groups were "pitiful remnants" of far-off wars that were either secret or that Americans wanted to forget. They were also, to put it gently, non-European. They did not have fellow Cubans in Miami, or lobbyists patrolling the halls of Congress, or access to American television, even in ill-fitting suits. The human stakes represented by the Cubans of Brigade 2506 or the Nicaraguan Contras were powerful sources of momentum behind covert action.

Momentum and Mistakes

The Nicaraguan intervention, like SUCCESS and the Bay of Pigs, was dotted with operational mistakes that can only be understood in light of the momentum of major covert actions. In retrospect the bombing of the *Springfjord* off Guatemala seems incredible; so does the landing of Brigade 2506 at the beaches of the Bay of Pigs, where it had no mountains in which to melt, only swamp in which to become mired.

By the same token, the CIA mining of Nicaraguan harbors two decades later seems unaccountably stupid. When, inevitably, it became known, no purpose in Nicaragua could justify the international opprobrium that would fall on the United States. All this seemed perfectly predictable before the fact. After the fact, when Nicaragua brought suit against the United States in the International Court of Justice, Washington felt compelled to deny jurisdiction—thus reversing U.S. policy of long standing and tarnishing the U.S. image as a nation committed to international order and the rule of law.

Or in 1983, when the Contras were dogged by allegations of human rights abuses, the CIA took the lead in producing a new operations manual for them.[69] Called *Psychological Operations in Guerrilla Warfare,* it was written by an American under contract to the CIA and reviewed by a dozen or so junior DDO officers. The author, a former Green Beret, apparently borrowed from old U.S. Special Forces lessons. In any event, the manual raised the possibility of hiring professional criminals and even of creating Contra "martyrs," arranged, if need be. Most damningly, it spoke of selective assassination of Sandinista leaders in order to intimidate villages—this despite laws and executive orders forbidding assassination, the products of congressional investigations less than a decade earlier. Compounding the folly, the manuals were then dropped by balloon to the

Contras, thus ensuring that some would fall into Sandinista hands!

It is not that CIA officers are less capable than their counterparts elsewhere in the foreign affairs agencies of government. Quite the contrary, the CIA's reputation for competence has led president after president to look with favor on it by contrast to the more ponderous military or diplomatic bureaucracies. Rather, mistakes inevitably result when the pressures to produce results are coupled with the secrecy of planning. Secrecy limits those who have a chance to review the details of operations; as in Cuba, sources of judgment at arms' length from the operation, either outside or inside the CIA, either go unconsulted or feel the terms of their assessment are constrained.

The limits of review, and the illusion of secrecy, may also tempt covert operators to take risks they would not take if they were more openly accountable. At best, under pressure, those CIA officers may be prone to wishful thinking: "We've succeeded before despite the odds, so why not again?" At worst, both pressed for results and haunted by their responsibility to those they are aiding, they may make calculations, like those that led to the mining of Nicaraguan harbors, that they later regret. So may their political superiors.

4

The Problem of Control: "Our" Purposes and "Theirs"

Major covert interventions, once begun, are difficult to stop. The very fact that the interventions are meant to be covert gives rise to special problems of control. The link between U.S. intentions and the actions of those foreigners the United States supports is often tenuous at best. They are acting; the United States is only helping. "Their" purposes may not be "ours." They have every incentive to hear from their CIA liaisons what they want to hear or construe it to suit their own purposes. Since their relationship to the United States is meant to be secret, the CIA is often in a weak position for compelling them to act to suit American purposes.

Moreover, the United States becomes associated with "their" purposes. Like it or not, American covert support for foreign groups inevitably identifies the United States with those groups, if and when the relationship becomes known. U.S. officials have sought, honestly no doubt, to draw fine distinctions between what covert support was and was not permitted to do, what it was and was not intended to achieve. Yet those distinctions cannot be sustained inside a messy foreign reality, where U.S.-supported groups pursued ambitions of their own and where connections among groups and causes were fleeting, often ambiguous.

Hearing the Message

Sometimes, the groups the CIA supports do not hear the message because they do not want to. Consider the case of hapless Colonel Díaz in Guatemala in 1954. Díaz thought he was leading a nationalist revolution, not serving American purposes as relayed through the CIA. He had been no part of American plotting with Castillo Armas. Indeed, while he was prepared to abandon Arbenz, he opposed Castillo Armas.

PBSUCCESS had succeeded almost too well, and success created a new problem for the United States. Castillo Armas, still far from the capital, had to be flown in with his followers. More to the point, senior U.S. officials were not sure they could trust Díaz. So far, PBSUCCESS had only presented the presidency to the revolution's senior military officer. Ambassador Peurifoy—who had earlier told Arbenz's foreign minister, Toriello, that he had no way to control Castillo Armas—assured Díaz that he would contact the rebel leader to arrange a cease-fire.[1] What Peurifoy did not know but soon learned, however, was that Díaz intended to continue fighting if Castillo Armas did not cease his attack. He pledged never to surrender to the rebels and, to bolster his support from the military, appointed Colonels Elfego H. Monzón and José Angel Sánchez to his governing junta.

Peurifoy consulted Washington. What he heard was that the Dulles brothers wanted to "get [Díaz] out and a better army officer in."[2] Thus, in the early morning of June 29 Peurifoy met with Díaz, who greeted him with a friendly summary of his first day in office, including a list of members of the previous regime who had been arrested. Peurifoy, however, responded with sharp criticism of Díaz for letting Arbenz use his resignation speech for one last criticism of the United States. He added, according to his report to Secretary of State Dulles, "This being the case, I did not see how we could work together toward bringing about peace."[3] Lest the point be missed, the same pilot who had dropped the bomb on June 25 was ostentatiously preparing for another mission.

Díaz soon got the point: the United States would not tolerate opposition to Castillo Armas; that was not why it had engineered Arbenz's downfall. Díaz reluctantly told Peurifoy that he and Sánchez would withdraw from the junta. At this point, Monzón, waiting outside, joined the meeting. Díaz left, escorted by Monzón's guard, and the new leader announced that Díaz had resigned and that he, Monzón, would form a new junta.

Yet power was still not in the hands of America's chosen successor. Peurifoy was initially unsure whether Monzón might not do; he had a record of loyal service in the army and had made no deals with Arbenz. On the other hand, Washington did not regard him as the sort of dynamic leader the situation required. And he suffered from another defect: he was not Castillo Armas. The United States could not risk alienating the leader of the rebel forces, and Peurifoy doubted that Monzón could govern without the acquiescence of the rebels, who had shown no disposition to recognize any government other than their own.

The Dulles brothers decided to bring Monzón and Castillo Armas together, and a conference was hastily arranged under the good offices of the president of El Salvador. The two Guatemalans arrived in El Salvador on June 30. Both Secretary Dulles and the responsible assistant secretary of state, Henry Holland, thought Peurifoy should not attend, and Peurifoy was inclined to agree; he had been extremely visible in the previous days, running back and forth among Arbenz's military with his shoulder holster, and the role of the United States was becoming harder to cover. In the end, however, Dulles wired Peurifoy: "If in your judgment conference agreement and consequent stabilization anti-Communist government can only be assured by exercise your personal influence on the spot, you may proceed to participate."[4]

Peurifoy immediately joined the conference, regarding himself as "authorized to 'crack some heads together.' "[5] He offered a bargain to break the deadlock: Monzón would save face by initially merely bringing Castillo Armas into his junta, but that would be accompanied by a promise of elections soon. And, as Peurifoy's cable to Washington made clear, there was little doubt who would win those elections: "Without actually stating it, the implication was that Castillo Armas would be elected."[6] The junta made Castillo Armas Guatemala's provisional president on July 7, and in early October he was confirmed in office in a "landslide" electoral victory.

Overwhelming the Message

In other cases, the fact of support overwhelms the attempt to convey a sense of the limits of that support to its recipients. Once the United States had set the Bay of Pigs invasion in motion, it was hard for the men of Brigade 2506 not to believe that America would do what was necessary to make it succeed. The Brigade's CIA advisers' efforts to whip up morale with lavish estimates of the chance of success only encouraged the Cubans' misperception.

In the second week of April 1961, White House aide Arthur Schlesinger's rear-guard action against the planned invasion was swept aside by the momentum of the project. But he did make a difference with the president on one point. His memorandum of April 10 argued that the exiles should be clear that under no circumstances would the United States intervene militarily: "We must tell the Revolutionary Council that it cannot expect immediate U.S. recognition; that recognition will come only when they have a better than 50–50 chance of winning under their own steam; that this is a fight which Cubans will have in essence to win for themselves."[7] Kennedy agreed and two days later told a press conference: "There will not be, under any conditions, an intervention in Cuba by the United States armed forces. . . . The basic issue in Cuba is not one between the United States and Cuba. It is between the Cubans themselves."[8]

It scarcely occurred to the exiles that the president might be telling the truth. Given the stakes the United States had acquired in success, both the Cubans and their CIA officers presumed the United States would intervene with military force if need be. To the CIA advisers no less than the Cubans, Kennedy's press conference remark seemed "a superb effort in misdirection."[9]

To reinforce his point, that same afternoon Kennedy sent Schlesinger and Adolf Berle, FDR's assistant secretary of state for Latin America and a Kennedy family friend now serving as an informal adviser, to make sure the exiles understood the U.S. position. They did not. According to Schlesinger, the provisional president of the exiles, José Miro Cardona, "displayed resistance and incredulity at the statement that no United States troops would be used."[10] Schlesinger and Berle could not convince him that Kennedy meant what he said, and they reported that back to the president. Kennedy then told Bissell, the DDP, that the invasion was off unless the exiles agreed to the U.S. terms. Bissell sent his own emissary to Miro Cardona, who finally professed to agree. The emissary left, however, unsure whether he had heard sincere agreement or merely Miro Cardona going through the motions of what he felt was required of him.

CIA enthusiasm for the invasion, and the resulting disregard for cautionary pieces of intelligence, fed the exiles' misperceptions. Four days before the invasion, on April 13, Kennedy received a report on Brigade 2506 from Jack Hawkins, an experienced marine colonel. A glowing report, it was, Robert Kennedy said, the "most instrumental paper in convincing the President to go ahead":[11]

> My observations have increased my confidence in the ability of this force to accomplish not only initial combat missions, but also the ultimate objective, the overthrow of Castro. The Brigade and battalion commanders . . . are young, vigorous, intelligent and motivated by a fanatic urge to begin battle. . . . [T]hey have supreme confidence they will win against whatever Castro has to offer. I share their confidence.[12]

Unhappily, much of that confidence, it turned out, was based on CIA misinformation, some of which cut directly across the president's insistence on limiting the American role. The brigade was only a small part of the landing force; the Cuban underground would destroy bridges throughout the island and call a general strike; hundreds of guerrillas would rush to join the invaders. This is what the exile force heard from its CIA advisers.[13] Perhaps the most encouraging part of the message was also the most contrary to the president's intent: "The United States would recognize the Cuban government-in-arms and assist it with whatever might be necessary to overthrow Castro. American ships would be standing near Cuban waters so help would not be unnecessarily delayed."[14] This message was not necessarily direct disregard for Kennedy's orders. Rather, his eleventh-hour decision to limit the U.S. role could not overturn the presumptions in the heads of the CIA officers who ran the project—and in the heads of the Cubans themselves.

One CIA adviser told the brigade that they would not even need the United States: "You will be so strong, you will be getting so many people to your side, that you won't want to wait for us. You will put your hands out, turn left, and go straight into Havana."[15]

Yet underlying the confidence was a safety net: if needed, the United States would be there. That presumption continued into the battle. As the brigade steamed toward Cuba, one exile tried out the ship's deck-mounted machine gun. The mounting broke and the firing mechanism stuck. Brigade members relaxing on the surrounding deck scattered for cover, but one was killed and two wounded, one seriously. The ship broke radio silence to call for help. Within hours an American destroyer pulled alongside to take the wounded men. The sight of that American ship gave a big boost to morale. "Everyone felt confident we were not alone," one brigade member recalled later.[16]

Onboard the brigade's ships, exiles tried to catch a few minutes' rest. One poignantly captured the mix of anxiety and confidence—and misinformation—in an entry in his diary:

> Final briefing said opposition would be weak as there were only about 5,000 militia anywhere in the area. The local populace would come in and we could expect large defections to us from the militia. All this bucked us up immensely. Men talked as if it was over and won and how splendid to be back in Havana. Myself, I wondered; I had a slightly sinking feeling about the battle ahead. I kept thinking: someone is going to be killed.[17]

Supporting . . . and Trying to Withdraw

Covert support, once given, is hard to withdraw when circumstances change. The United States cannot easily disentangle itself. The groups the United States supports may feel they continue to have American sanction even after the tangible assistance is ended. Or if they do not, the United States still will be implicated in the purposes and subsequent actions of those groups. If the fact of support becomes public, as is likely, so will American complicity. That was the sad outcome of Track II in Chile.

By the beginning of October 1970, three weeks before the Chilean congress was scheduled to settle the presidency, it was clear to U.S. officials in both Washington and Santiago that outgoing President Frei would not engineer a scheme to deny Allende the presidency, nor would the top military leadership, especially the commander-in-chief, General René Schneider, be party to a military intervention. The focus of attention along Track II thus shifted to divisions within the military and, in particular, to the second echelon of Chilean officers.

Track II caught the CIA unprepared. In July 1969 the station had secured headquarters' approval for developing a number of agents within the Chilean military to gather information on coup-plotting. At various times CIA assets in the military included men up and down the ranks in all three Chilean services. The project, however, had stayed close to its intelligence-gathering function, and by the autumn of 1970 the station's two assets in the military were not in a position to spark a coup.[18]

The station thus improvised. The U.S. Army attaché in Santiago, Colonel Paul Wimert, was particularly well connected to senior Chilean army officers. For the CIA, those connections were good fortune, not good planning. It turned out that Wimert shared with his Chilean counterparts a traditional military keenness for horsemanship, and so went riding nearly every morning with senior Chilean officers. On the station's request, the CIA deputy director asked for and received permission from his counterpart at the Defense Intelligence Agency (DIA)—the reporting channel for attachés—to use Wimert in Track II. The message Wimert then received through CIA channels evokes the pressure and secrecy surrounding Track II. Wimert was directed:

> to work closely with the CIA chief, or . . . his deputy, in contacting and advising the principal military figures who might play a decisive role in any move which might, eventually, deny the presidency to Allende.
>
> Do not, repeat not, advise the Ambassador or the Defense Attaché [Wimert's immediate superior in the Embassy] of this message. . . .
>
> This message is for your eyes only, and should not be discussed

> with any person other than those CIA officers who will be knowledgeable. CIA will identify them.[19]

As for Guatemala or the Bay of Pigs, the CIA established a special, highly compartmented task force to manage Track II. David Phillips, the CIA officer who had worked on propaganda for PBSUCCESS in 1954, was called back from an overseas assignment in Brazil to run the task force. Other than task force members, only four CIA men knew of its existence: Thomas Karamessines, the DDP, William Broe, the Western Hemisphere division chief, Broe's deputy, and the head of the Chile branch. The task force had a separate communications channel to Santiago and Buenos Aires.[20] Phillips, Broe, and Karamessines, who met daily during Track II, made most of the operational decisions.

To complement Wimert's contacts with Chilean officers, the task force at the same time sent four agents to Chile posing as nationals of countries other than Chile or the United States—"false flag" officers, in tradecraft terms. "We don't want to miss a chance," as headquarters put it to the station.[21] These agents received their instructions from headquarters, not the station. In Santiago they were compartmented from one another, reporting separately to an operative who in turn relayed their reports to the station chief.

The task force's marching orders, as relayed to the station, were to:

> a. Collect intelligence on coup-minded officers;
> b. Create a coup climate by propaganda, disinformation, and terrorist activities intended to provoke the left to give a pretext for a coup;[22]
> c. Inform those coup-minded officers that the U.S. Government would give them full support in a coup short of direct U.S. military intervention.[23]

In another cable on October 19, the task force offered its advice about how to create a "coup climate":

> It still appears that . . . coup has no pretext or justification that it can offer to make it acceptable in Chile or Latin America. It therefore would seem necessary to create one to bolster what will probably be their claim to a coup to save Chile from communism. . . . You may wish include variety of themes in justification of coup to military . . . : (A) Firm intel. that Cubans planned to reorganize all intelligence services along Soviet/Cuban mold thus creating structure for police state . . . (B) Economic situation collapsing . . . (C) By quick recognition of Cuba and Communist countries Allende assumed U.S. would cut off material assistance to Armed Forces thus weakening them as constitutional barriers. Would then empty armories to Communist Peoples Militia with task to run campaign of terror based on alleged labor and economic sabotage. (Use some quotes from Allende on this.)[24]

To say that many of the CIA officers closest to Track II were unenthusiastic about it would be to understate the point. Not that those officers were fond of Allende; quite the contrary. Nor were they necessarily opposed to a coup if that was what it took to prevent his accession. However, the circumstances were unpromising in the extreme: Frei would not act; Schneider would block any coup-mongering if he could; and those officers who wanted a coup were unorganized and unpromising. For example, the station chief in Santiago was moved to caution his superiors several times:

> Bear in mind that parameter of action is exceedingly narrow and available options quite limited.
> Feel necessary to caution against any false optimism. It is essential that we not become victims of our own propaganda.
> Urge you not to convey impression that Station has sure-fire method of halting, let alone triggering coup attempts.[25]

For his trouble, the chief was cabled on October 7: "Report should not contain analysis and argumentation but simply report on action taken."[26] To reinforce the point he was recalled to Washington, where the message was explicit: we are all under pressure to produce, so take your orders as we take ours.

Such prospects as existed for a coup centered on loose groups of plotters around two men. One was Brigadier General Roberto Viaux, an erratic character who had led the abortive "Tacnazo"—after Tacna, the Chilean city in which it occurred—revolt in October 1969. The Tacnazo, ostensibly intended to dramatize the military's demand for better pay but widely interpreted as a coup attempt, was amateurish but even so came close to success. After being cashiered from the army, Viaux still retained the support of many noncommissioned and junior officers, and he was the leader of several right-wing "civilian" groups.

The other group centered on General Camilo Valenzuela, commander of the Santiago garrison. This group, unlike Viaux's, was led by active duty officers, although one active officer may have been a member of the Viaux inner circle. The two groups, comprising perhaps a dozen officers, were, however, in contact with each other.

The Track II effort began in earnest on October 5, when Wimert approached an army and an air force general to inform them that the United States would support a military coup both before and after it happened. Between October 5 and 20, the station and Wimert, mostly the latter, recorded some twenty-one contacts with military and Carabinero (national police) officers.[27] On October 7 Wimert met with members of the War Academy, who asked him for light weapons. This was the first contact with the officer to whom Wimert did pass three machine guns on October 22. These officers stressed Schneider as the obstacle. They were trying to get "Frei to eliminate him, to replace him, send him out of the country. They had even studied plans to kidnap him."[28]

By the end of the second week of October, the task force regarded prospects as bleak. It and the station arrived at Viaux as "the only military leader willing to block Allende," but that choice had been reached "by process of elimination," even though his own colleagues, including Valenzuela, described him as "a general without an army."[29] The station's frustration was apparent in a cable it sent to Washington during this period, although the message's punch was diminished by the propriety of CIA communications officers: what we need, the station cabled, is not weapons, what we need is a Chilean general with b---s.

Wimert made the first contact with Viaux through a military attaché from another country; because of the risk of disclosure, the third-country agents took over the contact. As early as October 5 Viaux wanted several hundred tear gas grenades to launch a coup on October 9. Then and several days later, the CIA turned down those requests, essentially buying time while encouraging Viaux to refine his plans. To ensure some U.S. influence with him, the station was authorized on October 13 to pass him $20,000 in cash and promise him $250,000 in life insurance.[30]

By October 15 it was clear that Viaux, who had met with Valenzuela at least once, would deal with his "Schneider problem" by kidnapping him. The station had reported on October 13 that Viaux would do so within forty-eight hours, but Viaux evidently had postponed his coup attempt, and the next day the task force began to see "signs of increasing coup activity from other military quarters, specifically an Army General [deleted] and Admiral [deleted]."[31]

On October 15, nine days before the congressional vote, Karamessines met with Kissinger and his deputy, Alexander Haig, at the White House to review the bidding. They agreed to "defuse the Viaux plot, at least temporarily," because the CIA judged it could not succeed and to pass Viaux a message: "We have reviewed your plans . . . and come to the conclusion that your plans for a coup at this time cannot succeed. Failing, they may reduce your capabilities in the future. Preserve your assets. We will stay in touch. . . . You will continue to have our support."[32]

This message was relayed to the station the next day and passed on to a Viaux associate the day after. However, Viaux could not be defused at Washington's whim; the United States had lost whatever control it had. At meetings on October 17 and 18 the associate stressed that they would go ahead on October 22, "and that the abduction of General Schneider is the first link in chain of events to come."[33] At this point the CIA broke off contact with the Viaux plotters but did sustain what it called an "emergency channel"—that is, a way to get a message to him should the need arise.

Task force attention had shifted to plotters around Valenzuela, perhaps a general *with* an army. On October 17 Wimert met with an army and navy officer of that circle, who asked him for eight to ten tear gas grenades, three machine guns, and five hundred rounds of ammunition. Headquarters was puzzled by the request: "Find our credulity stretched by Navy officer leading his troops with sterile [not traceable to their source] guns. What is special purpose for these guns?" The plotters had told Wimert the guns were for "self-defense," and despite its puzzlement, headquarters said it would try to "send them whether you can provide explanation or not."[34]

As a first installment intended to demonstrate U.S. support, six tear gas grenades originally designated for Viaux were passed to the army and navy officer late in the evening of October 18, and the guns were sent from Washington by diplomatic pouch on the morning of October 19.

Valenzuela told Wimert, also on October 18, that he and three other senior officers were prepared to lead a coup. It was a complicated plan beginning with the abduction of Schneider at a dinner in his honor the next night. He would be flown to Argentina, Frei would resign and leave the country, and a military junta would dissolve the congress. Viaux, who knew about the plan but was "not directly involved," would be safely—and visibly—out of Santiago for a few days. The military would not admit to the kidnapping but would instead blame it on leftists.[35]

This bizarre plot failed when Schneider left the dinner in a private car, not his official one, and the police escort remained with him. Wimert's army contact assured him another attempt would be made the next day, and Wimert was authorized to pay Valenzuela $50,000, "the price agreed upon between the plotters and the unidentified team of abductors," but only after the kidnap was completed.[36] The second attempt also failed; given the second failure, the task force concluded that "the prospects for a coup succeeding or even occurring before 24 October now appear remote."[37]

Nevertheless, at 2 A.M. on October 22 Wimert met his army contact in an isolated section of Santiago and passed the machine guns and ammunition.

Shortly after 8 A.M. that same day Schneider's car was intercepted as he was driven to work. He pulled his handgun to defend himself, was shot, and later died.

The station was uncertain, but its first reaction was that the guns it had passed were those used in the abduction. It informed headquarters that it had instructed Wimert to "hand over $50,000 if Gen. Valenzuela requests," which also suggests that it believed the killing was the work of Valenzuela's paid abductors.[38] Later in the day, with Schneider still clinging to life, the station added: "All we can say is that attempt against Schneider is affording Armed Forces one last opportunity to prevent Allende's election if they are willing to follow Valenzuela's scenario."[39]

In the event, while martial law was declared, with Valenzuela himself as chief of Santiago Province, the station's prediction of October 9 proved on the mark: if Schneider were shot in an attempted kidnap, that would "rally the Army firmly behind the flag of constitutionalism."[40] Allende was confirmed as president on October 24, and Schneider died the next day.

It is probable that in fact the CIA-supplied weapons were not used in the killing and that the officers to whom they had been passed were not directly involved in the shooting. The Chilean Military Court investigation found that Schneider had been killed with handguns, not machine guns, and neither the army officer who had received them nor his navy ally were present at a meeting of the abductors before the shooting. Viaux received a twenty-year sentence for being the "author" of the kidnapping, along with a five-year exile for plotting a military coup. However, Valenzuela was also convicted of the latter charge and sentenced to three years in exile.

Yet the United States could hardly escape some complicity in what had occurred, even if, in this case, that complicity did not become public knowledge at the time. It had signaled its encouragement to Viaux, breaking with him because it judged he could not succeed, not for any other reason. It had done the same with Valenzuela, knowing that his plans, like Viaux's, included kidnapping. And it had passed weapons as tangible symbols of its support, knowing that they might be involved in the kidnapping. Killing Schneider was not the CIA's intention, any more than it had been the plotters'. But both knew the attempt might result in killing.

Collecting Information and Sending Signals

It is not just those clandestine activities labeled covert action that send signals to foreigners. In that sense, there is no tidy distinction between covert action and the covert collection of intelligence. That fact bedevils all practice of espionage, for those from whom information is being collected, secretly, are seldom passive purveyors of facts. They have their own agenda.

Nor are they disinterested in establishing a link to their CIA case officers. Often their interest is money, perhaps coupled with the promise of an eventual escape from their own countries. In those cases there is a certain shape to the transaction. But sometimes the purposes of those information-givers is political, as is their reason for establishing a CIA connection, so they are likely to interpret the winks and nods of their CIA case officers to suit their own purposes.

The Problem of Control

That problem is pronounced if the information-givers were once supported to act, not report. Then, they can hardly avoid looking for hints that the United States still may support their political purposes. After Allende was seated as president, the CIA began to rebuild its contacts in the Chilean military; again, as before September 4, the purpose was gathering information on coups, not fomenting them. Viaux and Valenzuela had both passed from the scene, but some of the officers from whom the CIA now sought information no doubt were aware of earlier American support for a coup, so they must have been particularly sensitive to any signals that they again had that support.

Moreover, as Karamessines later testified, from his perspective, "Track II was never really ended."[41] It just petered out in changed circumstances; the task force was disbanded, and Phillips returned to Brazil. Nixon and Kissinger turned to other matters but retained their distaste for Allende. Aware of their feelings and knowing their boss, Karamessines, to be a man who played by the book, his subordinates did not put him on the spot with the White House by seeking confirmation that, yes, the United States was no longer interested in a coup.[42]

Communications between station and headquarters in the autumn of 1971 testify to the fact that there was no clean end to Track II. By September the station had built a new network of agents and was receiving almost daily reports of coup plotting. The station requested guidance about how to use this new network, noting that developing more military sources would make the United States "a bit pregnant" by inevitably signaling some encouragement to plotters.[43]

In November the station cabled, suggesting that the ultimate goal of its penetrations of the Chilean military was a coup. At CIA headquarters, Broe's deputy, who still wishes his name not to be made public, was in charge of the Western Hemisphere division while awaiting Broe's successor. Instead of sending a telegram, which would have gone to Karamessines and put him on the spot with the White House, the deputy sent a written dispatch to Santiago. It was more philosophical than most bureaucratese, and also pithier.[44]

Its basic message to the station was: report history, don't try to make it. The CIA did not have 40 Committee authorization for coup plotting, which implied that the Track II authority finally had lapsed, a year after Allende assumed power. The deputy expressed the view that Chilean commanders could not be pushed into a coup but had to make the decision on their own. At the same time, he acknowledged the fuzzy line between monitoring coups and appearing to support them, and he recognized that the mere existence of contact with the military plotters, for whatever purpose, might be construed by them as American support for their future political purposes. That said, however, the station was still authorized to put the United States in a position to "take future advantage of either a political or a military solution to the Chilean dilemma," depending on how events played out.[45]

The blurring of the line between espionage and action became a reality in a more specific exchange between station and headquarters, one parallel to their dialogue about the purpose of military contacts. This concerned a "deception operation" intended to alert Chilean officers to—real or purported—Cuban penetration of the Chilean armed forces.

Strikingly, the new U.S. ambassador in Santiago, Nathaniel Davis, who arrived as both sets of internal CIA discussions were taking place, was informed of neither.[46] The first set of discussions was regarded as internal housekeeping, making sure that station and headquarters agreed on the standing instructions. In the instance of the deception operation, the CIA apparently exploited some combination of the transition between Korry and Davis and a loophole in the then-White House instructions for informing ambassadors of covert activities. Since the deception materials were actually passed outside Chile, they became a third-country operation, not one on which the ambassador in Santiago had to be informed. And, significantly, with Track II shelved but not dead, it, too, might have provided authority for keeping Davis in the dark. Or so CIA headquarters may have believed.

In September, the station proposed to provide information, some of it disinformation prepared by the CIA, to persuade senior Chilean officers that, with Allende's connivance, the Carabineros' investigations (that is, intelligence) unit was working with Cuban Intelligence (DGI) to gather information prejudicial to the Chilean high command. Headquarters responded the next month by suggesting that, instead, the station pass "verifiable" information to the coup plotter both it and headquarters then regarded as most likely to succeed.[47]

In the end, headquarters agreed to another station request, and in December a packet of material, including a fabricated letter, was passed to a Chilean officer outside Chile. The station never reported what effect, if any, the "information" had, and, contrary to initial plans, no further packets were passed. During the same period, however, the station did briefly subsidize a small antigovernment pamphlet distributed among the military.

At other points during the Allende government, the station compiled what it regarded as operational intelligence necessary in the event of a coup—arrest lists, key government locations that would need to be taken over, other places and people that would need to be protected, and government contingency plans in the event of an uprising. According to the CIA, none of this information was ever passed to the Chilean military.[48] Nor, since the information was regarded as CIA housekeeping, was the ambassador informed.[49]

Through 1972 and into 1973 the station focused on the group it earlier had judged most likely to bring off a successful coup; by January 1972 the station had penetrated it and was in contact through an intermediary with its leader. Rumors of coups swirled around Santiago. The station's monitoring peaked during two periods, June 1973 and the end of August through the first two weeks of September before the coup that succeeded.

It did worry some Washingtonians that the United States would be held responsible for a coup it had not promoted. At CIA headquarters, the same deputy who had written the philosophical dispatch in November 1971 was again minding the store in an interim between two chiefs. Apparently on his own initiative, he sent two cables to the station in May 1973. The first, on May 8, represented "a rather abrupt departure" from CIA custom in pointing out "the probability of an opposition move against Allende and the inevitability that CIA would be blamed as the instigator of any coup." The second, responding to a station reply, told the station to do the best it could at "ringing the gong"—predicting the coup—but stressed that it was more important to keep "the CIA's record clear."[50]

Involvement and Responsibility

The United States, through the CIA or the military, was not *directly* involved in the coup of September 11, which resulted in Allende's sad death. That was my conclusion in 1975 after having looked at all the government's classified documents. No evidence I have gathered in the interim has changed that conclusion.

Of how much the United States *knew* in advance I am less certain. The station did receive regular reports throughout July, August, and September on what was afoot among the group of plotters that acted on September 11, so the United States had *some* foreknowledge. The Chilean plotters, however, decided to proceed only a few days before acting; they apparently also decided not to inform the United States of their plans.[51] On Saturday, September 8, the embassy had indications of a coup on Monday, which over the weekend was postponed until Tuesday, a change of which the United States had clearer and clearer intimations during Monday.[52]

The Problem of Control

Yet even if the CIA neither supported the coup directly nor had precise forewarning of it, the United States still bears some responsibility for it. Acquiring information without sending signals is a problem as old as intelligence services. In Chile from 1971 through 1973 it was a problem that no amount of tradecraft—for example, receiving reports from assets through third parties, "cut-outs" in trade language—could resolve. CIA contacts with the Chilean military existed in the shadow of past efforts to overthrow Allende and in the context of deep official hostility to him. That was true no matter how scrupulous the CIA was in walking the fine line between monitoring and stimulating coup-plotting. And in several instances prior to the coup the United States stepped over that line.

The words of the CIA officials themselves are on the mark. In testimony before the Senate Select Committee in 1975, Karamessines, when noting that Track II never really ended, said: "I am sure that the seeds that were laid in that effort in 1970 had their impact in 1973. I do not have any question about that in my mind."[53] Or as William Colby, the DCI in 1973, put it: "Certainly in Track II in 1970 it [the CIA] sought a military coup. . . . Certainly, having launched such an attempt, CIA was responsible to some degree for the final outcome, no matter that it tried to 'distance' itself and turn away well before 1973."[54]

Fine Distinctions and Messy Reality

In all attempts by one nation to influence the actions of another, the chain between intention and effect is imprecise. Efforts to punish Soviet misbehavior by embargoing critical technology may cause more disruption in U.S. relations with allies than in the Soviet economy. Bombing Libya to deter its leader from supporting terrorism may make that leader a hero in the Arab world.

However, the circumstances of covert action are particularly unpromising for neat calibration of effect. Revolutions and counterrevolutions are seldom tidy. Usually they are chaotic. Those who plot coups or plot to stop them have reason not to reveal their purposes to anyone, much less to their CIA case officers. Moreover, any links among groups may be fleeting, and so the participants themselves may not be sure at any given moment what is afoot, who are their enemies and who their allies.

I recall long conversations during 1975 with Orlando Letelier, the urbane man of the left who had served Allende as minister of defense and ambassador to Washington. Then living in exile in Washington, Letelier was later killed—almost certainly on the orders of the Pinochet government in Chile—in a car bomb that also took the life of his American research assistant. Letelier was eloquent in describing the confusion of the Allende government's last months: Things would happen, he said, and he could never figure out how or why. It didn't add up. There seemed to be things going on that he didn't know about.

In these circumstances, Washington is hard-pressed to keep up. By the time the CIA is authorized to take a particular action, the situation in the foreign country may have changed to make it inappropriate. On the ground, once the CIA has passed money or weapons to those it supports, it loses a good measure of control over what then happens with either. It is not that the CIA is careless. Under pressure it, like any organization, makes mistakes.

Yet I have been struck by the contrast between the free-wheeling image of covert action and the accountantlike auditing that is CIA practice. The CIA use of unvouchered money may have been free-wheeling early in the cold war, but it is not now. One product of organizing by projects is tidier accounting, a tidiness reinforced by executive branch budgeteers and, more recently, by close congressional overseers. Notice that the classified record of covert action in Chile accounted for expenditures down to tens of dollars.

Rather, it is the messy foreign reality in which covert action takes place that frustrates precise control. In November 1970, after both Tracks I and II had failed, Salvador Allende was seated as president of Chile. The following February, in his State of the World message, President Nixon set the public line of U.S. policy toward Allende Chile: "We are prepared to have the kind of relationship with the Chilean government that it is prepared to have with us." This "correct but minimal" line had grown out of the earlier interagency study, National Security Study Memorandum (NSSM) 97, and set forth secretly in National Security Decision Memorandum (NSDM) 93 in November 1970.

Assistant Secretary of State Charles Meyer elaborated that line in testimony before a Senate committee, although he skated just to the edge of a lawyer's fine distinction in describing previous U.S. actions about which he did not want to speak, particularly before Congress in open session:

> The policy of the Government . . . was that there would be no intervention in the political affairs of Chile. We were consistent in that we financed no candidates, no political parties before or after . . . September 4. . . . The policy of the United States was that Chile's problem was a Chilean problem to be settled by Chile. As the President stated in October of 1969, "We will deal with governments as they are."[55]

The policy sought to put pressure on the Allende government to prevent its consolidation and contain its effects in the hemisphere, while the "correct" posture on the surface would deny Allende a handy foreign enemy against which to rally domestic support. One instrument of the policy was economic pressure, both overt and covert—aid cut off, credits denied, and efforts, partially successful, to enlist international financial institutions and private firms in tightening the squeeze on Chile.

The other instrument was covert action. During the Allende presidency, the 40 Committee authorized over $7 million in covert support to Chilean opposition groups, $6 million of which was actually spent. Adding project funds that did not require 40 Committee approval, the CIA spent a total of about $7 million dollars on covert action in Chile between 1970 and 1973.[56]

In broad outline, the covert support was intended to keep opposition parties and media, especially the Christian Democrats (PDC), the National party (PN), and *El Mercurio,* alive to fight another day. Yet, within that shared objective, the policy debate—in Washington, within the U.S. embassy in Santiago, and between the two—was narrow but frequently sharp: where to draw the line between supporting opposition forces and assisting those who actively sought to overturn the Allende government?

Within that narrow debate, the "doves"—those who resisted covert involvement with the antigovernment agitators—generally won the day. For instance, during Track II the CIA had passed $38,500 through a third party to Patria y Libertad (Fatherland and Liberty), a right-wing paramilitary organization, as part of the effort to build tension in Chile and thus a pretext for a military coup. After Allende assumed the presidency, the CIA occasionally passed the group small amounts of money for demonstrations or other specific activities. That support, which totaled only about $7,000, was ended in 1971 as Patria y Libertad became more and more militant.

The debate among U.S. officials over the limits of covert action grew heated in 1972 and 1973 as strikes by Chilean shopkeepers and others became the focal point of antigovernment protest, and the question arose whether the United States, through the CIA, should support private-sector groups that might be involved in strikes. In September 1972 the 40 Committee authorized $24,000 in "emergency support" to a business organization, the Society for Manufacturing Development

(SOFOFA), then in serious financial difficulty.[57] At the same time, however, on Ambassador Davis's recommendation, the committee decided against support to other private-sector organizations "because of their possible involvement in anti-government strikes."[58]

The next month, however, the 40 Committee did approve $100,000 for SOFOFA and two other private-sector groups, the Confederation of Private Organizations (CAP) and the National Front of Private Activity (FRENAP). For the CIA, this support was part of the larger project to influence the March 1973 legislative elections and was limited to voter registration and get-out-the-vote drives. When those elections failed to produce the two-thirds opposition majority in the Chilean senate that might have led to Allende's impeachment, the focus of opposition shifted away from votes and toward strikes—and the policy dilemma for U.S. officials reemerged.[59]

The CIA did, however, begin to support a research organization that was spun off from SOFOFA, and in 1973 provided three-quarters of its funding. This project was justified as research, not political action. The organization provided a steady flow of economic and other analyses to opposition groups; it actually drafted many of the bills submitted by opposition parliamentarians.

In the middle of July 1973 Chilean truckers began a strike that lasted until Allende's overthrow on September 11. The point of the strike was explicitly political: to paralyze the country so that the military would have to intervene—or at least reenter the Allende government—to restore order. In this context, official Washington reviewed a number of proposals for covert assistance to private-sector groups.

Again, Davis and the Latin Americanists at the State Department were reluctant, for those groups were known to hope for military intervention, and so support for them would take the United States across the line between supporting the opposition and seeking a change of government. On the other side of the argument were many CIA officers, who found themselves with high-level support from Davis's boss, Henry Kissinger, then about to move from White House assistant to secretary of state.[60]

On August 20 the 40 Committee approved a million dollars for opposition parties and private-sector groups, although passage of the money was contingent on the ambassador's concurrence. None of that money actually was passed to the private sector before the coup intervened, three weeks later.

In the middle of these discussions, the CIA station in Santiago asked headquarters to take soundings in Washington to see if support to the opposition could be stepped up to include groups like the truck owners. The ambassador, Davis, agreed to the soundings but opposed a specific proposal for $25,000 in support to the strikers that was forwarded by the CIA at the same time. It is unclear whether that proposal came before the 40 Committee. On August 25, sixteen days before the coup, headquarters cabled the station that it was taking soundings, but the specific proposal for aid to the truckers was never approved.

The pattern of deliberations within the U.S. government suggests a careful distinction between supporting opposition forces and funding groups trying to promote a military coup. The attempt to draw that distinction was, so far as I can tell, an honest one; certainly the arguments about it were real, sometimes passionate. Yet, given the reality of Chile, it was a distinction built of sand. The political parties, the militant trade unions (*gremios*), and the paramilitary groups prepared for violence were interconnected in a number of ways, many of them known to the CIA. It is thus probable that Patria y Libertad and a kindred group, the Rolando Matus Brigade, received CIA money secondhand, through the parties.

By the same token, it was clear to all observers that the two lengthy truckers' strikes, and particularly the critical one in the months before Allende's downfall, could not have been sustained with union funds alone.[61] The truckers got money from *somewhere*. Their strikes were actively supported by several of the private-sector groups that did receive CIA money, and some CIA money surely found its way through them to the strikers.

The first strike, in October 1972, coincided with the American decision to support the private groups, although the intended purpose of that assistance was the elections, not strikes. The next month the CIA did learn that, contrary to its stipulations, one private group had passed $2,800 to the strikers. It rebuked the group but still passed it more money the next month. The fact that the CIA discovered that passage of money can be taken either as a commentary on its tight auditing procedures or as evidence that if some money was caught, much more must have gotten through to the strikers—although we will never know how much.

In retrospect, though, what is most striking is how artificial was the distinction between supporting the opposition and seeking a change of government. It was a distinction in the minds of Americans, not Chileans. Those Chileans in the opposition did not want merely to exist; they wanted to succeed, although they differed in what actions they were prepared to take in that quest. Moreover, as Nathaniel Davis puts it: "The U.S. government wished success to opposition forces."[62] Even if those forces the United States supported abided by CIA strictures on the use of its money, the result still freed their own resources for other purposes. And *their* paramount purpose was the end of the Allende government. There was simply no way the United States could support them for any purpose without also buying into that overriding aim.

"Their" Purposes and "Ours"

Something of the same attempt to make a distinction that could not stand seems to have run through the first years of covert American assistance to the Nicaraguan Contras in the 1980s.

Executive branch officials justified covert support to the Contras in terms other than overthrowing the Sandinistas; that was the purpose that, as Robert R. Simmons, then the staff director of the Senate Intelligence Committee put it, "everyone discussed but few admitted."[63] The aid would slow the infiltration of arms from Nicaragua to the rebels fighting the U.S.-backed government of El Salvador, or it would focus the Sandinistas inward, away from the export of their revolution, or it would pressure the regime into serious negotiations with its neighbors and the United States. Yet the Contras, like the opposition in Chile, did not have limited purposes, much less ones that suited American convenience. They wanted not to constrain the Sandinista government but to replace it.

What the available evidence does not settle is whether the Reagan administration misled itself *and* Congress or just Congress. Did it sincerely hold the limited objectives for covert intervention it apparently professed to the congressional oversight committees, or was it dissembling in response to their insistence that American objectives be limited? Different parts of the administration emphasized different purposes, so, from the perspective of Congress, the objective was a moving target. The military stressed interdicting arms, with photographs to show progress, whereas the CIA gave pride of place to turning the Sandinistas inward and the State Department was more likely to emphasize regional negotiations.

Certainly, the administration's preoccupation with arms aid through Nicaragua to the rebels in El Salvador was apparent. That aid was first priority for Reagan's first secretary of state, Alexander Haig. In February 1981, the State Department released a white paper on the subject, presenting captured documents and other intelligence intended to prove that the Soviet Union and Cuba had been supporting the Salvadorean rebels and that Nicaragua had been the active conduit for the aid.[64] Washington tried to rally American allies in Europe against the

Sandinistas, and Haig spoke vaguely, but menacingly, of "going to the source"—that is, Cuba.[65]

Even before the president's November 1981 decisions about covert action against Nicaragua, Reagan reportedly had issued, on March 9, a "finding" for an operation intended to inderdict the flow of arms from Nicaragua into El Salvador.[66] In light of that finding, however, the November program seemed very broad—the first of a number of disputes between the administration and the intelligence committees of Congress over the precise purpose of the Nicaraguan project. The November language—"engage in paramilitary . . . operations in Nicaragua and elsewhere"—seemed to permit almost anything.

The series of congressional responses suggests that the committees, particularly in the House, where Democrats held a majority, did not believe the administration was sincere in professing limited objectives, that the committees and administration did not agree on what the objectives were, or both in some combination. The congressional committees first made clear in their classified reports on the CIA budget that they opposed covert efforts to overthrow the Sandinistas, then, at the end of 1982, put that language as the Boland Amendment publicly into the appropriations bill.[67] Named for Representative Edward P. Boland, chairman of the House Intelligence Committee, it stipulated that no money could be used "for the purpose of overthrowing the Government of Nicaragua or provoking a military exchange between Nicaragua and Honduras."[68]

The aims of America's covert intervention remained in dispute. In January 1983 Senator Patrick Leahy of the Senate committee, visiting Central America, met with Contra leaders who told him, of course, that they wanted to overthrow the Sandinistas. The Senate committee then stipulated that it would approve no more funding for the program without a revised finding, one that was specific about objectives. In August DCI Casey appeared with a new finding, which still seemed to license a more ambitious covert war. It was revised to meet committee objections and presented to the committee again on September 20 by Casey and Secretary of State George Shultz.

This new draft still posited a halt to the flow of support to the Salvadorean rebels as the American aim.[69] That limited objective seemed less and less plausible, especially after the revelations early the next year of direct CIA operations against Nicaragua. When Congress cut off aid to the Contras in October 1984, it set down conditions for resuming it that again came back to the question of objectives. The president was required to report "that the Government of Nicaragua is providing material or monetary support to anti-government forces . . . in El Salvador" and to "explain . . . goals of United States policy for Central America."

Over time the administration itself was more and more explicit about its objectives for U.S. policy—and for covert action. As Secretary of State Shultz put it in October 1985:

> Can we . . . accept the existence of the [Nicaraguan] regime in our hemisphere even if we find its ideology abhorrent? Must we oppose it simply because it is Communist? The answer is we must oppose the Nicaraguan dictators not simply because they are Communists, but because they are Communists who serve the interests of the Soviet Union and its Cuban client, and who threaten peace in the hemisphere.[70]

In February 1986 President Reagan put the point more colorfully, speaking of his desire to "remove" the "present structure" in Nicaragua and to make the Sandinistas "say uncle." In August he told the Mexican newspaper *Excelsior* that if Nicaragua did not become more democratic, "the only alternative" would be for the Contras to "have their way and take over."[71]

Even if the administration sincerely held only a limited aim for covert action, at least initially, no neat distinction between that objective and trying to overthrow the Sandinistas could stand in light of the Central American reality. It was plain for all to see that the Contras, while perhaps sympathetic to the limited American purpose, cared most about Nicaragua, not El Salvador. In assisting them, the United States could not escape identification with "their" purposes. Moreover, operationally, as in Chile a decade earlier, actions in pursuit of the two objectives could not be distinguished. Guerrilla attacks and sabotage against Nicaraguan ports and oil depots might distract and harass the Sandinistas, making it harder for them to help their comrades in El Salvador. Those actions would, however, also put pressure on the government itself, ultimately threatening its survival.

The distinction appeared to dissolve in the minds of policy makers themselves. By 1985 the United States appeared to have succeeded at its limited objective; there were no repetitions of the broad administration charges of 1981, and so the flow of arms from Nicaragua to El Salvador seemed to have slowed to a trickle. Either the motivation for covert action against Nicaragua had changed, escalating from limited to broader aims, or events had made it possible for the administration to admit that although it had stated limited goals under pressure from the Congress, it always had hoped for more. In either case, the covert intervention would be judged—by citizens in both the Americas and beyond—in light of its effects on Nicaragua, not El Salvador.

5

Covert Action and Unintended Results

In early 1975, during the investigations of the Church Committee, we asked for briefings on existing CIA paramilitary activities. We did so mostly for the sake of tidiness, not expecting to find much. What we were told confirmed our expectations: the "dummy" companies, or proprietaries, that had provided cover for much of the CIA's paramilitary activity during the war in Vietnam had been wound down; all that remained was a little residual training capability and small stocks of "sterile" weapons. What we did not learn because the Ford administration had not yet decided to tell us, but what we did soon learn, was that CIA paramilitary activities were moving sharply upward again, this time in Angola.

Covert intervention in Angola led to results quite different from what American policy makers had in mind. When South Africa intervened on behalf of the U.S.-supported factions, the FNLA and UNITA, a covert action intended to counter the Soviet Union and Cuba signaled something else: an alliance with the apartheid regime in Pretoria. The result was defeat, in the eyes of both Washington policy makers and the rest of the world.

The messy, half-secret circumstances of most covert interventions do little to help clearly calibrate the signals from American actions. The United States finds it difficult to control those it supports and to set limits on that support. It also may not have much choice over who becomes its partners in secret operations. For these reasons, history's assessment of a covert intervention can be strikingly at odds with what the United States intended.

Background to Intervention

A Portuguese colony for five centuries, Angola was, as one close observer put it, "an improbable locus for a superpower collision."[1] For fifteen years the Salazar dictatorship in Lisbon had fought a bloody war against Angolan liberation movements, but Portugal was a poor country, and the war—and a parallel one in Mozambique—was a drain on its finances and its young manhood. Throughout the early 1970s defections from Portugal's colonial armies gradually increased. In fact, the African experience was an important factor in the radicalization of the Portuguese military, which in April 1974 overthrew the Portuguese government of Marcello Caetano, a Salazar acolyte. The military council had neither the desire nor the resources to continue the war in Angola, or even to manage a lengthy transition. Angola would become independent, and soon.

Inside Angola, in anticipation of independence, three factions, fierce competitors during the war of liberation, jockeyed for position in a complicated power struggle. The three groups had their own regional and tribal bases, and their own external attachments; the Portuguese had exploited these differences during the colonial war, while the Organization of African

Unity (OAU) labored fruitlessly through the years to overcome them.

Of the three, the Popular Movement for the Liberation of Angola (MPLA), led by Agostinho Neto, was the most cosmopolitan, with links to Portuguese Socialists and Communists, and it had the best position in the capital, Luanda. Its tribal base, less marked than for the other groups, was Mbundu, concentrated in urban areas and in the north central part of Angola around Luanda. The three groups did not differ all that much in ideology or political program, and all three had received support from Communist countries. Still, the MPLA seemed the most clearly Marxist of the three, and it had been more openly critical of the United States for supporting the colonial regime.[2]

The National Front for the Liberation of Angola (FNLA) was the most formidable military force of the three. Anti-Marxist in the same way that the MPLA was pro-Marxist, it had been founded in 1962 by Holden Roberto. Its base was the Bakongo of northwestern Angola and into neighboring Zaire, and its patron was Zaire's strongman, Mobutu Sese Seko, a staunch U.S. ally and himself the beneficiary of U.S. covert action in the 1960s. For the FNLA, however, the link to Zaire, a military strength, was also a political weakness: many of the FNLA leaders were isolated by their French language, and their nationalist credentials were suspect. For reasons that had much more to do with China's competition with the Soviet Union than with any affinity between it and the FNLA, the FNLA had received arms from China since 1973, and those arms had been accompanied by a hundred-odd Chinese advisers in mid-1974.[3]

The third group was the National Union for the Total Independence of Angola (UNITA), founded by Jonas Savimbi in 1966. Savimbi had been a member of the FNLA but broke with Roberto, denouncing him as an agent of the United States and criticizing his refusal to cooperate with the MPLA. UNITA's support was mostly rural and in southern Angola. It lacked for organized military cadres and foreign sponsors, but it did have the largest ethnic base of the three groups—the Ovimbundu, comprising 31 percent of Angola's population. Its credo stressed self-sufficiency in a vaguely Maoist way but in the power struggle it was flexible, seeking to take advantage of necessity and so calling for a political solution to the conflict that would let it capitalize on its numerical strength.

In the wake of the April coup, Portugal's new leaders made sincere efforts at conciliation, bringing the three groups together twice in early 1975. In the Alvor agreement of January the three factions agreed to form a transitional government to be followed by elections; November 11, 1975, was set as independence date for Angola, Portugal's last African possession.

Predictably, however, that agreement was short-lived. The three sought, and received, both support and arms from their external allies. To sort out exactly which of those foreign sponsors acted first is virtually impossible. The Zairean press reported in August 1974 that the FNLA had received a large shipment of military equipment from Romania, and in September the FNLA publicly acknowledged its assistance from China.[4] The Soviets, who had cut off aid to the MPLA prior to the coup, announced in August that they regarded that group as the spokesman for the Angolan people. With the Portuguese military council tilting toward the MPLA, quantities of Soviet weaponry were permitted to enter Luanda in September and October, although exactly how much remains unclear.[5]

For its part, the United States had been in contact with Roberto of the FNLA since 1960, through the station in Kinshasa, Zaire's capital and near the southeastern corner of the country from which Roberto operated. Until 1969 he reportedly received money and weapons; after 1969 his support was reduced to a yearly $10,000 stipend for "intelligence gathering." The CIA stepped up its links to him in July 1974 and began passing him small amounts of money.[6]

The April coup in Portugal had taken Washington by surprise, and it was ill prepared to confront the Angolan tangle. In its review of policy toward southern Africa in 1969, National Security Study Memorandum 39, the incoming Nixon administration had expressed doubts about "the depth and resolve of black resolve" in Angola and "rule[d] out a black victory at any stage." Thus, there were no "realistic or supportable" alternatives to continued colonial rule,[7] and the United States had proceeded to reaffirm its support for the Portuguese colonial regime. As part of that policy, the CIA had withdrawn from Angola in 1970. What information on events in that country it did receive came through Angola's neighbors, particularly Zaire—and much of that came from Roberto.

With the transitional government in Angola visibly drifting toward civil war, the 40 Committee met in Washington on January 22, 1975, exactly a week after the Alvor agreement. The CIA proposed support, in the first instance political, for both the FNLA and UNITA. The committee authorized $300,000 for Roberto and the FNLA, which used the money to buy a radio station and a newspaper, but turned down the $100,000 for UNITA. Roberto was a known quantity, clearly a member of the "home team"; by contrast, UNITA appeared unreliable.[8]

The power struggle escalated throughout late 1974 and early 1975. The FNLA moved troops into Angola, along with elements of the Zairian army, and began contesting the MPLA in the northern part of the country. By March the Soviet Union had resumed supplies to the MPLA in earnest and transferred to it large quantities of AK-47 rifles, machine guns, bazookas, and rockets.[9] In March, the FNLA fought its way into Luanda, where it massacred some fifty MPLA members. By July, however, the MPLA had regained control of its Luanda bastion, the transitional government had collapsed entirely, and Roberto and Savimbi had joined forces—reluctantly, an alliance born of necessity.

A Modest Proposal

The impending collapse of opposition to the MPLA impelled Washington to act. The 40 Committee met in June, and an NSC task force on Angola was established. The key decision was taken in July, based on an options paper prepared by the Clandestine Service's Africa Division. The final version, submitted to the 40 Committee on July 14, outlined four options, not just the ritual bureaucratic trinity: (1) limited financial support for political activity, such as the CIA's January subvention to Roberto; (2) support designed to redress the military and political balance, with a $6 million price tag; (3) more support, $14 million, intended to give Roberto and Savimbi superiority over Neto provided the Soviet Union did not escalate; and (4) enough support to match Soviet escalation, estimated at $40 million, although there was no indication of how the Soviet response had been assessed.[10]

Official Washington was divided. In its briefing paper for the DCI, the Africa Division argued that, while a large shipment of weaponry to Roberto and Savimbi would not guarantee that they could establish control of all Angola, it would permit them to sustain a military balance that would both discourage further resort to arms and avoid a *"cheap Neto victory."*[11] In that way it would also reassure key African leaders in the region, like Mobutu and Kenneth Kaunda of Zambia, who were, in different ways, worried about an MPLA victory with Soviet backing even if diplomatic proprieties prevented them from saying so openly.

For the secretary of state, Henry Kissinger, the $14 million commitment was a minimum necessary to meet the Soviet strategic thrust. He outlined his view at a press conference in December: "The basic problem in our relations with the Soviet Union is the emergence of the Soviet Union into superpower status." In the 1960s "the disparity in strategic power" was "overwhelmingly" in America's favor; now, however, Moscow was "on the road to achieving effective strategic equality." That made "conscious restraint by both sides" imperative. But in Angola the Soviet Union was demonstrating no such restraint; on the contrary, it was trying to "impose on two-thirds of the population its own brand of government."

By contrast, Kissinger's assistant secretary of state for African affairs, Nathaniel Davis, who had moved to that job the previous April, having left the embassy in Chile in 1973, opposed covert involvement in the Angola civil war. His arguments, made in memos to the State Department representative on the 40 Committee, Undersecretary Joseph Sisco, reflected the views of most of the members of the NSC task force. At present, there was "no irrevocable commitment of U.S. power and prestige in Angola."[12] The CIA paper itself noted that the Soviets "can escalate the level of their aid more readily than we," and so "if we are to have a test of strength with the Soviets, we should find a more advantageous place."

Davis also ventured criticisms of the CIA's operational assumptions. The CIA paper, addressing the risks of exposure, located them mostly in the United States. It suggested that the CIA supply the FNLA and UNITA only with equipment that had belonged to the Zairian army, not with equipment that could be identified as having come only from the United States. To this, Davis argued that U.S. support would change military capabilities in a way that would be plainly visible. Moreover, "plausible U.S. official denial is no longer the recourse it might once have been thought to be—so the distinction the CIA paper makes between possible disclosure from authoritative or non-authoritative sources loses much significance."

The 40 Committee reviewed the options paper on July 14 and requested that an ad hoc interagency group submit a plan for spending $14 million in covert action, which the CIA submitted on July 16, code-named IAFEATURE. Under the Hughes-Ryan Amendment to the Foreign Assistance Act of 1974, President Ford was required to send Congress, in secret, a "finding" for any covert operation other than clandestine intelligence collection.

His "finding" for Angola, issued on July 18, 1975, the same day he authorized the first $6 million for the operation, was general. It did not mention Angola, only Africa, and it found the operation—described as "provision of material, support and advice to moderate nationalist movements for their use in creating a stable climate to allow genuine self-determination in newly emerging African states"[13]—to be important to the national security of the United States. Colby did, however, brief the Senate Foreign Relations Committee, and intelligence subcommittees of the House Armed Services and Appropriations committees—but not yet my Senate select committee.

On July 27, Ford authorized the additional $8 million. Two days later the first planeload of arms flew out of South Carolina, bound for Kinshasa, to replace Zairean weapons transferred to the FNLA and UNITA. Nathaniel Davis resigned as soon as he heard of the president's decision, in fact, as it turned out, before Ford actually signed the finding.

Stakes and Signals

In many respects, the Angolan episode runs parallel to the Bay of Pigs or Nicaragua. Under the heat of perceived threat, diplomatic action alone did not seem enough. The NSC interagency task force had recommended such an approach in June—a combination of pressure on the Soviet Union to reduce its support for the MPLA plus support for mediating initiatives by Portugal, African states, the U.N., or the OAU. The goal, in Davis's words, was to shift the "factional competition within Angola . . . back toward the political arena, thereby improving FNLA and UNITA prospects."[14]

Whether June was already too late for such an approach is

unknowable. In any case it was not tried. The task force recommendation became an option, one among three.[15] The United States did not approach the Soviet Union over Angola until the eleventh hour, in October. By that time it was too late.

Yet limited commitments, undertaken with the presumption of secrecy, conduced to larger ones. Washington first opted, in July 1975, for a limited program with limited objectives; at that point, the goal was only to deny the MPLA and their Soviet backers an easy victory. Yet it was tempting to hope for more. As the fighting in Angola escalated, it was also tempting to believe that just a little more would convert that hope into a reality. President Ford authorized another $10.7 million in covert assistance on August 20 and another $7 million on November 27.[16]

The very escalation of fighting, however, meant that the presumption of secrecy could not be sustained. The conflict became open warfare. Which external power was backing which internal factions could not remain secret. From Washington's perspective, the whole affair became a self-fulfilling prophecy. For the United States, defining the conflict in terms of the superpower rivalry made it all the more likely that arms would determine the outcome. In that escalation, the United States was, as Davis had suggested in the summer, ill positioned to compete. It was fighting what John Stockwell, of the CIA Angola task force, called an "economy-sized war." By contrast, U.S. estimates put the amount of Soviet assistance to the MPLA between March 1975 and February 1976 at $300 million.[17]

The contrast is illustrative even if the Soviet figure was too high and that for covert American assistance, $33 million, too low—it did not include salaries for the eighty-odd CIA personnel on the ground, nor assistance to Zaire and Zambia, which passed weaponry to the FNLA and UNITA. For its part, however, the MPLA could count on the Cubans, who began appearing in numbers in August and in large numbers in late October, totaling 3,000–5,000 by the end of November but some 12,000 by February.[18]

What the United States had was South Africa, and like it or not, that fact was decisive. South African troops frequently had entered Angola under Portuguese rule to confront Southwest Africa People's Organization (SWAPO) guerrillas operating into South African-controlled Namibia.[19] South African military and intelligence officers met with FNLA and UNITA leaders, including Savimbi, a number of times over the summer of 1975. In August South African troops occupied an area on the Cunene River in Angola near major hydroelectric installations developed by South Africa in cooperation with Portugal. By September South African officers were training UNITA units.

South Africa entered the war in force in October. The exact timing remains in dispute, but the outline of the intervention is clear.[20] In the middle of the month a "mystery column" of white mercenaries, FNLA and UNITA troops, and some South Africans entered Angola, armed with helicopter gunships and Panhard armored cars. Later on this force, code-named Zula, was joined by regular South African units. They pushed the MPLA out of the southern half of Angola, marching 650 miles north before being stopped 150 miles from Luanda as Cubans poured into Angola. South African advisers participated in an FNLA march on the capital from the north. By the time the South Africans withdrew, they numbered, according to the official account, some 2,000.

How closely South African and American actions were related is still a matter for conjecture. Certainly South Africa had its own reasons for intervening. Its concrete stakes in projects on the Cunene was one; its relationship with Savimbi another. More important, contiguity made Angola critical to the war on SWAPO. Moreover, events seemed to validate forebodings expressed by South Africans—often in language that seemed a caricature to outsiders—of a Communist thrust in Africa. As

John Vorster, the prime minister, put it of the Soviets and Cubans: "We know that the aim is not simply the establishment of a Marxist state in Angola, but to endeavor to secure a whole row of Marxist states from Angola to Dar-es-Salaam."[21]

By the end of November, P. W. Botha, then defense minister, was criticizing the "free world" for not showing a more direct interest in "getting the Russians out of southern Africa."[22] Kissinger labeled untrue any charges of American "collusion" with Pretoria, and Colby insisted that the CIA operation and its supply lines had been kept scrupulously separate from South Africa's.[23]

Yet American and South African policies were at least running in parallel. South African leaders hinted at consultation. For example, Botha told his parliament in January that South Africa's action "had the blessing of several African countries as well as at least one 'free world' power."[24] There were reports aplenty of contacts between the militaries and intelligence services of the two countries, and the operational requirements of aiding the anti-MPLA forces would have required contact, if not collaboration, in any case. Daniel Moynihan, the U.S. ambassador to the United Nations, while denying explicit coordination, admitted to a "convergence in policy" between the two governments. "We are doing the same thing, sort of," he said.[25]

Whatever the extent of consultation, the South African intervention identified both the anti-MPLA forces and U.S. assistance to them with the white regime in Pretoria. The game was over. It ended first in the United States, where the link to South Africa undermined the fragile acquiescence of those senators and members of Congress who had been informed of IAFEATURE. The $7 million passed to the FNLA and UNITA in November had exhausted the CIA Contingency Fund. Congress first blocked a proposal to transfer $28 million in Defense Department funds. Then, in December, the Senate voted the Clark Amendment banning further covert assistance—for the first time in American history cutting off a "covert" program with an open vote. The House of Representatives followed suit in January.

In the region, the South African intervention destroyed any possibility of collective African support for a compromise and isolated the "moderates," especially Zaire and Zambia. Most African states had adopted a wait-and-see approach to events in Angola after independence. Even as late as January, a special OAU meeting divided, 22–22, on the question of whether to recognize the MPLA as the legitimate government of Angola. By this time Savimbi was already fearful that South Africa was about to withdraw, and arranged, through Kaunda, to meet with Vorster directly.[26]

However, soon after the summit, with fighting escalating, tension between FNLA and UNITA breaking into open conflict, and FNLA positions collapsing in the north, the OAU did recognize the MPLA after a majority of its members had done so. South African troops began to depart in late January, and by late March the exodus was complete, Pretoria having received assurances from the MPLA that the Cunene works would be allowed to proceed.

South African intervention made the outcome a foregone conclusion. Even those African leaders who fretted about Cuban soldiers and a Soviet-backed regime on their borders had no choice but to accept it. The United States became not a force for a broadly based government in Luanda but an ally of Pretoria. That was what American covert action signaled. For the MPLA it was a stroke of good fortune, as important politically as Soviet assistance was on the battlefield. For UNITA and the FNLA it was correspondingly bad fortune; UNITA was—to paraphrase the Mexican saying about the United States—so far from God yet so close to South Africa. Savimbi felt he had no choice in its allies, saying he would take help from anyone who would give it.

Even if it did not encourage South Africa to intervene, Washington was by then the prisoner of its own conception: no retreat from the conflict could have been graceful. Stakes had been created, building pressure to up them. Having defined the conflict in East-West terms, the MPLA victory was a defeat, so proclaimed by the United States. The South African intervention sealed the "defeat."

Falling into Bad Company

In Angola, the United States found itself in the company of South Africa, and the signal conveyed by that fact outweighed all other American purposes, an outcome much different from what policy makers had intended. In the instances of Iran and Guatemala, private interests were deeply intertwined with the making of public policy. In both, and especially in Guatemala, the interventions suggested commercial interests, not strategic ones. They seemed to be interventions on behalf of United Fruit or Anglo-Iranian.

In neither case was that perception entirely wrong. Anglo-Iranian's role in developing AJAX remains a tangled question, and one that involves British more than American policy making. Nevertheless, Roosevelt did meet with representatives of the company. In inheriting Britain's operation, the United States could not escape the image of inheriting Britain's stakes. And Anglo-Iranian appeared large in those stakes, especially to Iranians.

United Fruit's position in Guatemala was even more dominant than that of Anglo-Iranian in Iran, being entangled with U.S. policy making to an extraordinary degree—from Foster Dulles to "Tommy the Cork" to "Beetle" Smith. It takes no special penchant for conspiracy theories to see the American intervention in the light of *la frutera*'s near stranglehold on the Guatemalan economy. Small wonder, then, that Guatemalans and other Central Americans saw it precisely in that way. The

United States could not escape the image of overlapping private and public interests.

That was the case even if, in retrospect, the fairest conclusion is that American officials acted because they believed strategic interests were at stake, not commercial ones. What American officials saw in the nationalization of Anglo-Iranian and in Arbenz's actions against U.S. economic interests was confirmation that both were tools of the Communists. That confirmation weighed more heavily in their calculations than the specific economic stakes. Recall Dulles's defense of Eisenhower administration policy: for him, the problem was "Communist infiltration in Guatemala," not United Fruit.[27]

Take Dulles at his word. In Washington, United Fruit's access to senior officials got it their attention. Once attentive, they construed United Fruit's arguments in light of *their* concerns—security, not commercial monopolies. Yet it is worth noting that in the 1950s Washington saw Arbenz's and Mossadeq's nationalizations as evidence that they were Communists or at least tools of the Communists. Certainly, Latin Americans and Asians and Africans did note that fact.

Moreover, having chosen to act, the United States cannot easily avoid identification with the interests of its partners, like it or not. For Howard Hunt, that identification diminished the success in Guatemala: "We did the right thing for the wrong reason. And I always felt a sense of distaste over that. I wasn't a mercenary worker for United Fruit."[28]

The problem of bad company, and the signals sent by American identification with it, arises even if the partner is less a caricature than United Fruit and even in times more recent than the 1950s. In March 1970 the 40 Committee approved the "spoiling operations" aimed at the 1970 Chilean elections. The next month a group from the Business Council on Latin America met with Assistant Secretary of State Charles Meyer, who had joined the administration from a career as a Sears Roebuck executive in Latin America. The group sought positive support for Alessandri, the only candidate who opposed expropriations. The chairman of the board of Anaconda, one of the giants of the Chilean copper industry, C. Jay Parkinson, said his and other interested companies were willing to put up $500,000 to block Allende's election.

Meyer was noncommittal, and Korry expressed his opposition in characteristically colorful language when he heard of the meeting.[29] Alessandri, the candidate of the rich, could afford to fund his own campaign. Moreover, in Korry's view, for the United States to move beyond the covert anti-Allende "spoiling operations" to actual support of the Chilean right was bound to backfire.

Over the summer, John McCone—the former DCI but now a member of the board of directors of ITT, of which in 1970 Chile's national telephone company was a subsidiary—approached Helms about a joint CIA–ITT program to assist Alessandri. In 1964, during McCone's tenure as DCI, a group of private companies had offered a million and a half dollars to support Frei against Allende. The offer went to the 40 Committee's predecessor, the 303 Committee, which rejected it, thus setting a precedent. To the committee, as to Hunt in 1954, the mingling of private motives and public purposes did not seem quite honorable. Moreover, CIA officers worried that the collaboration would make it harder to keep the election operation secret.[30]

Nevertheless, contacts between ITT and the CIA continued. In July, after a colorful ITT public relations man named Harold Hendrix had met with a CIA official in Santiago, McCone again contacted Helms. He arranged for the ITT head, Harold Geneen, to meet William Broe, the CIA's Western Hemisphere division chief. Geneen in turn offered Broe a million dollars for a pro-Alessandri campaign. The CIA rejected the offer but did advise ITT how to pass the money, in secret, to Alessandri. Later, the CIA also advised ITT how to pass money to the National party, a channel comprising two CIA assets who were at the same time getting Agency money to carry out the "spoiling operations."[31]

As the September elections approached, CIA officials remained in contact with ITT, both in Santiago and in Washington, and continued to provide advice. In all, some $250,000 in ITT money went to the Alessandri campaign, $100,000 to the National party; according to CIA documents, the station informed Korry of the CIA role in the former but not the latter. (Other U.S. businesses contributed another $350,000, but the CIA had no role in those subventions.)

By advising ITT, the CIA was, in effect, helping implement a policy the government had rejected. However, the episode seems less an example of the CIA-out-of-control than yet another instance of neat distinction in the minds of Washington policy makers—in this case between anti-Allende "spoiling operations" and pro-Alessandri support—being frustrated by the reality of a foreign country.

These private–public contacts continued after the elections. Several days after the election, a concerned Geneen asked McCone to get in touch with Helms again. Before Helms responded, however, Track II was set in motion. Agustín Edwards, the publisher of *El Mercurio,* was also a Pepsi-Cola bottler and longtime friend of Pepsi-Cola's president, Donald Kendall, who was in turn a friend and political ally of Richard Nixon. Edwards came to Washington to predict doom and plead the Chilean opposition's case (and his own). Kendall, impressed, arranged for Edwards to meet Helms. He also arranged a breakfast with Henry Kissinger and Attorney General John Mitchell for the morning of September 15, the day of the meeting at which Nixon opened Track II.

By his testimony, Helms thought these contacts made a difference: "I have the impression that the President called this meeting [at which Track II was started] because of Edwards' presence in Washington and what he heard from Kendall about what Edwards was saying about conditions in Chile and what was happening there."[32] These comments do not settle the question of how important these private contacts were in setting either Track I or Track II in motion, but that is not the point.

The central point is simply that the United States cannot escape being identified with the interests of those who become its partners, whoever they are. Both United Fruit and ITT were unusual companies, but the problem also obtains when the partners are less bizarre.

Covertness may compound the problem. Because the United States was not prepared to make public what it *was* doing, it could not make clear what it was *not* doing. What ITT and the other American businesses were up to was an open secret in Santiago. In those circumstances, Chileans were bound to assume that the CIA was in cahoots with them; no doubt that assumption would have prevailed in Santiago even if the CIA had been doing nothing. Later, however, when the shape of American covert action was revealed, the nuances of that program were lost, and the revelations were more likely to validate than to diminish the signal that the United States had conspired with American business to prevent Salvador Allende from being elected president of Chile.

Sending and Receiving Signals

In other ways as well, the signals sent through covert action diverge from what policy makers intended. We mislead as well as inform foreigners. Sometimes, indeed, we mislead ourselves. I was in Washington early in the Reagan administration for a CIA conference on developments in Western Europe. After the session, I joined several analysts from the intelligence side of the house for a beer. They grumbled about a National Intelligence

Estimate (NIE)—the intelligence community's premier assessment—then being prepared on terrorism.

The first draft had been skeptical about the extent of Soviet support for international terrorism. That conclusion did not square with the preconceptions of the Agency's new political masters, so the draft was returned with the suggestion that the analysts consult Claire Sterling, whose just published book had cited a number of examples of Soviet support for terrorism.[33]

The analysts did not appreciate the suggestion that they had been upstaged by a writer using only public sources, but did check her many examples. It turned out that virtually all of them were CIA disinformation—articles planted by covert operators in various media. It obviously was not her fault; she had cited them in good faith as evidence in support of her argument. Yet the right hand did not know what the left was doing, even within the Washington machine. Attempting to influence foreigners, we had misled ourselves.

The terrorism example is relatively minor. Others are not so minor. Iran 1953 remained an official secret in Washington even though the American role spread almost immediately through the entire political class in Teheran, and so American officials later dealing with Iran might have acted in ignorance of that critical particular. At the very extreme are the CIA attempts to kill Fidel Castro—at least eight plots between 1961 and 1965.[34]

Imagine the signal these plots conveyed to Castro. The plots remained secret in the United States for ten years after the last of them, but Castro must have known of them. He certainly suspected that the CIA was trying to kill him. In August 1975 he gave Senator George McGovern a list of twenty-four alleged attempts on his life that he believed had been undertaken by the CIA.[35] Castro was right to suspect anything the United States said to or promised him.

Worse, senior U.S. policy makers—who included, by what evidence is available, presidents of the United States—would have remained ignorant of one specific, powerful ground for suspicion on Castro's part. His reactions to American proposals would have seemed to them exaggerated, impossible to account, even crazy. Yet Castro certainly would have assumed that American presidents knew the CIA was trying to kill him: foreigners always assume the U.S. government is more coherent and purposive than it is, and third world leaders under attack are, understandably, especially prone to see method in our incoherence.

To be sure, American hostility to Castro's Cuba was overt as well as covert. Castro may have assumed the CIA was trying to kill him even if it had not been. Nor was the United States prepared to negotiate with Castro about much of anything other than the terms of his capitulation. Yet in other, less dramatic cases, the mixed signals being conveyed foreign leaders mislead American officials, especially if they do not know of the covert signal.

In the instance of Nicaragua during the 1980s, for example, the covert signal, the Contras, was not secret. Publicly, the United States supported negotiations through the Contadora process; aid to the Contras was intended to push the Sandinista government toward the bargaining table. Perhaps aid to the Contras did serve as that kind of stick; Sandinista aid to the rebels in El Salvador did trail off after 1981. Even then, however, the fact of an external enemy, especially one supported by the giant to the north, not only was useful as a rallying point for the Sandinista revolution; it also justified—in the eyes of many Latin Americans, including those who found the regime distasteful—the Sandinistas accepting help from Cuba.

But perhaps the signal to the Sandinistas was quite different. For the U.S. administration, the character of the Sandinista regime, and not just its international behavior, clearly was on the agenda. Moreover, that administration more than hinted that its real objective was replacing the Sandinista government, not merely constraining its actions.

In those circumstances, it would not have taken much paranoia on the part of the Managua government to construe the signals it received from the United States thus: they say they want to see us overthrown, they give money to the Contras, whose purpose is precisely that, so what is there to negotiate about—just the terms of our surrender? It may be that was precisely what the administration intended to signal; so its critics, within and beyond the United States, feared. If not, its actions ran the risk of belying its intentions: trying to overthrow a government while also seeking to negotiate a *modus vivendi* with it may push it to negotiate more seriously, but it may also only convince it there is nothing to negotiate save its demise.

Threats and Responses

These issues of signaling run from covert action as an instrument to the broader foreign policies from which it emerges and in which it is embedded. One way to judge the decision to intervene covertly is to assess it in the light of the threat to which it was a response. In the case of Angola, for instance, no one in official Washington argued that an MPLA victory with Soviet backing would pose a direct threat to American national security. Rather, the argument for intervention was based on an indirect threat of two sorts. First, such a victory would represent a negative for the United States in the global competition with the Soviet Union. It would be a blow to America's credibility. Second, more specifically, it would also represent the extension of Soviet power into a new area, and was thus, in American eyes, a violation of the spirit of the 1972 Soviet-American agreed "code of conduct" about the third world. For Kissinger, in particular, credibility was crucial, and so covert action offered a way to demonstrate that Moscow had to reckon with the prospect of U.S. involvement, even in Africa.

In the instance of Angola, it is evident that at least the Africanists at the State Department were skeptical—that the threat posed in Angola justified intervention or that covert action was an effective response, or both. In the case of Chile before and during the Allende presidency, it is possible to compare a series of American decisions about covert action with the government's simultaneous assessments of developments in Chile as they affected U.S. interests.

Those assessments came in several forms, of which NIEs are the best known. NIEs were, and are, joint agreed assessments produced by the entire American intelligence community; dissenting agencies register their views in footnotes.[36] Before 1973 a formal Board of National Estimates supervised the production of NIEs; subsequently they became the responsibility of national intelligence officers, senior analysts drawn from the CIA and other agencies. American intelligence produced one NIE on Chile per year between 1969 and 1973; in addition, Chile was the subject of several Intelligence Memorandums and Intelligence Notes, prepared by the CIA and State's Bureau of Intelligence and Research, respectively.

NIEs have the predictable defects of the quasi-judicial process that produces them: they often are least-common-denominator compromises, with disagreements obscured in woolly language, not highlighted. They are seldom decisive for senior policy makers, who, for better or worse, are more likely to pay attention to special analyses prepared for them or even to single bits of raw intelligence. Yet they do represent "the government's" best assessment and, while classified, receive a wide circulation within officialdom.

NIEs offer few explicit assessments of the threat posed by an Allende Chile. Intelligence analyses shy away from such conclusions because they depend on definitions of American interests—the competence of policy makers, not intelligence assessors. Rather, the NIEs focus on developments in Chile and so provide the wherewithal for inferences about the threat.

An Intelligence Memorandum issued just after the September

4, 1970, Chilean elections was, however, explicit about the threat. Although written by the CIA, it reflected the views of the Interdepartmental Group for Inter-American Affairs, which had prepared the response to NSSM 97 and included representatives from State, Defense, and the White House in addition to the CIA.

This memorandum concluded that the United States had no vital interests within Chile, that the world military balance of power would not be significantly altered by an Allende regime, and that his victory would not pose a threat to the peace of the region. What an Allende victory would do was threaten the cohesion of the hemisphere and represent an advance for Marxist ideas, a psychological setback for the United States.

Reading between the lines of the NIEs, it is possible to assess the threat posed by particular developments. One example is the likely course of Chile's relations with the Socialist world, in particular Cuba and the Soviet Union. The 1969 NIE predicted than *any* new Chilean administration, Socialist or conservative, would broaden Chile's foreign relations. However, it noted that Allende in particular would be deterred from moving too far toward the Communist countries by Chilean nationalism, which would oppose the tutelage of Moscow or Havana as much as that of Washington. The next year's NIE predicted that Allende would recognize Cuba (he did) and expressed concern about the possible growth of Soviet influence, including the possibility of a major Soviet military presence.

Over Allende's tenure, the tone of assessments on this issue indicated less, not more, cause for concern. For example, as Chile expanded its links to the Communist nations, the 1971 NIE stressed that Allende was careful not to subordinate Chile's interests to them or to risk a rupture with any non-Communist nation on which Chile depended for aid. The 1971 and 1972 NIEs both emphasized Allende's independent, nationalist course and his commitment to nonalignment.

By 1971, the NIE described Cuban-Chilean relations as distant ideologically but closer economically. Despite Allende's long friendship with Fidel Castro, he had refrained from dramatic overtures to him. The next year's NIE judged that Havana had been circumspect in using Chile as a base for revolution in the hemisphere.

With regard to a Soviet military presence, the 1971 NIE shifted ground from the previous year, expressing the view that "probably"—the fudge words for which NIEs are famous—neither Allende nor the Chilean military would tolerate a permanent Soviet military presence in Chile. The Soviet Union would continue to cultivate Allende through the Chilean Communist party, but it "probably" would continue to doubt its ability to make much of a dent in Allende's independence. In 1972 the NIE addressed Soviet attitudes, characterizing them as cautious and restrained, lest Moscow antagonize the United States or incur an open-ended economic commitment to Chile. Those same themes, and particularly Soviet unwillingness to make a Cuba-sized economic commitment to Chile, were underscored in a State Intelligence Note written after Allende's December 1972 visit to the Soviet Union.

Another element of the threat was the possibility of Chilean subversion in the hemisphere. The CIA Intelligence Memorandum of September 1970 noted that Chile long had been relatively open to extreme leftists and would become more so under Allende. On the other hand, the Chilean Communists themselves opposed violent groups; that fact, plus Allende's care not to provoke a backlash in his own military, would limit assistance to extremists.

Those predictions were confirmed in a State Intelligence Note of June 1971, which said that contrary to earlier indications that Allende might provide some assistance to insurgents in neighboring countries, he had been careful to avoid actions that would strain relations with those neighbors. Latin American expatriates residing in Chile had been warned they could do so only if they did not engage in political activities; some of the more zealous expatriates had been asked to leave.

In sum, the note concluded, Allende was unlikely to assist the export of insurgency. The 1972 NIE said that Allende had taken pains to convince his Latin American neighbors that he did not share Castro's revolutionary vocation. While some revolutionaries in Chile had received arms and money from groups in Allende's coalition, that probably had not occurred at Allende's behest (though perhaps not without his knowledge).

It is intriguing to compare what the intelligence community wrote about Chile with the presumptions on which the covert action was based. The 1970 Chile NIE, written in July before the September elections, was controversial within the community, the division paralleling that over covert action: the Latin Americanists at State were more hopeful, the U.S. ambassador and CIA station chief much less so.

The view of the latter group prevailed, with some qualifications, in the NIE: an Allende victory would mean the gradual imposition of a classic Marxist-Leninist regime in Chile. Democracy would survive for several years, but Allende could, the NIE noted, take Chile a long way down the road toward a Soviet-style Eastern European Communist state in the six years of his tenure. He would face obstacles—the military, the Church, the Christian Democrats, the Congress, and some unions—yet a temporary consumption boom would give him a chance to secure control of Congress in the 1983 elections. Chile was headed toward socialism of the Marxist type by the *vía pacífica* ("peaceful road").

The 1971 NIE, issued in August when Allende had held power for nine months, was less shrill. Allende was popular but had a long, hard way to go to consolidate a Marxist leadership; that outcome was not inevitable. In fact, while up to that point he had taken great care to observe constitutional forms and would want to continue doing so, he was judged likely to have to use techniques of more and more dubious legality to perpetuate his control.

The next NIE came out in June 1972. By then the prospects for the survival of democracy in Chile appeared better than at any time since Allende's inauguration. The system had been remarkably resilient. Elections of all sorts had continued normally, and progovernment forces had abided by results that went against them. Opposition parties in Congress had been able to stall government initiatives and curb Allende's power; opposition media had survived government intimidation and sustained their criticism. The NIE predicted that over the next year Allende was likely to slow the pace of his revolution to accommodate the opposition and so preserve the gains he had made.

One final NIE was prepared before Allende's overthrow in September 1973. It did not predict that coup: it noted the polarization in Chile was eroding Chile's tradition of compromise but gave only an "outside chance" to a move by the military. Its best bet was a political standoff, for Allende had not consolidated power even though he was able and popular and even though low-income Chileans believed he had advanced their interests.

The irony of these intelligence assessments is that they were written in ignorance of American covert action. Given the compartmentation of the CIA, the analysts who wrote NIEs did not know of the operations their DDO colleagues were forwarding to the 40 Committee. Hence the 1972 estimate that the Chilean opposition was durable was written without knowledge that precisely that opposition was receiving covert U.S. funding. There was no estimate of whether the opposition would survive *without* that funding.

And so quite opposite conclusions can fairly be drawn. On one hand, the NIEs undercut the presumption that the opposition was in danger of extinction and, undercutting the presumption, also undercut the argument for covert action. Forty Committee appropriations for opposition groups were growing just as the intelligence estimates were becoming more optimistic about the survival of those groups. On the other hand, the vitality of the Chilean opposition, and especially the sharp improvement in its prospects as assessed in NIEs between 1970 and 1972, can be seen as evidence of the success of U.S. covert action in Chile.

In any case, nothing in the assessments suggests that an Allende government posed a serious threat to the United States or to the region. Assessments written before he came to power expressed some concern about subversion and a Soviet military presence, but that waned once he was in office. Overall, the assessments matched Kissinger's famous quip to reporters "Chile is a dagger pointed at the heart of Antarctica!"—though for Kissinger the line was in jest, not a serious assessment of the threat: Allende was an annoyance and a blow to U.S. hopes for governance in Latin America. He and his government were not a serious threat to U.S. national security. Whatever the rationale for covert action against him was, it was not that.

In Chile in the period 1970–73, U.S. officials evidently did not consider covert action a last or next-to-last resort, to be used only in dire circumstances menacing the United States. For them, it was a more normal means—an instrument of middle resort.

Toting up Effects

Assessing covert actions in light of the threat as assessed at the time is one way to judge them. Hazarding evaluations in retrospect is, of course, even more speculative. Almost by definition, "failures" at achieving intended purposes are easier to discern than are "successes." The Bay of Pigs was a failure all around: lives of brave Cubans were spent; the United States was seen to be intervening; and the intervention failed. On the surface, Angola 1975 is similar: the MPLA was installed while the American role in trying to prevent that outcome was exposed.

However, the "failure" in Angola might be argued to be more ambiguous. If the purpose of covert action was to raise the price of victory for the MPLA and its Soviet and Cuban backers, then it might be counted a short-run success. Yet U.S. officials did not convey the impression that their aims were so limited, either at the time or later. And that aim does not seem commensurate with the likelihood that U.S. intervention would become public.

"Successes" in the short run are still harder to assess for it is never clear what would have happened *without* the covert action. History admits of no controlled experiments, nor does it permit a rerun to see what would have happened "if." It may be that the action, while marginal, was just the bit of "support for our friends" that tipped the balance in the internal politics of a foreign country. On the other hand, it may be that the U.S. support was entirely superfluous, that the same "successful" outcome would have ensued without U.S. involvement. Thus, all the covert action accomplished was to implicate the United States and tarnish the "success" by labeling it "made in America" when the existence of the covert action became known.

Consider again the instance of Chile under Allende. There is no question that opposition parties and media were the objects of pressure from the Allende government, ranging from fomenting labor disputes to withholding advertising and credits to a variety of legal harassments, including periodic arrests of editors. What is harder to assess is how far these tactics by the Allende government departed from business-as-usual in Latin America when the political "outs" become "ins," especially in deeply polarized politics. And since the opposition forces did survive to fight another day, there is no telling whether CIA support for them was decisive or irrelevant.

What *is* clear is the signal conveyed to history by U.S. covert action. In retrospect, most reasonably objective observers conclude that Salvador Allende's experiment in Chile would have failed on its own terms.[37] Ariel Dorfman, a Chilean poet and Allende sympathizer who spent a dozen years in exile after the

1973 coup, believes that U.S. covert action was a factor in Allende's downfall but grants that when the coup came it "was welcomed by an enormous number of Chileans, perhaps even by a majority—as salvation from a future dictatorship."[38]

Yet history's lesson is not that Allende would have fallen of his own accord. History's lesson is that the United States overthrew him in 1973. That is the lesson even if it is untrue in the narrow sense: Washington did not engineer his coup, nor did the CIA or the U.S. military participate in it. The fact of U.S. covert action muddied history's lesson. At a minimum, as I put it a decade ago—with the understatement of someone before the TV cameras for the first time—at a press conference on the Senate select committee's findings: "It is fair to say that the United States cannot escape some responsibility for his [Allende's] downfall."[39]

Seen in the longer light of history, even those cases, like Iran 1953 and Guatemala 1954, that seemed clear-cut "successes" at the time, are difficult to judge. Again, we do not know what would have happened without the covert action; too many events have intervened between then and now. With the perspective of three decades, neither Mossadeq nor Arbenz seems a tool of the Communists, much less the Soviet Union. Mossadeq was above all a fiercely anti-British nationalist. Although the competition was not challenging, he was more of a democrat than the shah. Arbenz seems a committed reformer, albeit perhaps a fairly weak man.

Both sought to preserve links to and even the good will of the United States. In terms of arms and strategies, both were ill prepared for confrontation with the United States. Had they not been under attack, covertly, might they have retained links to the United States, not turned the other way? The same question has been posed with regard to Castro's Cuba. It might be stretched to Sandinista Nicaragua.

The answers are unknowable. An affirmative answer seems more plausible in the instances of Mossadeq and Arbenz, less so in Castro's. Historians will continue to argue whether that is true because Castro had learned *his* lessons from history, because he was a committed Communist all along (even if he did not quite realize it), or some combination of the two. A "yes" answer is also less plausible for the Sandinistas, who seemed determined to make a revolution in opposition to the United States and who were, to boot, distinctly hotheaded, enough so to worry their ally, Fidel Castro.

For my purposes, however, the attitude of the United States is more important than those of nations targeted by its covert action. The United States almost inevitably would have become hostile to them in any case. That hostility was expressed openly as well as covertly; no doubt the American attitude would have been hostile had there been no covert action. In that sense, it is unfair to make covert action carry too much of the weight of U.S. foreign policy.

Washington did not immediately turn to harsh opposition to Castro Cuba, and it provided some economic assistance in the first years of Sandinista Nicaragua. Yet at each stage, the minimum requirements of their revolutions probably were more than the United States were prepared to countenance. U.S. limits were defined much more by broad attitudes toward the world than by the availability of covert action or any other policy instrument. And so the spiral of hostility continued, almost inevitably. Probably it was inevitable also in the instances of Mossadeq and Arbenz, given prevailing American attitudes of the times.

Similarly, AJAX and SUCCESS cannot fairly be ascribed too much credit—or too much blame—for what happened afterward in Iran and Guatemala. On one hand, AJAX restored the shah of Iran to his throne, where he remained for nearly a quarter century, a pro-Western bastion in a turbulent region. Twenty-five years of stability is no mean feat in international affairs.

On the other hand, U.S. covert action identified Iran and the shah more closely with the United States than was good for either of them. It also set in motion a kind of psychological dependence by the shah on the United States that Americans no doubt liked initially but came to lament in 1977 and 1978. It could also be argued that AJAX may have frustrated an evolution of Iranian politics that would have served long-term U.S. interests better than the shah did. Mossadeq's National Front might have become the democratic nationalists that Washingtonians so earnestly hoped for in Iran a quarter century later. Dealing with Mossadeq would have been uncomfortable in the short run but perhaps preferable in the long.

We will never know. Yet the aspects of U.S. policy that loomed so large in the shah's downfall in 1979 were overt, not covert: his image as a U.S. client, the waste and corruption associated with his massive U.S. arms purchases, and his own dependence on the United States—all of which owed much more to U.S. policy during the 1970s than to the events of 1953.

A similar conclusion applies to Guatemala in 1954. In retrospect, the "success" of SUCCESS looks more ambiguous than it seemed at the time. Perhaps Arbenz would have turned out to be a modernizing nationalist. He might have begun to wrench Guatemala away from the feudal oligarchs who controlled it and set his country on a happier, more stable path than it has experienced. Or suppose Arbenz's actions actually had provided more confirmation of Washington's fear than it appears in retrospect; suppose he had moved far to the left. That might at least have compelled the United States to get serious about Central America—in the 1950s not the 1980s.

Instead, the success of covert action permitted official Washington to do just what it desired with regard to Guatemala—forget about it. The squeaky wheel was eliminated, not greased, but the cart seemed able to move without it. Guatemala, like the rest of Central America, dropped out of sight in U.S. foreign policy, its position throughout most of history. Covert action dealt with the problem quickly and tidily.

As with Iran, however, most of the blame or credit lies with U.S. foreign policy, not with covert action. PBSUCCESS did not make it inevitable that Washington would forget about Guatemala; it only made it possible. David Phillips laments, "Castillo Armas was a bad President, tolerating corruption throughout his government and kowtowing to the United Fruit Company more than his own people." But, he argues, the United States "could have prevented this with the vigorous exercise of diplomatic pressure . . . to assure that he pursued social reform for the many rather than venal satisfaction for a few. Instead, Washington breathed a collective sigh of relief and turned to other international problems."[40] We do not know whether or not Phillips is correct in his belief that the United States might have exerted leverage on Castillo Armas; we do know he is right that it did not try.

The easy success in Guatemala also contained a lesson for would-be revolutionaries, a lesson about U.S. policy, not just covert action, although covert action was that policy's most vivid symbol. For a twenty-five-year-old Argentine doctor who was with Arbenz in Guatemala and who fled with him to Mexico, where he met a young Cuban named Raúl Castro, the lesson was

> that no Latin American reform, no matter how justified, would be accepted by the United States, not if it impinged on American economic interests. He was also convinced that Arbenz' failure to arm the peasants had caused his downfall. . . . Latin revolutionaries, he argued, must build an army whose loyalty is to the government, not independent of it, and they must spurn moderation, because moderation in the face of American hostility is futile. When, seven years later, the CIA went to Cuba to do to Castro what it had done to Arbenz, Guevara and the Castro brothers would be ready.[41]

That young Argentine was Ernesto "Che" Guevara. Phillips recalled starting a file on Guevara as a matter of routine, a file that eventually "became one of the thickest to be maintained by the CIA."[42]

6

Lessons for the Future

From the start, there was nothing much covert about the covert U.S. intervention in Nicaragua. Neither the November 1981 options nor the decision were very secret. Reporters were passed copies of both documents. After one major story in the Washington *Post* in March 1982, Senator Barry Goldwater, Republican chairman of the Senate Intelligence Committee, confirmed that "everything in the *Post* story was true," and in July the DCI, William Casey, told the New York *Times* that the president had approved covert operations toward Nicaragua the previous November.

This "overt" covert action was something new, even if not without precedent in postwar history. It was overt not just because it, along with broader U.S. policy toward Central America, was controversial, or because Congress openly voted to fund it. It was overt because the Reagan administration itself was not much interested in secrecy. It regarded aid to the Contras as good policy, an element of its global program to put pressure on Marxist governments in the third world, especially those aligned with the Soviet Union.

In November 1986, however, it turned out that the Reagan administration had been conducting a covert operation that *was* secret—selling arms to Iran. In a strange twist, it also turned out that the Iranian operation had crossed—in a way that was apparently kept secret even from the president—with aid to the Contras. "Overt" covert action of a new type in Nicaragua intersected with a covert operation in Iran that repeated old patterns: it became public sooner rather than later, and the result was quite different from what Washington had had in mind.

From Geostrategic Opening to Hostages

In November 1986, a pro-Syrian Beirut newspaper, *Al Shiraa*, published a bizarre account of a secret visit made to Iran the previous May by former national security advisor, Robert McFarlane.[1] The account would have been dismissed as another piece of partisan Middle East nonsense, except that it was true. The visit was first confirmed by Ali Akbar Hashemi Rafsanjani, speaker of the Iranian parliament, then by McFarlane.

The story became stranger and stranger. McFarlane, it seemed, had arrived in Teheran, with little advance planning, on a plane carrying U.S. spare parts for HAWK anti-aircraft batteries. His party was said to be bearing a key-shaped cake to symbolize an American opening to Iran. McFarlane and his group were spirited to the top floor of the former Teheran Hilton for several days of on-again, off-again negotiations. McFarlane had expected to get all the hostages released in exchange for more weapons deliveries. When his Iranian interlocutors would have none of it, negotiations were broken off. One American hostage was released in July, and the president subsequently approved shipping the remainder of the May weaponry.

The McFarlane delivery of U.S. weapons to Iran was part of a sequence dating to August 1985. The first two shipments, of TOW antitank weapons in August and September 1985, had been made by Israel, through middlemen, with U.S. approval and assurance that depleted Israeli stocks would be replenished.

Another American hostage was released in September. The operation, very closely held in Washington, was managed on a daily basis by Lieutenant Colonel Oliver North of the NSC staff; his primary contact was Manucher Ghorbanifar, an Iranian businessman living in France. Washington's obsession with secrecy meant that normal procedures for approving covert actions were circumvented; critical meetings were held with no analytic papers prepared beforehand and no record of decisions kept afterward.

The United States became directly involved in the third shipment, HAWKs again, in November 1985. In a comedy of errors, a contact of North's, retired U.S. Air Force General Richard V. Secord, first could not get landing rights in Portugal for the shipment coming from Israel, then could find no aircraft to transship them to Iran. North got in touch with Duane Clarridge, the CIA division chief for Europe, who put Secord in touch with an air charter company previously owned and used by the CIA.

When he heard of the CIA involvement, John McMahon, the Agency's deputy director, upset, asked his aides to prepare a formal presidential authorization, a "finding," for the past and any future CIA role in the operation. The president eventually signed a finding, though not until January—after the operation almost came to an end. In December, McFarlane, who had resigned from government November 30, met with Ghorbanifar, apparently for the first time, in London and came away unimpressed. He recommended against another arms-for-hostages plan and the president agreed. However, North's Israeli contacts, in particular Amiram Nir, an advisor to Prime Minister Shimon Peres on counterterrorism, revived the operation just when it seemed to be dying—a role the Israeli connection played more than once.

The January finding committed the United States one step further: American arms, bought by the CIA from the Pentagon, would be shipped directly from the United States, by Secord to Israel for transfer to Iran. President Reagan wrote in his diary on the 17th: "I agreed to sell arms to Iran."[2] Two such shipments, of 500 TOWs each, were made in February, but, contrary to the premises of the January finding, no hostages were released and no meeting with Iranian officials was arranged. Nonetheless, the McFarlane mission ensued in May.

That mission marked the end of reliance on Ghorbanifar. McFarlane had doubted him since their first meeting, and Ghorbanifar had failed a CIA lie detector test in January. His record seemed to American officials one of errors and broken promises. In July, an Iranian living in London suggested to Albert Hakim, a business associate of Secord, the opening of a second channel—through the relative of a powerful Iranian official, presumably Rafsanjani. North, Secord, and George Cave, a retired CIA Iran specialist, met with the second channel several times over the summer and into the fall. The operation became more and more bizarre. At one meeting, in October, North presented the Iranian a bible inscribed by the president. The inscription had been suggested by North, through Admiral John Poindexter, McFarlane's successor as national security adviser. It was from Galatians: "All nations shall be blessed in you."[3]

These efforts came to fruition just as the whole operation was revealed. No Americans had been taken hostage between June 1985 and September 1986, but three more were taken in September and October. Against this backdrop, the president approved another shipment of TOWs and HAWK parts on October 29; the Iranians promised the release of one hostage, perhaps two, and to continue their efforts on behalf of the others. Only one was released on November 2. Two days later the operation blew.

The transfers arose out of earlier Israeli dealings with Iran—ironically, the United States bought into an Israeli operation with regard to Iran, just as three decades earlier it had bought into a British one. The arms sales reflected a confluence of U.S. strategic interests in Iran and the president's fervent commitment to releasing the six Americans being held hostage in Lebanon. Of that commitment there is no doubt: the president's chief of staff, Donald Regan, reported that the president began each morning's intelligence briefing by asking Poindexter if there was anything new on the hostages. Along the way, the notion arose that the position of "moderates" in and around the Iranian regime might be bolstered if the United States were forthcoming.

In May 1985 American intelligence reappraised the situation in Iran. A controversial assessment, written by Graham Fuller, the national intelligence officer for the near East and south Asia in an unusual collaboration with the NSC staffer responsible for Iran, Howard Teicher, stressed Iran's strategic importance and the proximity of a Soviet threat. While the United States had little direct influence, it might ease its arms embargo and encourage its allies to sell some military equipment to Iran: "the degree to which these states can fill a military gap will be a critical measure of the West's ability to blunt Soviet influence."[4]

For its part, the CIA's interest in an opening was spurred by desperation to free William Buckley, its station chief in Beirut, who had been kidnapped by pro-Iranian extremists in Lebanon in May 1984. When TWA flight 847 was hijacked in Beirut in June 1985, more American officials became persuaded that Iran was a key to releasing American hostages being held by the Shiite group Hezbollah.

When the story broke, however, the president first denied that his administration had swapped arms for hostages. He said on November 13: "We did not—repeat—did not trade weapons or anything else for hostages—nor will we." Rather, he first insisted, the American purpose had been to establish a dialogue with Iran, the arms deliveries had been a token of sincerity—what intelligence officials would call *bona fides*—and the release of hostages was a happy by-product. In his words:

> It's because of Iran's strategic importance and its influence in the Islamic world that we chose to probe for a better relationship between our countries. . . . Those with whom we were in contact took

> considerable risks and needed a signal of our serious intent if they were to carry on and broaden the dialogue.[5]

Whatever the initial motivation, however, the hostage dimension came to predominate. On January 17, 1986, the president's approval for the operation argued for the sales in terms close to the president's later language: "to establish contact with moderate elements within and outside the government of Iran by providing these elements with arms equipment." But the accompanying background paper prepared by North was explicit about the link to the hostages: " . . . this approach may well be our *only* way to achieve the release of the Americans held in Beirut. . . . If all the hostages are not released after the shipment of the first 1,000 weapons, further transfers would cease" (emphasis in the original). The president himself later admitted in a speech to the nation that he let his "preoccupation with the hostages intrude into areas where it didn't belong."[6]

The tale became more bizarre when it was revealed that the profits from the arms sales had been diverted to support the Contras. The arms had been sold to Iran for nearly $20 million more than the CIA had paid the Pentagon for them. In a scheme masterminded by North, the profits were then laundered through Swiss bank accounts, to be drawn on by the Contras. When the scheme was revealed, North was fired, and his boss, Poindexter, resigned, replaced by former Deputy Secretary of Defense Frank Carlucci.[7]

How Secret?

The whole episode underscored one important lesson. Major covert actions will become public—sooner rather than later, and perhaps even before the operation is over. While this is especially true in the post-Watergate era, it applies to other actions as well. In reflecting on the Bay of Pigs fiasco a quarter century earlier, Richard Bissell noted:

> The argument was [not] made that this is now a very public business, and we'd better treat it as such, and either cancel it if we can't stand the publicity, or else do some of the things that will increase the chances of success if we are going to go forward with it.[8]

Once the plan changed (without anyone outside the CIA quite noticing it), from a guerrilla operation into a full-fledged amphibious invasion, the chance of maintaining tolerable secrecy diminished to the vanishing point.

As they grew, the paramilitary operations in Guatemala and Angola also became noisier. They required bases in foreign countries, arms shipments, and training by CIA officers. None of that was easy to keep secret, at least not for long, once the scale of the operation began to increase. Moreover, training an army, even a ragtag lot like Castillo Armas's "liberators," took time. As time passed, the chances increased that pesky journalists would inquire or that information would leak from participants in the operation: the operation might be penetrated by its intended target, as was PBSUCCESS; participants might simply boast about their exploits in bars; or they might have a change of mind.

Still, several brief and small—in people if not purpose—interventions did manage to stay secret for some time. During the 1950s, several operations remained secret for a long time: the CIA's secret war in Tibet still is almost unknown; that against President Achmed Sukarno of Indonesia only slightly more discussed.[9] Track II was not revealed for five years after it happened, and the plots to assassinate Castro stayed buried for ten.

The CIA's election projects in Chile were tolerably secret even though they were large compared to the size of the electorate and the amounts of money spent in the campaign overall. But these interventions were concentrated. What advance planning they did require could be done largely within the station in ways not all that different from the station's usual activities. Moreover, elections are by their nature chaotic; money moves around with great abandon.

It was harder to hide continuing large-scale support for opposition groups. Chile under Allende was also turbulent. But the fact that opposition groups were much more active than their financial difficulties would have suggested was noticed. That was true even though there were other sources of money for these groups, sources ranging from wealthy Chileans to Brazilian capitalists.

In the 1980s and 1990s, large secret interventions almost inevitably will spill into print at some point. Today, Americans, sadder but wiser in the wake of Watergate, are more skeptical of their government. (When Ronald Reagan, the most popular president in some time, first denied in 1986 that his administration had traded arms for hostages, most Americans did not believe him.) This skepticism has been reinforced by other developments. One is investigative journalism, which now is everywhere; more media people now are asking hard questions, probing for leaks, unprepared to take the government at its word. In the 1960s, a few words from the president of the United States sufficed to induce the editors of the New York *Times* not to go public with the details of covert operations. Today, those few words seldom suffice.

If reporters are more likely to seek information on "secret" operations, they are also more likely to find it. "Leaking," always present, has become routine and almost acceptable in Washington. Officials sometimes leak information merely for the gratification of being pandered to by journalists more famous than they. More often, they leak for the sake of policy, to rally opposition or, more rarely, support. Administration after administration, regardless of its political persuasion, declares war on leakers, but those wars always fail, and for a simple reason; as my colleagues and I joked in the Carter administration, the ship of state is like no other for it leaks from the top. Top government officials are precisely the ones who know of covert actions and thus are most likely to take their opposition to particular programs into the open. What is true of the executive branch is all the more true of Congress, where it is reinforced by institutional pride and, often, by partisan politics. On the whole the intelligence committees of the House and Senate have kept secrets at least as well as the executive branch. Yet their role in overseeing covert action means that those who might oppose a particular project are more likely to know of it. The process creates a set of frustrated opponents who will, on occasion, go public with their frustration.

Moreover, if the leak does not originate in Washington, the American press overseas will pick up the scent—even if, as in 1986, the first article is published in Beirut in Arabic. Despite heavy-handed attempts by many third world governments to control information, their nations' media are more active—and more sophisticated—than three decades ago. Moreover, leaders and media in the third world may have a powerful incentive to reveal a U.S. covert operation, especially if their nation is its target.

Why Secret?

Not every exposé, however, has created controversy to which the American government had to respond. Some stayed in the tabloids or the back pages of major dailies. In the instance of Guatemala, the leaks, not the operation, were discredited. The vivid prose of *Time* magazine reflected the temper of the times in Washington: the revelations were "masterminded in Moscow and designed to divert the attention from Guatemala as the Western Hemisphere's Red problem child."[10] Curiously, despite all the public information about it, even the Bay of Pigs—uncontroversial among those insiders who knew of it, save for a few presidential advisers and a senator or two—did not become a major public issue before the fact.

Now, however, more covert operations are controversial inside the governing establishment—and outside when leaks occur. The series of events titled "Vietnam" has made Americans more skeptical about assertions that every upheaval in the poor countries of the world threatens U.S. interests enough to warrant intervention, covert or open. The U.S. public's ambivalence toward Nicaragua reflected that skepticism: on the one hand, the drift of the Sandinista government was worrisome, still more so if it took Managua closer to Havana or Moscow; yet, on the other, there was no conviction that the threat justified American blood. CIA intervention was preferable to a military commitment, but even that was controversial.

Certainly, as ever, there will continue to be cycles in American attitudes. Concerns over Soviet power coexist with worries about nuclear war and peace; one predominates, then the other. In the early 1980s, most Americans evidently shared their president's concern with the Soviet threat, and their congressional representatives went along with huge increases in defense spending—and in covert action. So, too, Ronald Reagan was able to rebuild considerable authority and discretion in the U.S. presidency, thus ending a cycle begun by Vietnam and Watergate. Indeed, the saddest consequence of the Iran-Contra debacle may be that it will undermine that achievement.

Even now, not every covert action is controversial. Of the forty or so covert actions underway in the mid-1980s, at least half were the subject of some press account. Yet only a few of these were controversial enough to make the first leaks result in extended coverage. Most of the rest were open secrets, more unacknowledged than unknown; most members of Congress thought they made sense, as did most Americans who knew or thought about them—and, no doubt, most of the journalists who reported them. Former DCI Colby characterized the reaction to revelations of U.S. assistance to the resistance in Afghanistan: "Afghanistan was a two-column headline in the Washington *Post* for one day, then almost nothing."[11]

The point is not that the 1990s will bear no resemblance to the 1950s, and that every covert action will immediately be leaked, still less that it will be controversial when it does. Yet, almost every covert action will become known eventually. If *Time*, like the rest of the American media, will continue to dismiss most of what the Soviet Union says as propaganda, it is hard to imagine that it will so dismiss every revelation about a U.S. covert operation. And when the operation finds its way into the media, more often than in the 1950s it will be controversial.

Intervening and Succeeding

These changes, primarily in U.S. domestic politics, make it more difficult for the United States to achieve its purposes *secretly*. A second set of changes, primarily in the third world nations that have been the targets of U.S. action, make it harder now than in the 1950s for the United States to intervene successfully at all, covertly or openly. Despite the controversy and mystique that surround covert action, history suggests that there is no magic to it. It means providing foreigners, secretly, with money or weapons or training or indications of U.S. support.

Most covert actions were conceived in secrecy and began small, so the initial assumption of covertness was reasonable. What was often forgotten is that operational necessities for success required them to grow. That meant more of everything: more CIA officers more visible in the foreign land, more airfields or training bases, more meetings in Washington, more channels for passing money in foreign capitals, more propaganda assets—all of which, in turn, diminished the chances that the operation would remain secret.

Even the early successes were closely run operations, their

sponsors reckoning their chances as less than fifty-fifty. And, as time went on, a little money or a few weapons were less likely to achieve grand foreign policy purposes. In the Congo in the early 1960s, the CIA had spent a million dollars a day to achieve an ambiguous "success" through a series of actions so tangled that today even foreign policy experts cannot recall them in broad outline. To think in 1975 that a few million dollars might alter the fate of Angola was a faint hope at best, an illusion at worst, all the more so since the CIA recognized that the Soviets and other external actors might counter U.S. support with assistance of their own.

Or notice the contrast between two Central American cases three decades apart—Guatemala and Nicaragua. Castillo Armas's liberators numbered no more than several hundred. Their "invasion" was more conjured than real. Yet they had control of the air, in large part because Arbenz, unsure of the loyalty of his air force, was unwilling to risk putting his own pilots in the air. "*Sulfatos*" and rumors of invasion were enough to induce Arbenz to capitulate. In the case of Nicaragua, the Contras numbered as many as ten thousand by the mid-1980s, yet not even the most ardent advocates of their cause would argue that U.S. assistance would soon induce the Sandinistas to "say uncle," much less cause the regime to be overthrown by force of arms.

The makers of revolutions have learned their own lessons from the history of U.S. covert action. Like Guevara, they are determined not to repeat the mistakes of Arbenz and Mossadeq and to assure themselves of the loyalty of the army or, failing that, to build revolutionary armed forces loyal to them. And they have also learned a related lesson: if the United States threatens or tries to impose an arms embargo on the revolutionaries, there are other sources of supply, including the Soviet Union if need be, to which they can turn. And unlike Arbenz or Mossadeq, they have turned to those sources sooner rather than later. Even the CIA officials who planned the Bay of Pigs knew that to delay the invasion until after Cuba had received deliveries of advanced Soviet fighter planes would be to condemn the plan to failure. In the event, when Brigade 2506 hit the beaches of Cuba, it found disciplined Cuban revolutionary armed forces, not a thin military rabble that would crumble, or even defect to the invaders, at the first sign of fighting.

Some of the targets of U.S. concern in the 1970s and 1980s were real revolutionaries, with different attitudes toward friends and enemies. Guevara's lesson was that the United States would not tolerate real reform, and history did seem to indicate to many third world leaders that radical change was more likely to succeed than moderation. For these leaders, Chile under Allende confirmed the proposition that real reform within a democratic framework was doomed to fail.

Moreover, to some of these leaders, the United States was more useful as an enemy than as a friend. Arbenz and Mossadeq and even Allende sought Washington's approval, or at least its acquiescence. For Mossadeq, Washington's threat to warn Americans that they were not safe in Iran was also a threat to his ability to govern. By contrast, for Castro, the Sandinistas, and the Ayatollah Khomeini, if the United States had any use, it was primarily as a foreign demon against which the revolution could rally, even if the Sandinistas were prepared to accept U.S. aid as long as it was forthcoming and the revolutionary Iranians were not above seeking American spare parts for their military. In 1979 Iranians took Americans hostage and released them only when they ceased to be useful counters in the bargaining within the revolution.

Today few third world countries are caricature banana republics. Many, though not all, are more secure politically than when they faced the United States in earlier decades; they are no longer thin ruling establishments sitting atop indifferent or even hostile populations. Instead, they seek to mobilize their publics and so protect themselves. In 1953 it seemed virtually impossible for Iran to operate its oil fields without foreign technicians—

in any case, that was the expectation, inside and outside Iran. By 1980, both the fact and the expectation had changed.

When the Carter administration debated how to deal with revolutionary Iran in late 1978 and early 1979, its attention focused on the role of the military. There was no doubt that the military had enough force to contain the revolution; the question was whether it would hold together in attempting that task. What Washington did mattered. But the issue did not turn on a few brave operatives, a little training, a few weapons, or some whispered indications of U.S. support. Covert action of the sort discussed in this book was not an option, although it did become one later, as Washington tried to find ways to replace Khomeini in order to get the American hostages released.[12]

To be sure, a number of the third world regimes that are the objects of American concern in the 1980s do seem vulnerable. The list would include Angola, Mozambique, Kampuchea, and even Libya or Afghanistan, countries whose economies are in shambles and whose control of their populations is questionable. Several of these may be vulnerable to armed insurgencies. Yet it is unlikely that relatively small U.S. interventions could oust them, for armed conflict is precisely the terrain on which their Soviet and Cuban (or Vietnamese) allies can be the most helpful, providing arms and training for loyal militaries and security services. As paramilitary targets, they are more formidable than earlier U.S. opponents in the third world.

On the other hand, the economic vulnerability of some of these countries does offer opportunities for more patient American approaches, not necessarily to supplant regimes but to nudge them in directions more acceptable to the United States. With national borders more permeable than ever to information, it is harder for third world nations to hide their economic shortcomings from their own people, although many try. Angola and Mozambique may welcome Cuban and Soviet help in the military defense of their regimes, but they know that Soviet rubles will not rescue their economies, nor will the Soviet computer-chip industry show them the path to development. For those purposes they must turn to the West.

The Organizational Context

If intervening, let alone intervening secretly, is more difficult than before, why have U.S. administrations continued to resort to covert action at least as often in the mid-1980s as earlier? Part of the answer lies in the organizational behavior of the Central Intelligence Agency and the processes of review and decision under the presumption of secrecy. More of it rests in how presidents and senior officials have perceived their own stakes.

Many aspects of organization and process at work in covert action are common to major endeavors by any large organization, public or private, open or secret: officials managing particular programs develop stakes in their continuation; projects often grow and seldom shrink under the pressure of changing operational realities; and those officials also develop personal stakes in the people with whom they are working. What makes covert action different in degree, if not in kind, is the combination of secrecy with the special nature of the CIA as an organization.

Most obvious is the simple competence of the CIA, in both image and fact. President after president has turned to the CIA precisely because it could get the job done. I remember meeting in 1975 with Theodore Shackley, then chief of the Far East Division of the CIA and later the number two man in the Clandestine Service. Our meeting was about covert action in his region, but our conversation digressed to his career and the CIA: "I'm in the business of producing spies," he said with emphasis. "If I'd wanted to produce widgets, I'd be in private industry."

The "can do" spirit of the CIA, plus its emphasis on secrecy, has been reflected in a tolerance for special arrangements within the organization. The CIA has prized innovation: how many other government organizations can boast a "contingency fund" for use as circumstances change—thus serving as a goad to creative thinking? Successful officers in the field can be promoted without having to "punch their tickets" by serving in managerial posts in Washington. In virtually every case discussed in this book, the CIA assembled a special task force, which operated alongside the DDO division ordinarily responsible for the country in question and sometimes, for reasons of secrecy, even excluded officers who normally handled that country.

The first justification for these task forces was secrecy, but they also made for a special intensity of effort and for short lines of communication. The task force pulled officers back from overseas assignments to undertake particular tasks. Key decisions were made by a small circle of officials—the task force head, the division chief, the DDO, and the DCI. The DCIs were directly involved, sometimes on a day-to-day basis—a reflection not only of the pre-eminence of operations over analysis in the Agency, but also of the fact that, after all, these special operations usually were, for short periods at least, the Agency's most important business. They could make or break DCIs' reputations with political leaders.

The changes in the United States in the postwar period have not left the CIA untouched. With time, and under the pressure of congressional investigations into controversial operations, it has become an organization more like other organizations of government. If, in Colby's words, the "raw material is better now than earlier," the CIA is less freewheeling and more bureaucratic, a tendency encouraged by its physical remoteness from the rest of the Washington governmental machine. By the mid-1980s, its top management was all careerists; unlike the OSS generation that stopped at Wall Street en route to or from the CIA.

As a result, the CIA has come to behave more like other bureaucracies. Projects conceived in one year do not get approved until the next. Even minor operations require major paperwork. And despite renewed fondness for covert action on the part of U.S. administrations, CIA officers retain an anxious eye on their political masters outside the executive; none wants to be a subject of the next congressional investigation. The CIA is becoming more cautious; understandably enough, its officers, like McMahon, when he heard of the first CIA assistance in shipping arms to Iran, want authorization in writing.

In one instance, terrorists hijacked an airplane. The CIA, it turned out, had mastered a way to blow out airplane doors without harming the passengers inside, and so a counterterrorist team, one from a NATO country, asked for CIA assistance. The local CIA station cabled headquarters for permission to help. It heard nothing for two days. Fortunately, the intelligence service of one other Western country also had mastered the technique, and the team, unable to wait any longer on Washington, turned to that other service. It agreed to help over the telephone on the first call. Within hours, its specially trained commandos were en route to the hijacking and soon managed to blow the door off.[13]

Still, CIA officers do regard themselves as producing *something*. By contrast, the State Department's preoccupation with the process of foreign relations, while appropriate enough, may seem to political leaders only the pursuit of "good relations" with every nation for its own sake. So it has looked to a number of presidents: recall the possibility that Rusk forbore criticizing the Bay of Pigs plan lest he be regarded as soft and inactive. Twenty-five years later, his successor, George Shultz, absented himself from the Iranian operations nearly as much as he was cut out, perhaps because of a calculation similar to Rusk's.

Secrecy and the Primacy of Operations

Since the beginning, the CIA has given pride of place to operations over intelligence. When a careerist was made DCI, it was Helms or Colby—operators, not analysts. Given the sophistication of their craft, the Agency's operational side has remained a closed shop. When operations wind down, as after Vietnam, DDO operators are transferred to the analytic side. Movements in the opposite direction are much rarer.

Within operations, covert action, not espionage, has been the way to a career. To one observer, the "three CIAs"—espionage, covert action, and assessment—were integrated at Langley about as much as the army, navy, and air force were at the Pentagon.[14] Even today espionage remains a slow, undramatic process. The "assets" an officer develops will, most of the time, only become valuable much later on, if ever. By that time, the officer will be elsewhere, and the success will register not for him but for his successors.

By contrast, covert actions like those discussed in this book are quick and dramatic. Being involved in them puts young officers in touch with senior management. If they succeed, they make reputations. David Phillips, then a very junior officer, describes the rehearsal for briefing the president on PBSUCCESS, a rehearsal conducted in the garden of Allen Dulles's Georgetown home:

> Two limousines were waiting for us at Washington's National Airport. We were driven directly to the home of Allen Dulles on Wisconsin Avenue. . . . Dulles was casually dressed, fiddled with his pipe and occasionally touched his ample moustache. He was the actor central casting would have selected to play the role of spymaster. . . . We drank iced tea as we sat around a garden table in Dulles's back yard. The lighted shaft of the Washington Monument could be seen through the trees.[15]

Early planning for the Bay of Pigs was confined to the operational side of the CIA, the very place that had the largest organizational stake in seeing the project go forward. Each of the changes made as the plan developed evidently made sense to Allen Dulles and his colleagues. For them, the changes were operational, hence their business, not that of the government's senior political leaders. Yet the cumulative effect of those changes was dramatic. The result was far from the "Guatemala scenario" that had been the plan's original model. What emerged was a full-scale amphibious invasion, with no fallback, whose success or failure would soon be clear—as would the role of the United States.

Moreover, in assessing those changes, the government's senior officials were interlopers on arcane terrain. Who were they to challenge the tradecraft of professionals who had spent a lifetime in intelligence? The qualms they registered seemed hollow, even naive, against the assembled experience of the intelligence profession. In that sense, the problem for political leaders or top managers is similar to what they face with regard to the uniformed military.

Yet the secrecy of covert action makes political leaders especially unwilling to expand the circle of decision to include other sources of guidance. In the early stages of the Iranian affair the circle was narrow, although this time, apparently, it was the CIA professionals themselves who were cut out of an operation being run from the White House. In more open processes, even for military issues, the rivalry among the professionals involved, say in the uniformed services, often gives rise to competing points of view. Sometimes political leaders get wind of those disputes.

For covert action, however, the range of competing advice is also restricted by the compartmentation of the Central Intelligence Agency. In the earlier cases certainly, and to some extent now, the intelligence analysts in the Directorate of Intelligence may not even know what their nominal colleagues in the Directorate of Operations (earlier Plans) have in mind. Whatever else may be said of the Bay of Pigs operation, one of its key premises—that discontent in Cuba would translate into quick assistance for the invaders—was disbelieved by the CIA's intelligence analysts. Yet they never had the chance to register their dissent directly, for they never knew of the plan. Their belief was surely known to Dulles and Bissell, but for them it was an abstract view, not a comment on the plan, and so was brushed aside. Even if they had been given the chance to make their criticism directly, it probably would not have mattered since they were analysts, not operations specialists.

Similarly, the judgments that formed the basis for covert action in Chile just before and during the Allende presidency were not the assessments of the government's analytic fraternity as reflected in National Intelligence Estimates, which, for instance, while initially concerned over the implications of an Allende Chile, never painted a serious threat to U.S. national security. In fact, their general tone became increasingly sanguine during the course of Allende's rule. In the case of Angola, we do not know precisely what the intelligence estimates said, but the NSC interagency group doubted the premises of covert action, and even DDO officers were skeptical that a program big enough to make a difference could be kept secret.[16]

Pressure from the Top

In deciding on covert intervention, however, most presidents have not been captives of organizations they did not understand or processes they could not control. Far from it. More often they put pressure on the CIA rather than vice versa. Karamessines left no doubt about the pressure he felt during Track II, which had been set in motion by President Nixon and whose chances of success seemed remote to those CIA officers working on it. In the instance of Angola, President Ford and Henry Kissinger themselves sought out covert action as the "middle" option, and they did so against the opposition of the State Department's African Bureau and, once more, the dubiety of the CIA's own operators. The White House not only set in motion the covert sales of arms to Iran but ran the operation from the National Security Council as well, at least for a time. When John McMahon, the CIA deputy director, resigned in 1986, his own doubts about deepening U.S. interventions, in Nicaragua and Afghanistan, were part of the reason.[17]

In the context of this pressure from the top—plus secrecy, the CIA's emphasis on operations, compartmentation, and escalating stakes in particular operations—what appear in retrospect as obvious mistakes are easier to understand. Producing spies, not to mention overthrowing governments, is a risky business, much riskier than most. The CIA is in the business of taking risks. Kim Roosevelt turned what could have been a disaster into a stunning success. Castillo Armas's invasion of Guatemala was going nowhere until Agency officers decided on one final throw of the dice—the bombing raid accompanied by the propaganda blitz. From the perspective of the CIA, the decision to bomb the *Springfjord* or to move the Cuba landing site away from the mountains or to mine the Nicaraguan harbors appear less as mistakes than as risks that went awry, taken by an organization under pressure.

However, in some cases, especially earlier ones, organizational momentum did play a role in carrying planning to a "go" decision. For instance, Presidents Eisenhower and Kennedy were both careful to stress that, even after initially approving PBSUCCESS and the Bay of Pigs, they reserved the decision to go ahead. Yet in both cases that discretion was more apparent than real. In both cases the plans were well down the track when the time came for final approval. Armies had been recruited and foreign governments had been asked for training sites. The project had ceased to be merely a plan; it was flesh and blood in which the United States—and the president—now had a stake. In the case of the Bay of Pigs, there was even some doubt in the president's mind whether Brigade 2506 actually could be disarmed if he chose.

At that point it became particularly hard not to choose the "middle" option. At least until the Bay of Pigs the reputation of the CIA made it harder still. Why turn down an easy success? In Chile the fact of past covert interventions shifted the burden of proof in 1970. Not only was the operational machinery for covert involvement in the 1970 Chilean elections at hand, but the practice of intervention was established. It was up to those who opposed the covert action to make the case against it.

Yet presidents and their senior advisers have themselves set in motion the "middle option." The presumption of secrecy seems a crucial part of the reason. At the point of decision, covert action does not differ from other foreign policy issues because decisions are taken in secret. Most foreign policy decisions are so taken. What is different about covert action is that policy makers often presume that the action, not just the decision, will remain secret, or at least that the hand of the United States will be hidden. The decisions to prepare and then to authorize the raid to free the American hostages in Iran, in 1980, were taken in the strictest secrecy. The secrecy held; word of the preparations did not leak. Yet those decision makers all knew that the action itself would be public. They presumed they would be held publicly accountable for the operation's success or failure and thus for the decision's wisdom or folly.

Not so for covert action. There, the governing presumption is that the U.S. role will remain secret. That presumption makes it tempting to choose covert action. It is *something*: less than war but more than nothing. In that sense it resembles other "middle" choices, like economic sanctions. Yet sanctions, unlike covert action, offer no promise of remaining secret; they commit the government to a public course of action.

Under the presumption of secrecy, the first commitments, small and secret, are tempting to make. Once committed, even secretly, leaders are more likely to take the next step than to pull back—a feature of human behavior familiar to situations less unusual than covert action. The Iranian operation in 1985 slid, little by little, from a geostrategic feeler toward Iran, to the notion of moderates, to arms sales for hostages. It was not exactly a case of throwing good money after bad, for at each step it could be argued that the operation was succeeding and the next step was justified. Warning signals were clearer in retrospect to outsiders than they were at the time to those committed to the operation.

In the process, amid secrecy at the point of decision and against the pressure to do something, decision makers neglect the long-term costs of covert action. Again, that feature of decision making is hardly unique to covert action: short-term imperatives often overwhelm long-term considerations of any sort, perhaps all the more so in administrations whose time horizon seldom extends beyond four years and never beyond eight. Yet the presumption that covert action will remain secret makes it all the more tempting to ignore longer-term costs. The costs, even if they are recognized, may never have to be borne. Yet history teaches that they probably will be borne. In all likelihood, the operation *will* become known and the United States *will* be judged for having undertaken it. So the record shows.

If They Can Do It, So Can We

Thus, the practical lessons lead into moral issues. How we Americans act in the world will be judged both by the world and by us. I return to Americans' ambivalence about intervening in the affairs of other nations, especially secretly, the debate between the "realists" and the "idealists," between those who would take the world as they see it and those who would have the United States strive to reshape it, a debate as old as the Republic.

The issues in that debate are hardly unique to *covert* intervention, although they *are* powerfully present there, and they are often obscured in policy making by the presumption that covert actions will remain secret. Overt interventions, like the U.S. invasion of Grenada in 1983, or military attacks, like the bombing of Libya in 1986, raise similar moral and instrumental concerns. Those concerns are not absolute ones; they must be weighed against the gravity of the threat and the adequacy of other available responses.

In those two cases, the calculus was similar to that of covert action. In the instance of Grenada, would the image of intervention wipe out any possible short-term advantage? Would young Latin Americans or Europeans cite it as a particular in support of "equidistance" between the United States and the Soviet Union—two superpowers that were, if not identical, then at least difficult to choose between on the basis of their international behavior? Or would the image of intervention be muted by the evident cooperation of Grenada's neighbors and by the welcome afforded the American "invaders"? And were there good reasons to believe that the intervention could be brief, that the basis for democracy in Grenada was substantial?

For Libya, would the raid deter Libyan support for terrorism even if it could not much diminish Libya's capabilities? Would the raid demonstrate American strength and determination to keep its word? Would citizens of third world nations, even Arab ones, secretly relish the raid on an eccentric leader even if they could not say so openly? Domestically, would it reassure Americans, whatever its effect on Libya? These effects then had to be judged against the costs to the U.S. image—and the pains to U.S. allies—of acting alone and seeming to beat up on a small country. The risk was that the raid would make Colonel Qaddafi look good—hardly the result Washington had in mind.

This is a book about U.S. policy toward covert action, not Soviet policy. Still, if Soviet behavior is not decisive to the moral calculus of U.S. policy, it is relevant. By what evidence is available, the Soviets are active in the whole range of clandestine activities, including covert action.[18] Whether they are noticeably more effective at it than the United States is a subject of dispute. If Angola is counted a Soviet success, that is partly due to the availability of the Cuban cadres but mostly due to the fact that, once the South Africans intervened, the Soviets and their Cuban allies were perceived in Africa as on the "right" side, the United States on the "wrong."

Soviet influence also increased during a number of decolonization struggles, especially in Africa. Again, crucial here was not the brilliance of Soviet clandestine operations but the clear Soviet identification with the "right" side, while the Western nations remained saddled with the colonial legacy. The primary instruments of Soviet policy in these cases were open, not covert—rhetorical support plus some military assistance.

When coups in the third world have brought to power regimes friendlier to the Soviet Union—from Egypt and Iraq in the 1950s, to Peru, Syria, and Libya in the 1960s, to Grenada and Suriname in the 1970s—most of the time the Soviet role has been marginal. Only in Southern Yemen in 1978 and, more controversially, Ethiopia in the mid-1970s was the Soviet role central.[19] The Soviets have, however, been better at protecting friendly regimes once in power, which they have done through a combination of measures more half-covert than covert: military assistance; support for "vanguard" parties; and, most important, Cuban (and sometimes East German) training of intelligence services and militias loyal to the regime. Indeed, if the Soviet Union has any obvious advantage over the United States in the shadow wars of the third world, it is the Cubans.

Nonetheless, I believe that if a Soviet analyst were doing a net assessment of his country's covert action analogous to this book, he would, if honest, reach similar conclusions: seen in the long light of history, most successes of covert action look small, ambiguous, or transitory. A KGB defector listed his agency's goals for operations in Japan as provoking distrust between the United States and Japan, creating a pro-Soviet lobby among the Japanese and discouraging Tokyo from disputing Soviet control of the northern islands.[20] What is striking about these ambitious goals is how far they are from realization. Overall, covert means seem marginal by comparison to overt policies, such as Soviet unwillingness to return the northern islands to Japan.

A book about the Soviet invasion of Afghanistan by that same Soviet analyst would probably sound familiar. Based on what we know, the Afghanistan affair seems to have begun as a small, if not covert, operation, run by the Party and the KGB, an effort to replace an Afghan leader whom Soviets were coming to doubt with a more loyal ruler.[21] When that small plan was bungled, Moscow faced the choice of accepting a reversal or upping the ante by sending in troops in large numbers. The reversal might have meant acquiescing in the fall of a fraternal Socialist regime that bordered on the Soviet Union, and that was unacceptable, so Moscow escalated.

Suppose, though, as a baseline assumption for evaluating U.S. policy, that the Soviet Union is both active and ruthless in pursuing foreign policy advantage through covert means. Suppose also that common images are true—that as a closed society it does have some considerable advantages in carrying out secret foreign operations. At a minimum, its covert activities are less likely to be revealed at home than are America's. To put the point comparatively, all the Soviet government operates with the kind of insulation that the CIA enjoyed in the 1950s.

Still, symmetry with Soviet practice does not settle the argument. It does not suffice, either morally or practically, to say that we must engage in covert action because the Soviet Union does. In December 1976 I was in Washington working with several old friends who were making arrangements for the transition between the Ford National Security Council and Carter's. We had decided to retain the basic structure of the Ford operation, with its network of sub-Cabinet committees for particular purposes. Yet, as a new administration, we would of course have to change the names of those committees, and so we joked about names. The 40 Committee, the Ford administration's group for discussing covert action, would become the "If-They-Can-Do-It-So-Can-We" Committee.

In the idealist view, if-they-can-do-it-so-can-we is unacceptable both on moral and instrumental grounds. We are different from the Soviets, and we believe that difference is not only basic to what we are as a people but also a source of U.S. influence in the world. Although our actions often belie our words, we do believe that nations should not interfere in the internal affairs of their neighbors. That belief, as old as our distaste for the power politics that we associate with the old world, the European state system, we regard as part of our nation's moral armor.

In this perspective, nonintervention is not just a moral principle. It is also an instrumental value. It differentiates us from the Soviet Union and is thus a source of U.S. influence in the world. We believe the example of democracy is a powerful one, one toward which peoples all over the world will gravitate, given the chance. If we believe that, then we must also believe that the example is powerful in our external behavior, not just in our internal arrangements. If people do indeed prefer democracy, then democracy must be demeaned—perhaps doomed to fail—if it is imposed from the outside. There *is* something incongruous about overthrowing governments—even, on occasion, ones that came to power, as in Chile in 1970, in elections that we would define as tolerably fair—in the name of democracy.

By such actions we not only fail to live up to our own ideals; we also diminish the power of our example. There are important differences between the Soviet invasion of Afghanistan and U.S. support for the Contras, but those differences are mostly ones of degree, not kind. It is possible, if frustrating, to see how to Africans or Asians or Latin Americans, or even young Europeans, Soviet and U.S. behavior could look rather similar. To those people, the Soviet Union and the United States have more in common because of their status as superpowers than they differ in their international behavior. To the extent our actions appear to validate such views, that is a foreign policy loss for the United States.

In this view, even the "successes" of covert action seem ambiguous or transitory in retrospect, accomplished at some cost to what we hold dear as a people and to America's image in the world. In the longer view of history, success is more elusive and implicit costs more apparent. Worse, in more recent cases like Angola, we have been both interventionist *and* unsuccessful.

Nor do other comparisons settle the issue. Israel, for example, seems adept at covert operations. Many of its successes result from patient espionage—penetrating terrorist or other opposition groups—more than grand covert scheming. Perhaps, too, a frank Israeli assessment, like a comparable Soviet one, would be less enthusiastic about what has been accomplished covertly than it appears from outside.

Yet suppose the Israeli record is as good as it looks. Israel is not the United States. It is a much smaller society with a much more closed military and intelligence establishment. The sense of immediate and grave threat from its neighbors has attenuated over time but still remains strong enough to produce considerable consensus in providing room for covert operators. In none of these ways is Israel a model for the United States. Nor is it a model in another way: the Israeli record has earned it, however unfairly, the reputation as a pariah state. Surely we do not want to emulate that.

Helping America's Friends

The opposite case, that of the "realists," begins with the observation that the world *is* a nasty, complicated place. In that regard, Americans' historic ambivalence between the high moral view and the feeling that international politics is a dirty business is understandable. As Representative Stephen Solarz put it, "Given Soviet violation of . . . accepted international norms," for the United States, "perpetual indifference is neither politically practical nor strategically prudent."[22]

Moreover, nations affect each other's politics in so many ways that any overly tidy definition of "intervention" is suspect. In all my examples, covert action formed only part of U.S. policy. The United States decided whether or not to grant economic aid to Cuba or Chile or Angola and whether to release Iranian assets held in the United States. Most of these decisions were based on explicitly political criteria. Even if similar decisions toward other countries are not so explicitly political, the decisions in any case have political effects on the country in question; of that fact, foreign political leaders have no doubt.

The same is true of actions by "private" American actors. U.S.-based businesses either invest or do not invest in a country, and that decision too has not just an economic but also a political effect—even if the decision was not "political" in any narrow sense of the term. Most of the businesses or banks that chose not to invest in Chile under Allende probably did not do so for any specific political reason, despite Washington's pressure; ITT was an exception. Rather, their decision was a business one, based on the climate in Chile. They saw that judgment as an economic one, although the implications of political instability surely were a part of it.

The definition of intervention becomes fuzzier still in considering other actions that do have explicit political purposes. Nations of both East and West beam radio programs at each other in order to broadcast public information for political purpose. Until the late 1960s, two of the U.S. radio stations, Radio Free Europe and Radio Liberty, were operated covertly by the CIA. Now they continue operations under open appropriations from the U.S. Congress. The West German political party foundations receive grants from the government. They spend money on political and labor organizing on behalf of sister parties in the developing world. Links among the world's Communist parties have a quasi-legitimacy about them that seems to Americans a double standard; in a number of Western countries it may have even been common practice for a portion of the revenues from East–West trade to be skimmed off for the benefit of the local Communist party.

In this context a unilateral self-denying ordinance against intervention—open and, perhaps, at times covert—is too restrictive. Some threats to U.S. national security require responses. Some American friends in the third world deserve support. In 1961 President Kennedy enjoined his fellow Americans to "pay any price, bear any burden, meet any hardship, support any friend, oppose any foe to assure the survival and the success of liberty." Now that language seems an artifact of the times, too indiscriminate and too interventionist. Yet, if particular manifestations of the Reagan Doctrine were controversial, Americans and their representatives in Congress broadly supported the attempt to help America's third world friends. In the 1960s the issue was which "wars of national liberation" the United States would oppose; now it is which the United States will support—and how.

A Bias Toward Openness

Responsible people can, and do, differ about whether or not to intervene. Moreover, no matter how much Americans would like it to be otherwise, the messiness of the world frustrates clear, broad guidlines just as it frustrates attempts to draw boundaries around specific covert actions toward particular countries. As usual, much will depend on the case; decisions will be matters of judgment.

In deciding whether to intervene covertly, however, the judgment often is obscured by the presumption of secrecy. If the action as well as the decision remain secret, then it appears that the United States can have it both ways, reaping the benefits of the action but avoiding the costs of being seen to take it. Instead of ranking close to overt military action as a last resort, to be taken only if the threat to U.S. national security is grave and all other responses exhausted, it often is the "middle" option. It becomes a first resort, not one of the last.

The imperative of secrecy, so powerful in the minds of decision makers in a crisis atmosphere, may be less than it seems. If "covert" action is not going to remain secret anyway, why not act openly? To be sure, there are arguments against acting openly. In John Bross's words:

> Identification with foreign support can turn what looks like patriotic opposition into what looks like treason. Secrecy also helps to avoid confrontations with other powers who have a stake in the target country and might feel threatened by a change of regime (or no change of regime).[23]

If open identification with the United States is the kiss of death, then supporting our friends will only crush them in our embrace. (Indeed, by that logic we should try to support our enemies, something that has occurred to the CIA from time to time, at least as a propaganda ploy.) And, in Angola for instance, *if* U.S. support could have been kept secret *and* the Soviets and Cubans had not intervened, IAFEATURE might have succeeded.

Neither of these arguments can be summarily dismissed. From time to time one or the other might be decisive. Yet both turn on the presumption that covert aid can be kept tolerably secret, a presumption that is belied again and again by the examples in this book. *Maybe* Eduardo Frei was better off because U.S. money for his campaign was "covert" (and perhaps even unknown to him). Yet no one in Chile doubted that the United States favored him and opposed Salvador Allende. Whether his identification with the United States helped or hurt, it was a political fact in Chile, quite apart from covert action.

In other cases, especially more recently, the presumption of secrecy is plainly false. The FNLA and UNITA in Angola, the Contras in Nicaragua: covert rather than overt aid spared the first two identification with the United States for only the first few months of 1975; for the last, the "covert" form made not one whit of difference. Nor is it obvious that in any of these cases the recipients of U.S. largesse much minded the source of the money being known. There is also the risk that covertness creates a self-fulfilling prophecy: if the United States only aids its friends secretly, then any link to the United States may seem sinister, portending much more than is the fact.

The bias toward openness is a strong one, but it is not easy to implement. It requires an explicitness about influencing the politics of a foreign country that Americans find uncomfortable and hence is likely to be controversial. Moreover, governments that feel threatened by that open assistance can act to prevent it more easily than if it were covert. For this reason, the bias toward openness does not settle immediate, hard cases: What if the Sandinista regime prevents open assistance to opposition political forces or media in Nicaragua? What if the regime in Pretoria does likewise in South Africa?

Yet doing openly what might earlier have been done covertly is not out of the question. U.S. radio broadcasting into Eastern Europe and the Soviet Union from Munich, Radio Free Europe and Radio Liberty, were in form private organizations; advertisements exhorted Americans to contribute to them. In fact, they were created and financed, covertly, by the CIA as propaganda. When that support was disclosed, in 1967, the stations continued to operate, supervised by a board and supported openly by appropriations from the U.S. Congress.

A still more hopeful model is the West German political party foundations, which are instruments of the major parties but are supported, openly, by government money. They have openly assisted kindred parties and labor movements around the world. Sometimes, as in Central America, Washington has resented that German involvement as meddlesome; elsewhere, as in the chaotic days after the Portuguese revolution of 1974, it came to appreciate them. In both cases the United States has felt the lack of anything similar, certainly anything overt.

Two decades ago that something would have been the CIA. The Reagan administration was moved, in 1983, to create the National Endowment for Democracy, an American parallel to the German foundations. The endowment, with a 1985 budget of $18 million, channels money to the two American political parties plus the AFL-CIO and a business group, which then make grants in support of democratic institutions, mostly in the third world. So far, the record of the endowment is mixed but promising. Its grants, and those of its four constituent institutes, have been cautious and close to government policy: for instance, more than $400,000 over two years to the American Friends of Afghanistan to develop educational and cultural facilities inside those portions of the country controlled by the resistance groups—what might in other times have been called the "civic action" component of a paramilitary operation.[24]

Through much of the postwar period, the AFL-CIO has supported non-Communist labor movements, especially in Latin America—activities that might have been done covertly by the CIA and sometimes were. Much of that AFL-CIO effort was discredited by its ideologically heavy-handed image and by its association with the CIA—an instance, perhaps, of covert actions tainting overt ones. Open funding under the endowment may, over time, diminish that taint.

Inevitably, the endowment was quickly drawn into the hardest issues. It made several grants to support the Nicaragua newspaper, *La Prensa,* under pressure from the Sandinista government—exactly the kind of assistance the CIA provided covertly in Chile and probably in Nicaragua as well. Given the virtual war between the United States and Nicaragua, any support from a U.S. institution would not long have been regarded as tolerable by the Sandinistas.

It also remains an open question whether, given U.S. politics, public funding is compatible with creative, and thus controversial, acts by "private" groups. The endowment budget is only an eighth that of the German party foundations, in a country a fourth the size of the United States. In 1985 Congress halved the endowment budget and denied any funding to the Republican and Democratic institutes, although that prohibition was relaxed the next year.

It is a sad fact about U.S. politics, even in the 1980s, that it is easier for the CIA to get money from Congress secretly than for another institution to get it openly—even if the two purposes are kindred. If the CIA wants to finance, secretly, Latin American social democrats to attend a women's conference in Africa, it can do so. If the endowment wanted to do the same thing openly, it would risk winning Senator Proxmire's "Golden Fleece" award for wasting the people's money. Part of the difference is the image of CIA competence, by comparison to a new and inexperienced institution. Yet funding for the CIA remains wrapped in the cloak of national security. And it may be that members of Congress are quite happy to fund particular activities but are reluctant to be seen to vote for them lest their constituents ask "why that and not me?"

For the near future, open funding will be limited to small, political—and not very controversial—projects. Yet as a long-term direction for U.S. policy, a bias toward openness would reflect the realization that at century's end national boundaries are more and more permeable; in these circumstances, moreover, those groups the United States would like to support may not be so chary of accepting even—perhaps especially—if the support is open. The United States would say to them: We are prepared to support you but only openly. We think that is better for you. In any case, we know it is better for us.

Covert Circumstances

There are circumstances in which major "covert" actions make sense, but those are becoming more and more unusual. U.S. support for Afghan resistance fighters is a recent case in point. That U.S. assistance, reportedly begun in a small way in the last year of the Carter administration, escalated sharply in the mid-1980s, to an estimated $280 million for 1985, mostly for small arms, clothing, and supplies.[25] Americans, in and out of Congress, broadly supported the cause of the rebels—or freedom fighters, depending on your taste.

The secret was an open one; the U.S. role was not so much covert as, by tacit agreement, unacknowledged. Indeed, Egyptian President Anwar el-Sadat said on NBC News two weeks before he was killed: "Let me reveal a secret: the first moment that the Afghan incident [the 1979 Soviet invasion] took place, the U.S. contacted me here and the transport of armaments to the Afghans started from Cairo on U.S. planes."[26] The reason for circumspection was the touchy position of the Pakistani government, the only conduit for U.S. supplies to the rebels. It was prepared to support them but unwilling to be too visible in doing so lest it antagonize its powerful neighbor, the Soviet Union. In those circumstances, the resort to the CIA, rather than the U.S. military, was more a matter of discretion than secrecy.

The choice has become one of institutions rather than instruments, as was striking in the instance of Nicaragua, where there was nothing "covert" about that covert action. If, in 1984–85, congressional opponents of aid could not stop it, they wanted at least to limit it to "nonlethal" items and have the program administered by the State Department, not the CIA. For them the purpose was mostly political, something to vote *for,* thus avoiding being labeled "soft" on the Sandinistas.

The compromise that emerged in August 1985 was a strange one. "Nonlethal" was something of a fiction, since not only was the boundary hard to define—is a truck that can carry soldiers "lethal"?—but if the Contras could raise any money at all from sources other than the U.S. government, then any "nonlethal" U.S. assistance only freed resources to buy guns and bullets. Moreover, trying to administer the program was almost more than the State Department could manage. Chartering airplanes, arranging drops, fixing cover: these are hardly mainline diplomatic activities, still less so because the nonlethal assistance had to be provided quietly, if not covertly. The State Department soon found itself embroiled in charges that its deliveries had commingled "nonlethal" public assistance to the Contras with "privately" financed weaponry, or that a chunk of the money had disappeared en route to the Contras.

The choice of institutions raises issues of effectiveness and accountability both. If the United States is to provide enough help to warring factions in the third world so that the assistance cannot be secret, it seems logical to have the U.S. military do it, not the CIA. It seems strange that helping El Salvador fend off an armed insurgency in the 1980s was a military responsibility, whereas helping the Contras mount one in neighboring Nicaragua was a task for the CIA—even though the votes on the amounts of assistance were in both cases public. It seemed similarly strange in Vietnam: why build a CIA air force for Laos when the United States already had one air force?

Reflecting on the Vietnam experience, former DCI Colby argued that the reason for not using the military, even for "overt" covert paramilitary operations, was that "they would approach it as a military operation, to attack the enemy. Paramilitary operations are different—they call for constructing a political base first—and our military are non-political."[27] Indeed, large paramilitary operations have never been central to any service's mission, not even the marines; it and, especially, the army have moved only haltingly toward a capacity for unconventional war. Their special units are oriented toward commando operations in support of main force movements, not toward providing secret assistance for local armed insurgents.

It may also be that the quieter, although not secret, CIA paramilitary operations, instead of ones run by the U.S. military, carry lower risk of provoking a Soviet–American confrontation. The extent of U.S. commitment is less with the CIA, and so are the risks of inadvertent escalation. If an American CIA officer in Pakistan were killed in a Soviet strike on an Afghan resistance base, that would be sad. But the body would be less likely to return to the United States in a flag-draped coffin than if that American had been an army colonel. Thus pressure on American leaders to avenge the killing would also be less.

Yet the issue of accountability remains, for flexibility and accountability are opposite sides of the same coin. Part of the reason the CIA can be quieter is that detailed overseeing of its operations is mostly done in secret, not in the glare of public attention. Its flexibility, less than in the freewheeling days of the 1950s, is still more than that of the military. If its flexibility is greater, however, so may its freedom from being called to account. Or so the concern runs.

In rare cases, circumstances may justify providing money to friendly political parties or unions *and* make it impossible to do so openly, as in Portugal after the revolution of 1974. Contending political forces were in close balance, and a sharp turn to the left was distinctly possible. U.S. strategic stakes were major: Portugal is a NATO ally and home to major U.S. bases in the Azores. In these ways, Portugal differed from Chile, although the differences were matters of degree.

Some of what the United States wanted to do it could do openly. It conceded $20 million in loan guarantees to Portugal in late 1974, a measure intended in part to add to the prestige of foreign minister and Socialist party leader Mario Soares. However, the United States also sought to build up the Socialist party as it contended with Portuguese Communists, a purpose

Washington shared with its allies in Western Europe. In the spring of 1975, the CIA began passing money, several million dollars a month, to the party through its fellow Socialist parties in Western Europe, before it began receiving support directly from those fellow parties.[28]

When the story of CIA support leaked to the press, the State Department refused to comment, and Soares, for his part, said the United States had given him only "diplomatic support."[29] There the story ended; the operation was relatively brief, no doubt would have been supported by most Americans had they known about it and was supported by those in Congress who did, and was consistent with overt U.S. policy.

In a few cases, the politics of a foreign country may, like Iran's in 1953, be so finely balanced that a little U.S. assistance to one side will be decisive. A few other targets may be as vulnerable in the 1990s as Guatemala was in the 1950s. Both kinds of cases will be rarer and rarer, for all the reasons I have discussed: would-be revolutionaries have learned their lessons, and they can counter U.S. involvement with other support.

Choosing the Covert Option

In choosing to intervene covertly, prudent policy makers should ask themselves a careful series of "what ifs?" That injunction applies to all policies, foreign and domestic, but it applies with special force to covert action because of the presumption of secrecy.[30]

The most obvious "what if?" is "What if—or more likely, when—it becomes public? What if it becomes public in mid-stream?" Covert actions, if large, will not remain secret, a reminder that is easy to say but hard to embody in the making of policy when pressures all go in the direction of wishful thinking: witness Bissell's lament about the Bay of Pigs. Perhaps if that realization had been clear, the outcome would have been the same, but it might have induced Kennedy to think through the chain of publicity to U.S. responsibility for success or failure. That might have led him to cancel the operation, despite the pain of doing so. Or it might have led in the other direction, toward the determination that if the United States was to be seen as involved it should do what it took to succeed. In either case, it should have made it less like that the United States would get both public responsibility *and* failure.

If the Iranian operation of 1985–86 had remained secret for several years after all the hostages had been released, that success might have outweighed the costs of being seen to have traded arms for hostages when the operation became public. Perhaps. We cannot know for certain. It did not, however, take a sophisticated analysis to worry that a covert policy targeted toward some Iranians was vulnerable to being publicized by opposing Iranian factions if and when it suited their political purposes. When it was blown, trading arms for hostages, and with a nation the United States had denounced as terrorist to boot, would be deemed unacceptable—by America's allies, much of the rest of the world and, most important, the American people.

Whether a particular covert operation can bear the test of disclosure is apparent in retrospect but often far from obvious before the fact. For presidents, prudence suggests careful attention to such warning signals as the review process throws up—the view of Cabinet officers, people in the White House who attend to the president's interests, and congressional overseers as surrogates for public reaction.

One warning signal, however, *is* evident in advance: Does the intervention contradict overt U.S. policy? If it does, as with arms sales to Iran, it is especially improbable that the operation will withstand the test of disclosure. The arms sales were exactly the opposite of the administration's public policies, which had twisted the arms of U.S. allies not to sell arms to Iran, instead seeking an end to the war between Iran and Iraq with neither a victor nor a vanquished, and had pledged not to deal with terrorists over hostages, much less to sell arms to them.

A second "what if?" is, "What if the first intervention does not succeed? What then?" If covert action is to remain secret, most of the time it will have to be small. Its purposes will have to match its scale. It can accomplish no grand purpose; there is no magic to covert action. For instance, terrorists have been targets of U.S. covert action in the last decade. No doubt, if open votes had been possible on secret actions, the American body politic would have supported those operations. Many were undertaken covertly only because of the sensitivities of U.S. allies and others the United States wished to enlist in the effort. For these reasons, covert actions against Libya, much discussed in the mid-1980s, probably could have stood the test of disclosure. The rub, however, was that no small operation seemed practicable.[31]

It seems clear that covert action is only one instrument among many in combating terrorism. It may have registered successes on occasion; from the public record, we cannot know for certain. But we can be relatively certain that it has registered no major victories, for those have a way of becoming public. Iran's and Guatemala's architects found a way three decades ago; in the 1980s stunning successes do not remain secret. More likely, covert action against terrorism is secondary to grubbier instruments—good police work and tedious poring over intelligence.

Often, small operations began with grand purposes, objectives incommensurate with the instrument. When that purpose could not be achieved, leaders were tempted to take the next step and the next. So it was the Bay of Pigs or Angola or Iran in the mid-1980s. Sometimes, once a limited objective was achieved, hopes were raised further—witness Angola or Nicaragua. This "what next?" suggests, at a minimum, careful attention to the covert operators themselves, for signs of skepticism that operations as initially conceived can achieve their purposes. Such signs were there between the lines of Track II, Angola, Nicaragua. Some risks are worth running, but few are worth running in ignorance.

A third set of questions is, "What signal will be received, by whom and with what result?"—judgments that are also easier with the benefit of hindsight, for they involve calculations of threat and of U.S. interests. Intelligence assessments, by the CIA or the State Department, provide one set of indicators. In 1985–86, for example, U.S. intelligence on Iran was weak, but what there was offered precious little ground for believing there were "moderates" who might be detached from their revolutionary colleagues and later cast doubt on the imminence of a Soviet threat to Iran, one of the premises of the original CIA paper. These were cautions that intended signals might go awry.

Exactly who is to receive secret American assistance can provide warning signals. Since their relationship to the United States is clandestine, the CIA is often in a weak position to compel them to act to suit American purposes, yet the United States inevitably will become associated with their purposes, like it or not, if and when the fact of support becomes known. Aid to the Contras has been dogged by their origins in Somoza's hated National Guard and by continuing charges of human rights violations. Similarly, support for resistance forces in Afghanistan may be justified as a way to put strategic pressure on Soviet occupation of that country; given the character of the resistance forces, it cannot be said to be a way to bring "democracy" to Afghanistan.

The regional context, in particular the attitudes of American friends in the region, provides another set of indicators. In the instance of Afghanistan, U.S. assistance to the resistance was supported, although with varying degrees of publicity, by nations ranging from Pakistan to Egypt to Saudi Arabia to China. In Central America this indicator was ambiguous, for most of the nations of the region publicly expressed qualms about aid to the Contras while privately hoping the Sandinistas could be made to go away.

A second round of covert action in Angola raised these questions of signals given versus signals intended, questions for which the 1975 episode provided guidance. In July 1985, at the administration's urging, Congress lifted the Clark-Tunney Amendment passed a decade earlier banning covert aid to the Angolan rebels. At the time, the administration argued that the amendment was too sweeping and thus hampered its ability to deal with changing African events. Providing covert assistance to Jonas Savimbi's UNITA, with which the CIA reportedly had been in contact since 1979, was a controversial issue within the administration.

In January 1986, however, Savimbi visited Washington to rave reviews, especially from American conservatives, and met with Reagan. The visit swept away opposition from Secretary of State Shultz, who had argued that aid to UNITA would scupper negotiations for getting Cuban troops out of Angola. Similar doubts expressed by the congressional intelligence committees were also swept away, and the CIA was authorized $15 million in weaponry for UNITA—weaponry that included Stinger hand-held anti-aircraft missiles, a subject of special controversy because of their attractiveness to terrorists should they fall into the wrong hands.[32]

For the Reagan administration, the intended signal was anticommunism. For it, there was nothing incompatible about supporting anticommunism in Angola and anti-apartheid in South Africa. Alas, the reality of southern Africa frustrated the distinctions in the heads of Washington policy makers—as so often foreign reality has differed from Washington's conception. Whatever his attractions, Savimbi had one flaw, a fatal one: he was almost completely dependent on South Africa, his army almost a unit of South Africa's. Massive support might have enabled him to separate himself from South Africa, although it would have been difficult to supply him without going through

South African-controlled territory. To support him modestly was only to signal to Africans that the United States had thrown its lot in with South Africa.

These rules of thumb amount to setting a higher threshold for the use of covert action. The guidance is mostly negative, a series of cautions. It is unwelcome to men and women who are looking for something to do, not something to avoid—a trait that runs deep into the American character and is reinforced by the circumstances in which covert action becomes an option. Yet given how both the United States and the world it confronts have changed over the postwar period, the circumstances in which major covert action makes sense as policy are sharply limited.

Guidelines akin to these were articulated a decade ago by Cyrus Vance, later secretary of state, and were embodied in Executive Order 12036 of 1978. For Vance, the language of the 1947 act—"affecting the national security"—was too loose a standard for covert action. Instead, he recommended covert intervention only when doing so was "absolutely essential to the national security" of the United States, when no other means would do.[33] Decisions would still be matters of judgment, but no one has improved on the Vance standard. It bears remembering now when so much damage has resulted from less demanding guidelines.

7

The Ultimate Paradox: Covert Action in an Open Society

If the United States remains in the business of covert action, even under restrictive guidelines, it will continue to confront the paradox of secret operations in a democracy. That paradox is, if anything, sharper now because of the changes in the American body politic, particularly relations between Congress and the executive. The arms sales to Iran, the diversion of profits for the Contras, and the Administration's role in "private" funding for the Contras stirred up a brouhaha that underlines both the political changes and the continuing paradox.

Contras, Arms, and Hostages

When Congress first cut off CIA assistance to the Contras in 1984, then provided only "nonlethal" aid the next year, there were persistent charges that the administration, and in particular NSC staffer Lieutenant Colonel Oliver North, had circumvented those restrictions by organizing private or foreign assistance for the Contras. These concerns came to a head in October 1986, when a civilian cargo plane carrying ammunition and supplies to the Contras was shot down over southern Nicaragua.[1] The American pilot and copilot were killed, and a third American, Eugene Hasenfus, was captured, tried, and later sentenced to thirty years in prison by the Sandinista government before being amnestied. Hasenfus had been a CIA cargo handler in Southeast Asia during the Vietnam war; the plane was owned by Southern Air Transport, which itself had been a CIA front company from 1960 to 1973. Hasenfus denied being a CIA agent but said he felt the CIA supported the operation.[2]

The Reagan administration denied it had been responsible for the flight. It argued it had been scrupulous in obeying the 1984 ban on *direct* assistance to the Contras; in the words of Elliott Abrams, assistant secretary of state: "I deny it. The intelligence committees have kept looking at it and looking at it. They have never found anything."[3] Several House investigations of similar allegations of administration misconduct in 1985 did in fact end without result.

When the congressional intelligence committees first limited covert assistance to the Contras, to $24 million in the autumn of 1983, it also barred any resort to the CIA Contingency Fund. They did not, however, explicitly prohibit the executive branch officials, including the CIA, from seeking other sources of aid. In late 1983 and early 1984, as the $24 million ran out, the president approved DCI Casey's recommendation that new sources of funds be found. Casey and other officials approached governments, ranging from Israel to Brunei to Saudia Arabia, and quietly canvassed private sources in the United States, South Korea, Taiwan, and Latin America. That private support was estimated to amount to some $25 million during the period of the aid cutoff, much more over the longer period of Contra activity.[4]

When the $24 million authorized by Congress ran out in

March 1984, North became informal coordinator of the private support, and in October, when Congress barred any CIA involvement, the Agency issued a "cease and desist" order to its stations. By the fall of 1985, North was directing the operation, overseeing the logistics for shipping privately purchased arms to the Contras and including the construction of a secret airfield in Costa Rica.[5] In 1986, he established his own private secure communications channel with 15 encryption devices supplied by the National Security Agency. Some dozen CIA officers were involved in North's operations, apparently construing North's role to signify White House authorization.

North, who called his operation "Project Democracy," relied on a network of conservative organizations and ex-military men, including two retired generals, Richard V. Secord, who was also a key conduit for arms sales to Iran, and John Singlaub. Secord was a former deputy assistant secretary of defense familiar with the international arms trade; Singlaub, who had been dismissed by President Carter for his public opposition to the administration's policy on Korea, had been commended by President Reagan for the work of his private U.S. Council for World Freedom.[6]

Private assistance to the Contras raised issues similar to those that ran through other covert actions. Once having supported the Contras, the United States could not easily disengage even if it wanted to. Executive branch officials felt this responsibility particularly keenly over the summer of 1986 after Congress had resumed lethal aid to the Contras but before the money could flow. When it did cut off support, the Contras were able to sustain themselves from other sources, and the United States could not escape some responsibility for their actions. Fine lines drawn in Washington blurred in Central America: during the year when the U.S. government furnished only "humanitarian" aid, that aid, too, was furnished covertly, and so the same channels and the same airplanes might be used, literally, one day for government-financed food and medicine, the next for weapons and ammunition provided by private sources. In one case, some $15,000 in humanitarian assistance was diverted to buy weaponry.[7]

More strikingly, the episode also demonstrated the perils of congressional oversight, for if in withdrawing the CIA from the Contra operation, the administration had observed the letter of a law it opposed, it had remained firm—and public—in its support for the Contras. Of private aid to them, the president, who on occasion observed, "I'm a Contra," said: "We've been aware that there are private groups and private citizens that have been trying to help the Contras. But we did not know the exact particulars of what they're doing."[8] Or as North put it, more pithily, to Poindexter in a May 1986 secret message: " . . . President obviously knows why he has been meeting with several select people to thank them for their 'support for Democracy' in Cent Am [Central America]."[9]

Robert "Bud" McFarlane, then Reagan's national security adviser, believed the administration had complied with the law, but his argument echoed David Phillips's:

> We had a national interest in keeping in touch with what was going on, and, second in not breaking faith with the freedom fighters. What does it mean not to break faith? Nothing more or less than making it clear that the United States believes in what they are doing. We could not provide any support, but we made it clear we would continue seeking that support [from Congress]. We wanted to give a continuity of policy.[10]

The Hasenfus affair was, however, quickly overshadowed by the Reagan administration's most serious crisis, the Contra operation crossing with secret arms sales to Iran. The joint congressional investigation in 1987 was good civics and great theater—it made Oliver North a folk hero, though briefly. Both it and the investigation by a special prosecutor, however, were hampered in tying up the loose ends of exactly who knew what, when, by the death of William Casey in early 1987 and by the fuzzy memories of key participants, especially the president and Poindexter.

Nevertheless, the implications seemed clear—and familiar: despite the congressional investigations of a decade earlier and the reforms in their aftermath, despite the argument between the executive and Congress over the Contra operation and the tightened reporting that resulted, still, congressional oversight was fragile when confronting a president determined to proceed. And even the president's control of covert action could be as loose as it had been in the days of plausible denial.

Poindexter bespoke both the looseness and the misguided quest for deniability. For him, the diversion of funds was a mere "detail . . . a matter of implementation of the President's policy. . . . Although I was convinced that . . . the President would approve it if asked, I made a very deliberate decision not to ask the President so that I could insulate him from the decision and provide some future deniability . . . if it ever leaked out."[11]

The looseness pervaded the entire episode. Secretary of State Shultz indicated that he registered his opposition to the sales in two full NSC meetings on the subject, on December 6, 1985, and January 7, 1986, and on at least one other occasion as well. Secretary of Defense Weinberger—who had written, "This is almost too absurd to comment on. . . . It is like asking Qadaffi over for a cozy lunch" on the original memorandum, a draft National Security Decision Directive circulated the previous summer—also expressed his opposition on January 7.[12] Given McMahon's objections to CIA involvement without a formal presidential authorization, the president approved the January finding but explicitly indicated that the CIA was not to inform the congressional overseers of the project. In fact, the president did not actually *sign* the finding; rather Poindexter recorded the president's approval after an oral briefing.

Both Shultz and Weinberger left the December meeting believing of the arms sales, in Weinberger's words, that "this baby had been strangled in its cradle." In January Shultz was not even sure a decision had been made: "this was not a meeting in which an explicit decision was stated . . . it wasn't as though there was some sharp decision." On a number of occasions during the Iran-Contra affair, meetings occurred neither with options papers circulated in advance nor decisions recorded on paper afterward.

Shultz testified that he had not even known of the January finding until the following November, although he acknowledged that "bits and pieces of evidence float[ed] in." Shultz apparently expressed his view and then retreated to the sideline, cut out but also partly, it seems, preferring not to know. Weinberger seems to have fared similarly, even though the weapons came from Pentagon stocks.

Regan, perhaps seeing his boss's anguish over the hostages, was a cheerleader for the transfers. In this atmosphere of looseness, North, hearing his president enthuse over the Contras, could have connected the transfer and the Contras on his own, seeking authorization first from Casey, then from Poindexter. He adopted his own version of plausible denial, one long since discarded by the CIA and one it was unwilling to countenance in this case, seeking instead clear authorization from the president.

New Rogue Elephants?

The Iran operation differed from support for the Contras in that the administration was divided over the first but strongly agreed on the second. Yet even before the two operations crossed, they had much in common. Both were being run from the White House, and both were extremely tightly held; in May 1986, Poindexter cautioned North: "From now on, I don't want you to talk to anybody else, including Casey, except me about your operational roles." Both relied heavily on private citizens, and both were amateurish in the extreme: witness North's difficulty in getting arms for Iran shipped past Portugal, or the allegations that most of the diverted money from the sales disappeared en route to the Contras. And for both the paper trail of approval and accountability was almost nonexistent—reminiscent of covert operations of the 1950s and 1960s, except that this time the operators were NSC staffers and White House insiders. Indeed, for Casey, according to North's testimony before Congress, the diversion not only was "the ultimate irony, the ultimate covert action," it was the beginning of an "off-the-shelf, self-sustaining, stand-alone" fund for covert action outside the normal controls of government.[13]

In combination, the two operations raised the specter of new "rogue elephants," this time not in the CIA but in the White House, a specter like the one that had given birth to the Church Committee a decade earlier. When that committee began its work in 1975, it did so very much under the shadow of Watergate. Former intelligence officers—like E. Howard Hunt, the man in charge of propaganda for PBSUCCESS—were among the Nixon administration's "plumbers." The press was full of intimations, many of them unfortunately true, that intelligence agencies had been involved in a wide variety of activities outside the law—illegal wiretapping, domestic surveillance, harassment of antiwar and civil rights groups, and more.

Still more troubling was the impression that the intelligence agencies had become kingdoms of their own, operating beyond the ken of Congress and outside the control even of presidents. Some of the CIA's internal investigation into its own involvement in plots to assassinate foreign leaders already had found its way into the American media, evoking Senator Church's metaphor of the CIA as a "rogue elephant."

Then, we did not find much evidence of rogue elephants in the CIA. The rogue elephants we discovered were more likely to be wearing FBI crewcuts. In time we even came to joke about the metaphor with our CIA counterparts. Once, when then-CIA Director William Colby was coming to testify before the committee in executive session, a colleague and I found a picture of a family of elephants linked in a row, trunk to tail. We unveiled it at the session with the caption: "Director Colby and his associates arrive to testify before the Select Committee."

Instead of searching for rogue elephants at the CIA, most of our investigation raised a question akin to that of this book: Did, and do, particular CIA activities make sense as part of America's foreign policy? Yet then as now questions of process were inseparable from issues of substance. If we did not find "rogue elephants," we did find that plausible denial as it had been practiced did create a troubling looseness in the executive branch's review and control of covert action, even as in a pinch it seldom protected administrations in power. In the early days, the congressional role amounted to the "buddy system"—informal conversations between the CIA director and a few senior members of Congress. Plausible denial and the buddy system did not emerge because the CIA had broken free of its political masters. They emerged because that was how both administrations and Congress wanted it at the time.

"Plausible Denial" and the "Buddy System"

I recall Richard Helms testifying before the Church Committee in 1975 about charges that the CIA had tried to kill Fidel Castro. He was vivid in describing plausible denial and almost plaintive in drawing its implications:

> It was made abundantly clear . . . to everybody involved in the operation that the desire was to get rid of the Castro regime and to get rid of Castro . . . the point is that no limitations were put on this injunction . . . [but] one . . . grows up in [the] tradition of the times and I think that any of us would have found it very difficult to discuss assassinations with a President of the U.S. I just think we all had the feeling that we're hired out to keep those things out of the Oval Office.[14]

If he had ever thought he would later have to testify before Congress about what he had done, Helms reflected, he would have made sure that his orders were in writing.

By their own testimony, not a single member of the National Security Council outside the CIA knew of, much less authorized, those plots.[15] Even within the CIA, it remains unclear exactly how much John McCone knew of the plots while they were underway during his tenure as DCI.[16] As Richard Bissell, the DDP at the time of the first plots, puts it, even within the CIA "there was a reluctance to spread, even on an oral record, some aspects of this operation."[17]

As a result, CIA officials spoke with each other only in riddles about these operations. And if they spoke of them at all with those outside the CIA charged with approving covert operations, they did so "indirectly" or in "circumlocutions." Thus, in 1975 the select committee spent hours trying to unravel whether terse references in documents to "disappear" or "direct positive action" or "neutralize" referred to assassination. We could not be sure. And that was precisely the point of plausible denial. Those CIA officials who spoke in circumlocutions could feel they had done their duty as they understood it. Their political superiors could understand what they would, ask for more information if they desired, but also forbear from asking. If things went awry, they could, if they chose, disclaim knowledge and do so more or less honestly.

These effects of plausible denial are extreme in the instance of the Cuban assassination plots, but similar effects ran through covert actions of the 1950s and 1960s. Dean Rusk, who served Presidents Kennedy and Johnson as secretary of state, has observed that he routinely knew little of CIA operations: "I never saw a CIA budget, for example."[18] Of some thousands of covert action projects between 1949 and 1968, only some six hundred received consideration outside the CIA by the National Security Council body then charged with reviewing covert operations.

In practice, the CIA sought broad grants of authority for covert action, which spawned small projects, many of which, arguably, were sensitive enough in political terms to merit specific NSC approval. Through the time of Iran and Guatemala in the 1950s there was no NSC body charged with reviewing covert action, and even after the first such group, the 5412 Committee, was created in 1955, it met infrequently. Then, and later, the initiative remained with the CIA. Its officials were the only ones in a position to make judgments about whether a given project was covered by a previous authorization or was large and sensitive enough to merit special consideration outside the CIA.

When a project did come before the NSC body for approval, only the briefest of notations was recorded, in keeping with plausible denial. The president's special assistant for national security affairs—in the Eisenhower administration more of an executive secretary than the policy maker the holders of that job became in later administrations—would note in a memorandum: "CIA project number 75A was approved."

Beginning in 1959, the 5412 Committee's successor, the Special Group, began to meet weekly. Yet even when proposed covert actions came before NSC review, those outside the CIA were in a weak position to assess it. That fact seems evident before 1959, for instance in the critical meeting at which AJAX was ratified. It is even more striking in planning for the Bay of Pigs. The initiative remained with the CIA. Senior political leaders who had doubts about the project could hardly address its operational details; hence the Bay of Pigs grew from a guerrilla uprising to an amphibious invasion, and the invasion site changed.

They were only slightly better positioned to question the presumptions and implications of a particular covert action. In the few years leading up to the Bay of Pigs, those officials confronted the legacy of CIA success in Iran and Guatemala and the formidable personality of Allen Dulles. The CIA had succeeded; it had done so with tolerable "deniability." Who were they to say it could not be done again, particularly when Dulles said it could? Moreover, criticism, especially in the Kennedy administration, could easily be mistaken for insufficient energy in the war on communism—and so, perhaps, Rusk refrained from voicing any doubts he harbored.

For its part, the U.S. Congress was more interested in making sure the CIA had what it needed in the fight against communism than in overseeing its operations. The fate of several congressional initiatives for improving oversight that came to naught in these early years is eloquent testimony to that mood of the times and temper of the Congress. In early 1955 Senator Mike Mansfield, later chairman of the Foreign Affairs Committee, introduced a resolution calling for a joint oversight committee; his resolution grew out of a congressional review of executive branch procedures. The resolution had thirty-five cosponsors. It also had the strong opposition not only of the executive but also of the "club" of senior members. In hearings on the resolution, Mansfield elicited the following comment from Senator Leverett Saltonstall, the ranking Republican on the Armed Services Committee and its Defense Subcommittee:

> It is not a question of reluctance on the part of the CIA officials to speak to us. Instead, it is a question of our reluctance, if you will, to seek information and knowledge on subjects which I personally, not as a Member of Congress and as a citizen, would rather not have, unless I believed it to be my responsibility to have it because it might involve the lives of American citizens.[19]

In April 1956 the resolution was voted down, 59 to 27, with a half-dozen cosponsors voting against.

The debate did, however, result in the creation of formal CIA subcommittees in both Armed Service Committees. Yet the "buddy system" remained largely unchanged. Dulles, the near legend, was still DCI; relaxed and candid with senior members, he had their absolute trust. In the Senate Armed Service Committee, Senator Richard Russell appointed to the formal subcommittee those senators with whom he had been meeting informally on CIA matters—Saltonstall and Robert Byrd. Later he added Lyndon Johnson and Styles Bridges. When, in 1957, the Appropriations Committee formed a subcommittee for the CIA, its members were Russell, Byrd, and Bridges. They did both "authorization" and "appropriation," often at the same meeting.[20] Most CIA business continued to be conducted as before—by Dulles and Russell, meeting informally.

"Failure" and Its Aftermath

The Bay of Pigs marked the end of an era for the CIA. It was a stunning defeat for an agency that had been known only for success. President Kennedy took responsibility for the debacle, but Dulles and Bissell were eased out of their jobs, to be replaced by John McCone as DCI and Richard Helms as DDP. The Dulles era was over.

Yet neither executive procedures for nor congressional oversight of covert action changed all that much. Plausible denial seemed threadbare after the Bay of Pigs: Kennedy did not feel he could make use of it; nor had his predecessor, Eisenhower, when the Soviet Union shot down a CIA U-2 reconnaissance aircraft over Russia in May 1960. In the wake of the Bay of Pigs, the Taylor Report—after General Maxwell Taylor, who became the president's military adviser—redefined the membership of the Special Group to better coordinate paramilitary operations. Later, the administration created two additional variants of the Special Group, one for counterinsurgency and one to handle the covert war on Cuba.

By 1963 the CIA and the Special Group had developed criteria for which covert action proposals should come before the Special Group; until then, that decision had been left to the discretion of the DCI. The criteria were never written down and were not—could not be—all that precise. The Group and the CIA agreed on $25,000 as the dollar threshold, and CIA officers also estimated three kinds of risk—chances of exposure, chances of success, and degree of political sensitivity.

In February 1970, National Security Decision Memorandum

(NSDM) 40 replaced fifteen-year-old NSC 5412/2 as the governing document for covert action. Other than changing the NSC authorizing group's name to the 40 Committee, it affected process in the executive only by mandating a yearly 40 Committee review of projects previously authorized.

The Bay of Pigs and a decade of covert action afterward, including the big expansion in Asia as the war in Vietnam heated up, did lead to somewhat more formal procedures in the executive branch. The 40 Committee considered Chile on twenty-three separate occasions between March 1970 and October 1973.[21] Not all those occasions were meetings; some were merely the collection of clearances by telephone. Yet major decisions were debated. The range of that debate was constricted, but within those limits the debate sometimes was sharp: witness the decisions to opt for spoiling operations, not support for Alessandri in 1970, or to set limits on support to opposition forces later, or to intervene in Angola in 1975.

Still, in numbers of projects, most covert action projects continued to be approved by no one outside the CIA. One critical such case, Track II, was, like the Cuban assassination plots, unusual even within the unusual. Most were small, often propaganda projects, deemed not risky by the rough guidelines in effect. By the early 1970s only about a fourth of all covert actions were coming before the NSC review body.[22]

Moreover, the authorization process also was—and is—made more difficult by the fuzzy line separating covert action from espionage or counterintelligence. Covert actions of the political kind—support to labor unions, political parties, or media organizations—often used assets that had been developed to provide intelligence. That intelligence gathering provided wherewithal for covert action, yet typically it was not reviewed outside the CIA. In the extreme, it might itself *be* a kind of covert action: witness the grounds for concern in Chile after Allende was seated that the Chilean military officers being cultivated by the CIA for intelligence purposes would also construe that contact as implying support for *their* purposes—unseating Allende in a military coup.

How covert action, even "routine," was checked with the State Department and with the relevant ambassador continued to be an issue, as it had been in the earlier period. Station chiefs were—and are—barons of their own kingdoms, with special practices and communication channels of their own. (Indeed, since for security reasons the CIA handles all embassy communications, CIA personnel in the field are in a position to see all State Department traffic, save a few specially coded messages, whereas the ambassador and his State colleagues do not have comparable access to CIA communications.) In 1961 President Kennedy addressed a letter to U.S. ambassadors, charging them with responsibility to oversee all American activities in their countries. Later presidents issued similar directives, and in 1974 the guideline was embodied in statute.

Neither letters, even from presidents, nor legislative guidelines, however, could resolve the problem. The ambassador could exert the influence of his position as head of the "country team"; he could request but not compel the station chief. Some ambassadors preferred not to know too much lest they become too closely identified with the CIA; in other cases, mostly ambassadors who were political appointees, the CIA and the State Department tacitly agreed that they should not know too much. These considerations were reflected in internal CIA instructions, which indicated that before a covert action proposal was forwarded to the 40 Committee it *should* be reviewed by State, and "*ordinarily*" the concurrence of the ambassador would be required.[23]

In practice, then, CIA–State relations in the field depended on the personalities of the ambassador and station chief. Most ambassadors knew—and know—the broad compass of covert action and other clandestine activities underway in the countries to which they are accredited. They often did not—and do not—know operational details such as particular agents, recipients of money, or funding channels. Sometimes they did not want to know. Edward Korry's relations with his station chief in Santiago, Henry Heckscher, frequently were contentious, but Korry seems generally to have known what the CIA was up to. He often was active in suggesting or framing covert action proposals. The main exception was Track II, and of that Korry shared his ignorance with almost all the rest of the government. Korry's successor, Nathaniel Davis, was informed of some but not all of the disinformation efforts with regard to the Chilean military that the CIA was engaged in when he arrived.

However, both men worried that they might not know all they should, that their diplomacy would be hit from the blind side by some CIA operation of which they were unaware. They shared that concern with other U.S. ambassadors. Korry put it colorfully in discussing Track II:

> It [the CIA] could operate behind my back, not merely with the President of the United States, but with Chileans, and private Americans, because the whole process of espionage and intelligence, like knowledge, confers immense power, and because the CIA was the one permanent institution to tie the past to the present.[24]

More committees of Congress received more information from the CIA than in the early days. In 1967, thirteen committees in addition to the four with oversight responsibilities were briefed by the CIA.[25] Most of those briefings, however, concerned intelligence products, not clandestine operations. About those operations the CIA did not often volunteer information, and Congress did not frequently ask. The role of Congress had not moved from receiving information to overseeing operations. In 1961 after the Bay of Pigs, and again in 1966, Senator Eugene McCarthy attempted to revive the idea of a CIA oversight committee, but it still was an idea whose time had not yet come.

Chile both illustrates this pattern and suggests the beginning of a change in attitude, especially on the part of Congress. According to CIA records, Chile was the subject of fifty-three CIA briefings for Congress between 1964 and 1974.[26] Covert actions were discussed at thirty-one of these, and of those, twenty-three concerned special releases from the CIA Contingency Fund. Of the thirty-three covert action projects the CIA undertook with 40 Committee approval during that period, Congress was briefed in some fashion on eight; those eight comprised about half of the $13 million the CIA spent in Chile during that period. Many of those briefings did not come until quite long after the fact, and needless to say, Congress was not informed of sensitive operations that did not go before the 40 Committee—Track II, for instance, or projects labeled intelligence gathering, not covert action.

Before 1973 most of the meetings with Congress were confined to the designated oversight committees—the appropriate subcommittees of Armed Services and Appropriations in each house. After Chile passed into public scrutiny, both the frequency and scope of meetings expanded. There were thirteen meetings between March 1973 and December 1974, and these included congressional newcomers to the subject such as the Senate Foreign Relations Subcommittee on Multinational Corporations and the House Foreign Affairs Subcommittee on Inter-American Affairs.

The Climate Changes: A Tale of Two DCIs

If Congress did not much want to ask about covert action and the CIA did not much want to tell, Watergate and Chile, coming on the heels of the war in Vietnam, changed all that. First to change was Congress's disinclination to ask. In 1974 it passed the Hughes-Ryan Act, the operative paragraph of which reads:

> No funds appropriated under the authority of this or any other Act may be expended by or on behalf of the [CIA] for operations in for-

> eign countries, other than activities intended solely for obtaining necessary intelligence, unless and until the President finds that each such operation is important to the national security of the United States and reports, in a timely fashion, a description and scope of such operation to the appropriate committees of Congress.[27]

The presidential judgment required by the law came to be called a "finding"—a written document bearing the president's signature. As so often, Congress sought to change the pattern of executive action not by determining specific decisions but rather by changing the decision-making process. Hughes-Ryan reflected the demise of plausible denial, which seemed in the mid-1970s to have confused procedures within the executive—and deluded Congress—more than it protected anyone.

Hughes-Ryan required the president to put his name, and his reputation, on the line. It was meant to ensure against future wrangles such as those over assassinations: covert actions, wise or stupid, would reflect presidential decision; there would be no doubt that someone was in charge. It also tied the hands of members of Congress: they would find it harder to assert that they had been kept in the dark. Less often could they speechify in professed ignorance of covert action.

The change in the congressional climate, and the dilemmas posed for the executive in responding, is demonstrated by the contrast between two DCIs, Richard Helms and William Colby, in their dealings with Congress.

In February 1973, Helms, recently appointed U.S. ambassador to Iran, was called to continue his confirmation hearings in executive session before the Senate Foreign Relations Committee. Senator Stuart Symington of Missouri asked him: "Did you try in the Central Intelligence Agency to overthrow the Government of Chile?"[28] Helms replied, "No, sir." Symington then asked, "Did you have any money passed to the opponents of Allende?" Helms again replied, "No, sir." Symington continued, "So the stories you were involved in that war are wrong?" Helms: "Yes, sir. I said to Senator Fulbright many months ago that if the Agency had really gotten behind the other candidates and spent a lot of money and so forth the election might have come out differently." As a result of this testimony, Helms was convicted four years later on one of two counts of criminal information for failing to testify fully and accurately before the U.S. Congress.

A month later, in March 1973, Helms was back before the same committee, again in executive session. This time Frank Church asked him: "Following the [1970 Chilean presidential] election and up to the time that the Congress of Chile cast its vote installing Allende as the new President, did the CIA attempt in any way to influence that vote?"[29] Helms asked, "Which vote?" "The vote of the Congress," Church explained. "No, sir," Helms responded. For this testimony, Helms was convicted on the second of the two counts of criminal information, again for failing to testify fully and accurately.

The changing times caught Helms in a direct conflict of allegiances. On the one hand, it was the Foreign Relations Committee of the U.S. Senate. As Helms explained to the court: "I didn't want to lie. I didn't want to mislead the committee."

On the other, he had signed an oath of secrecy when he joined the Agency. He could not simply refuse to answer, for that would have implied a positive response. More important were his long years of service to the Agency, most recently as DCI. Revealing covert operations, even to a committee of Congress, ran against everything in his nature and training. Moreover, Foreign Relations was not the CIA's designated overseer. That was a particular problem in the March hearings, which Helms said he expected to be about another subject. Thus, Church's questions seemed to him both outside the committee's jurisdiction and beyond the scope of its hearing.

Helms decided his responsibility as he construed it to the CIA superseded his duty to Congress. He reckoned in the heat of the moment that disclosure could risk blowing the operations; in any event, with press accounts of CIA covert action in Chile in the air, for him to confirm those activities would at least embarrass the Agency and the administration—not to mention him personally in the midst of his own confirmation battle.

Two years later, Helms's successor as DCI, William Colby, faced a similar conflict of responsibilities. He reached a different decision, on the belief that the changing American circumstances in which the CIA found itself called for a change in how the Agency dealt with Congress. His decision cost him his job with the Ford administration. But it opened a new period in congressional oversight of the CIA—including covert action.

In the autumn of 1975 the administration and the two congressional investigations—the Church Committee and a parallel one in the House chaired by Representative Otis Pike of New York—were engaged in a guerrilla war over access to secret documents. For those of us on the staff, the war accentuated the hurry-up-and-wait that is characteristic of Congress even in normal times. We would work long days gearing up for hearings that then would be canceled at the last moment because the administration had withheld documents. Then the wrangling over which secret documents we would get access to, and under what terms, would begin again.

These lulls were frustrating, but they did offer us a chance to do interviews, cull public sources, and respond to the many, many offers of information we received over the transom. Most of those offers were plainly nuts; nothing like an investigation of intelligence to bring loonies out of the woodwork. Indeed, we had our own flak-catchers—kindly women of a certain age who sat outside our secured offices (a Senate auditorium recently vacated by the Watergate investigation) and specialized in knitting and dispensing gentle refusals to crazies.

Yet some of the stories we heard were not so easily dismissed. Some contained operational details—code names and the like—that their tellers should not have known. And so we found ourselves taking some unusual excursions during the lulls. One of the most bizarre was to the Queens house of detention in New

York to interview a man who claimed he had flown guns into Chile for the CIA. We had no reason to believe his story was true, and in general it did not strike us as plausible, but some of the details were troublingly accurate. What we found was a man accused of stabbing his wife twenty-odd times until she was very dead. We left with the troubling details—and with the sense that some attorney had in mind a murder defense more creative than the gun-running story.

The negotiations that created lulls for us on the staff cast Colby into a dilemma akin to Helms's. Colby had concluded that times had changed and that the change required new attitudes on the part of the intelligence services. In his words:

> There had been a time when the joint hearing held by the Senate's intelligence subcommittees would have been deemed sufficient [to] . . . end the matter. Senators with the seniority and clout of McClellan and Stennis then could easily have squelched any demands for further action on the part of their junior colleagues. But this was no longer the case.[30]

Colby was more resigned to the change than fond of it: "The lesson was clear. The old power structure of the Congress could no longer control their junior colleagues. . . . CIA was going to have to fend for itself." Yet in the end he regarded the changed congressional role as appropriate, a view that put him at loggerheads with many in the Ford White House: "I must say that, unlike many in the White House and, for that matter, within the intelligence community, I believed that the Congress was within its constitutional rights to undertake a long-overdue and thoroughgoing review of the Agency."[31]

Colby's conflict with his political masters came to a head in September 1975. The Pike Committee was prepared to publish its report criticizing the CIA for its past intelligence failures. That the report was mostly stitched together from the CIA's own internal postmortems was galling enough; worse, Colby believed, publication of excerpts from CIA documents could harm intelligence "sources and methods." Pike agreed to some deletions but not to all, the president cut the committee off from any further classified documents until the matter was resolved, and the committee, in turn, prepared to cite Colby for contempt of Congress.

Colby was feeling more and more isolated within the administration. While he had argued against disclosure in this instance, in his words, he "did not believe that, in the long run, the Executive could hold to a position that blocked a Congressional committee from pursuing an investigation of intelligence."[32] But the White House made no move to resolve the impasse, and Colby's position among the "doves" was more and more uncomfortable. In the end, the House itself resolved this issue. It voted to shelve the entire Pike report. Already the climate in Congress and the nation was beginning to shift again; in the press, stories fretting about the harm being done to U.S. intelligence were beginning to outnumber accounts of CIA excesses—a shift capped in December 1975 by the brutal murder of Richard Welch, CIA station chief in Athens. In this atmosphere, House members were becoming more and more uneasy over the bad publicity the Pike Committee was earning them.

Yet Colby was still odd man out within the administration. The final straw, he believes, came in September 1975, when the Church Committee held its first open hearing—on poisonous toxins that the CIA had at one time produced and had failed to destroy as stipulated by international treaty. The failure was bureaucratic oversight, not malice, but Colby found himself "with some wonderment describing the story about the poisons and dart gun before TV cameras."[33] The day was a bad one for Colby. No senator could resist the chance to be photographed holding the dart gun and making appropriately severe remarks. For many in the Ford administration, it was the final piece of evidence that the congressional investigations should have been killed aborning—and that Colby's willingness to cooperate bore much of the blame. Colby, however, continued to "believe in the Congress' constitutional right to investigate the intelligence community; and I believed that, as head of that community, I was required by the Constitution to cooperate with the Congress. I also believed that any other approach just wouldn't work."[34]

At eight o'clock on the first Sunday in November, Colby was called to the White House. This time, unlike others, it was not for a special meeting on a crisis then breaking. This time, Colby was fired.

Tending the "Government's" Secrets

Whatever their results, the committees, and the Church Committee in particular, were an innovation in constitutional relations between the executive and Congress.[35] Our own language mirrors the ambiguity about what constitutes the "government," particularly in foreign affairs. High school civics textbooks show the Congress as a coequal branch of the "government," yet often we use "government" more narrowly to refer to a particular administration in power. At the heart of all our wranglings with the Ford administration over access to classified documents lay the constitutional issue: Were those secret documents, written and classified by the CIA or State, the property of the executive only? Or were they the "government's" documents, to which Congress should have access on terms decided by it and which could be declassified by its decision as well as that of the executive?

We did not, in 1975–76, reach a clean resolution of this fundamental question. Probably, in the nature of our system, we could not have. But we did move a long way toward the view that, even in matters of clandestine operations, Congress has its own right to the "government's" secret documents—and bears the responsibility that goes with that right. In seeking to establish that position, the Church Committee was fanatic about leaks. So far as I am aware, not a single secret worth mention seeped out through the committee and its staff.[36]

The Ford administration was a grudging partner in reshaping the bargain between the executive and Congress. A few in the administration, Colby foremost among them, believed the reshaping was fundamentally correct; others, no doubt, simply felt the administration had no choice. The administration employed something of a dual approach to the Church Committee. At one level, as a matter of principle, it was opposed to the investigation and its results. It held, thus, that publication of the interim report on assassinations was a mistake, one that would harm the reputation of the United States.

At another level, however, it was prepared to work with the committee, particularly to protect intelligence sources and methods. In that regard, it and the committee shared an interest: the committee had no reason to want to endanger intelligence methods or agents' lives, quite the contrary. In the case of the assassination report, the issue boiled down to whether we would publish the names of some thirty-three CIA officers. The administration argued that publishing the names would tarnish reputations and might, in one or two instances, endanger the individuals in question. Colby even took the issue to district court.

In the end, the committee and the administration reached a sensible compromise. The committee agreed to delete the names of twenty of the officers. Neither the substance nor the credibility of the report required those names. The remaining names were left in. Most of those were senior officers whose names were already in the public domain. We felt, moreover, that as senior officials it was fair to hold them publicly accountable for their actions. Like most compromises, this one pleased neither side fully, but both sides could live with it.[37]

As the committee groped toward a changed constitutional

bargain, my most immediate concern was Chile. From the outset, the general sense of the committee had been that we ought to lay one covert action out in public. That seemed essential to this once-in-a-generation clearing of the air. As it was, the swirl of charges, many of them excessive, some of them untrue, did the CIA itself no good. If we were to make one covert action public, Chile was the logical candidate. Newspaper revelations about covert action in Chile were part of the reason the committee had been created in the first place. President Ford himself had stripped what remained of the fig leaf of plausible denial from the operation in September 1974, when he confirmed it at a press conference. By the middle of 1975, not much was secret about the operation except some particulars of truth.

The committee argued with the administration about Chile throughout 1975, an argument interrupted by the assassination inquiry. Against the administration's strong view that a public hearing on Chile would damage the national security of the United States, the committee reconsidered, eventually deciding to go ahead. As with the assassination report, the administration's approach was dual: in principle, it remained opposed to any hearing, and it refused to permit any sitting officials or retired CIA officers to testify in public; yet if we went ahead, it was prepared to work with us, again ostensibly to protect "sources and methods."

Given the administration's unwillingness to let those officials who had been closest to the Chile operations testify in public, the committee decided to issue a staff report to lay out that story. We did a draft based on CIA and State Department documents and supplemented by numbers of interviews with participants. The hearing was scheduled for December 4 and 5, 1975. The days just before it I spent with the draft in a secured room at CIA headquarters in Langley with Seymour Bolton, Walt Elder, and a shifting set of their CIA colleagues. Our topic of discussion was meant to be sources and methods. In fact, we argued through every line of the report. Was a particular conclusion, even if tentatively drawn, fair in light of the evidence? Did a particular verb overstate the point?

The argument went on and on. It was exhausting but also exhilarating. It seemed to me, then and now, to represent the American system working well. The executive had its position, the committee had its. Neither changed its mind. But we worked together to avoid needless damage to interests we both held dear. The process forced me and my Senate colleagues to think again about the evidence and to sharpen our prose. And in the end it was the committee itself that would decide whether it published the report or not, and with what included and what excluded.

As with the assassination report, the final issue of contention was names. On most of those we relented, yet a few seemed to us either appropriate to publish or so well known already that their exclusion would only convey the impression that we were trying to hide something. For instance, for "*El Mercurio*," our friends at the CIA wanted us to substitute "major Santiago daily." Their phrase was tantamount to naming the paper, given all the press play Chile had received. It seemed to us more likely to spread confusion or suggest deception than to protect anything. The committee accepted our advice on all the contended names, and the final report, *Covert Action in Chile*, contained them all.

The Shifting Bargain

Nevertheless, when I left the committee early in 1976, all our work seemed to amount to precious little. On the domestic side, in safeguarding the rights of Americans, the investigations themselves were valuable. Throwing a harsh light on past abuses diminished the risk that they would recur in the future. On the foreign policy side, I was left to hope that the same might be true of covert actions that looked, in that harsh light, unwise. Certainly, our legislative legacy was meager. Legislation prohibiting assassination was fine, but those sad and impotent assassination plots had emerged from so special a context that I did not then worry that they would be repeated even if we did not bar them.

The committee had hoped to draft charters for the various intelligence agencies, making clear in legislation, not just executive orders, what they were to do and not do. That was a sensitive and controversial task; it not only ran into the growing concern about hamstringing U.S. intelligence, but it also opened the long-simmering feud over how much authority DCIs should have over the bulk of the intelligence budget that is located in the Defense Department, not the CIA. What had seemed a sea-change in public and congressional climate in 1974 appeared by the time of the Chile hearings to be a window, fast closing. The charter issue had to await another Congress.

The committee's principal recommendation was that it be made permanent. We hoped it would in time absorb all the existing oversight functions and so provide a single focal point for the Senate's consideration of the intelligence community. That hope was realized. In the short run, however, all the permanent new committee did was increase the number of congressional overseers of intelligence from six committees to seven, or eight including the House Select Committee, albeit ones with more access to information.

Yet the institutional legacy of permanent select committees in each house of Congress has turned out to be an important one. The committees include members who sit simultaneously on the Armed Services, Foreign Affairs, Judiciary, and Appropriations committees, giving those committees the opportunity to relinquish their oversight function without feeling they have been entirely cut out. Moreover, the committees established the principle of rotating memberships, to broaden their representation within the Congress, thus guarding against a recurrence of the buddy system in image or in fact. An earlier innovation in congressional oversight, the Joint Atomic Energy Committee, was widely regarded as having become the captive of the very agencies it oversaw.

The procedural legacy, that messy constitutional bargain between executive and Congress, was at least as important as the institutional one. Congress secured its access to information about intelligence activities, including covert action, as a matter of right, not of executive courtesy. (Whether Congress always likes knowing about covert action is another matter.) Secret documents became the property of the "government," not just the executive.

Making the president sign on the dotted line for major covert actions and reinforcing that with congressional access to secret documents would, we hoped, induce administrations to think and think again before resorting to covert intervention. Prudent presidents, we thought, might come to use the overseers as a source of seasoned counsel about the political risks of an operation, and so as a check on the CIA's can-do mentality or the temptations of White House staffers. The process would also make Congress share the responsibility at the "takeoff," in one staffer's phrase, and so make it responsible also for the "landing," even if failure made the landing a hard one.

Campaigning in the wake of the congressional investigations, President Carter promised further intelligence reform. In office, he, too, shied away from legislative charters but did issue Executive Order No. 12036 in January 1978, covering the whole range of intelligence activities. It made the Carter NSC's Special Coordination Committee (SCC) the successor to the 40 Committee as executive branch reviewer of covert action. The formal membership paralleled that of predecessor committees, including the secretaries of state and defense, the DCI, the chairman of the Joint Chiefs of Staff, the director of the Office of Management and Budget, and the assistant to the president for national security affairs; the attorney general, however, was a significant addition. In an attempt to deal with the fact that clandestine operations not labeled covert action sometimes have political effects, the SCC was also charged with reviewing sensitive collection and counterintelligence projects.

The Carter administration also tightened executive branch procedures for reviewing covert action in other ways. It sought, in its first two years at least, to embody an inclination against covert action in the process of review. Within the CIA, proposals were passed to a number of offices outside the Directorate of Operations—the comptroller, the general and legislative counsels, and, continuing a practice begun during Colby's tenure, the Directorate of Intelligence, then called the National Foreign Assessment Center. The Agency's analysts would have some chance of knowing what its covert operators were up to.

Before the DCI signed off on any proposal, it was also reviewed two places outside the CIA—the State Department and a staff-level working group of the SCC, composed of representatives of all the agencies on the parent SCC. The working group was advisory, not decision-making. But many proposals never got beyond its review, while others were sent back to the CIA to be recast. As earlier—and later—much depended on the views of the individuals that reviewed proposals, but no longer were decisions about what merited SCC review, presidential finding, or consultation with Congress purely the province of the CIA.

The Carter administration's dealings with Congress over covert action were easy. With the administration using the instrument sparingly, Carter's continuation of the Ford practice of submitting blanket findings—covering, for instance, a range of covert actions against terrorist targets in a single finding—was not much of an issue. Nor was the fact that Carter's DCI, Stansfield Turner, rejected the notion of "prior notification"—that is, notifying the Congress before operations are underway.[38]

While the issue of legislative charters proved too hard, the administration and Congress cooperated in passing the Intelligence Oversight Act of 1980, the most important law passed by Congress in the realm of covert action.[39] The act did cut back the executive's reporting requirements for covert action to the two intelligence committees. It also made clear that Congress wanted to be notified of all covert actions, not just those carried out by the CIA; secret executive recourse to other agencies, in particular the military, was denied.

Congress also tiptoed toward prior notification of covert action. The "timely fashion" of Hughes-Ryan allowing notification after the fact (within twenty-four hours came to be the understanding) became "fully and currently informed," including "any significant anticipated intelligence activity," in the 1980 act. Yet notifying Congress still was not a "condition precedent to the initiation" of covert action. And the act gave the president another escape hatch, for in emergencies he was permitted to limit prior notice to eight members—the chairmen and ranking minority members of the intelligence committees, the speaker and minority leader of the House, and the majority and minority leaders of the Senate—the "Gang of Eight."

The Inherent Tension

Tension between the executive and Congress over covert action, muted when the administration in power and the congressional overseers shared the view that the instrument should be used sparingly, increased with the surge of covert actions in the 1980s. The Reagan administration came into office determined to make covert assistance to "freedom fighters" around the world a key element of its global pressure on the Soviet Union. In setting out what came to be called the Reagan Doctrine, the president said third world trouble spots "are the consequence of an ideology imposed from without, dividing nations and creating regimes that are . . . at war with their own people. . . . And in each case, Marxism-Leninism's war becomes war with their neighbors."[40]

Mr. Reagan's Executive Order, No. 12333, slightly expanded the definition of covert action, termed "special activities," over the Carter order. It is striking in light of what came later that it gave the CIA full responsibility for those activities except in time of war or by specific presidential instruction.[41]

The administration reshaped its internal review processes to manage the increase in covert actions. In place of the SCC, it created the National Security Planning Group (NSPG), which included the vice president, the secretaries of state and defense, the DCI, and the national security adviser, but, for reasons of secrecy, the other SCC members were dropped. In their place, three presidential advisers were added—the White House chief-of-staff, his deputy, and the president's counselor. The president himself was also a member. The intent was to make the process more responsive to the president's desire for more frequent resort to covert action. The risk was that sources of expert advice—the attorney general or Joint Chiefs of Staff, for instance—especially advice that might be cautionary, were lost.

By 1985 the administration had created a group to backstop the NSPG, somewhat parallel to the SCC working group in the Carter administration. Like its predecessor, it was composed of the deputies of the NSPG members. Formally nameless, it was dubbed the 208 Committee, after the room where it met in the Old Executive Office Building in the White House complex.

With the new administration, attitudes changed more than procedures. One congressional staffer referred to men like Oliver North as "field grades," people eager for action, long on energy but short on political savvy. William Miller, staff director of both the Church Committee and the first permanent Senate Intelligence Committee, observed that the CIA and its sister agencies were led in the late 1970s by people who had been through the experience of investigation and reform. They were "so immersed in the constitutional questions that they could recite chapter and verse. Questions of law and constitutional balance occurred naturally to them." By contrast, the Reagan leadership was dominated by "advocates, people who were always trying to get around the roadblocks of institutional and statutory limitations, who were looking for a way to get it done."[42]

Nicaragua was the first focal point of tension between executive and Congress; the long wrangle over the funding for aid to the Contras demonstrated that. The clash of interests was almost built into the process, for the Reagan administration, like the Ford and Carter administrations before it, preferred broad, general findings that would give the CIA room to adapt to changing circumstances, whereas Congress was wary of signing a blank check, particularly since the administration wanted to do more by way of covert action than at least the House committee was prepared to countenance. Carter's DCI, Turner, summarized the conflict:

> Under a broad finding, an operation can be expanded considerably; with a narrow one, the CIA has to go back to the President to obtain a revised finding if there is any change of scope. The Congress is wary of broad findings; they can easily be abused. The CIA is afraid of narrow findings; they can be a nuisance.[43]

McGeorge Bundy, who ran the 303 Committee for the Kennedy and Johnson administrations, commented on the difficulty reviewers outside the CIA confront, a comment that congressional overseers of the Contra operation would appreciate: "I think it has happened that an operation is presented in one way to a committee and executed in a way that is different from what the committee thought it had considered."[44]

Whether an operation that changed in midstream compelled the president to issue a new finding was a related point of tension. Hughes-Ryan required presidential findings for covert actions "important to the national security" but could not spell out how the "important" was to be distinguished from the "routine" in this special realm of covert action. Later provisions required every covert action to be covered by a finding, but whether an operational change required a new finding was a matter of judgment: Did the change increase the risks of exposure or harm if disclosed? Did it represent a marked shift in the nature of the operation? Did it substantially increase costs?

All these questions required congressional overseers to get deeply into the details of ongoing operations—hard for them and uncomfortable for covert operators in the executive branch. Critical details could fall between the cracks even with the best of wills on both sides. And suffice to say that wills were not always the best. The CIA's mining of Nicaraguan harbors is a case in point. The operation clearly was, at a minimum, risky since it threatened not only Nicaraguan vessels but also international shipping, including that of U.S. allies. It also represented a new phase in the covert war, albeit a phase suggested by the original CIA proposal. The president approved the recommendation in the winter, probably in December 1984.[45] The Sandinistas charged on January 3 that the Contras were laying mines in Nicaraguan harbors, and rebel leaders announced on January 8 that they would do so.

On January 31 DCI Casey met with the House committee, a persistent critic of covert action in Nicaragua, and mentioned the mining, although the meeting was primarily about releasing further funds for the overall Contra project. Several members of the Senate committee and its staff may also have been briefed. The Senate, however, was pushing toward its February recess, and the administration twice asked for a delay so that Secretary of State Shultz could attend. As a result, a full briefing of the Senate committee was delayed, and many, perhaps most members remained unaware of the operation, especially of the direct CIA role in it. So did the staff director.

Casey first met with the full committee on March 8, for over an hour, but this meeting, too, dealt primarily with authorizing the release of funds, over which the Intelligence Committee was fighting a jurisdictional battle with Appropriations. Only one sentence dealt with the mining, and it, like the rest of the briefing, was delivered in Casey's inimitable mumble.[46] Many on the committee did not learn of the mining until a month later, almost by accident on the floor of the Senate.

Casey honored the letter of the law with his brief reference, but the episode angered even Senator Barry Goldwater, the committee chairman, and a man not opposed to covert action. He had not understood the reference. Once the committee staff received a full briefing on April 2 and he learned about the operation, he was furious. His letter to Casey, which leaked to the press, was notable for its unsenatorial prose as well as for its displeasure: "It gets down to one, little, simple phrase: I am pissed off!"[47]

It may be that committee members, like Goldwater, were not paying attention. The episode also demonstrates another peril of oversight, for if the two houses share a distrust of the executive, no matter which party is in power, they are jealous of each other as well, and so the two committees do not automatically share information. However, as Turner concluded, Casey's performance, if it squared with the letter of the law, was "hardly the intent. . . . The CIA did go through the motions of informing, but it wasn't speaking very loudly."[48]

Most of the time, getting members of Congress to pay attention to covert action was not, and is not, a problem. They have little political reason to become involved, much less to take responsibility for particular actions, but the mystique of clandestine operations remains a powerful tug on their attentions. Time and again during the work of the Church Committee, I was struck by the prospect of committee members listening, in secret session, to long disquisitions about code breaking or satellite reconnaissance while their political aides fretted, their constituents waited, and other hearings dealing with business that was less romantic but more relevant to their political stakes went on without them. At the beginning of the 100th Congress in 1987, sixty members of the House had signed up for four openings on the Intelligence Committee.

Still, even for members of the intelligence committees, the assignment is one among many. Even their staffs are hard-pressed to keep up with the details of forty-odd covert actions. As one staffer close to the process put it: "How can you know which detail will jump up and bite you. Things move fast. How long did the mining take from beginning to end? A few weeks. Even the manual [for the Contras] took only three months from printing to distribution."[49]

And oversight is something of an unnatural act. Members have little political reason to become involved in it, more reason not to. Sometimes, they feel they know more than they want to know. As Senator Daniel Inouye, the first chairman of the permanent Senate Intelligence Committee, observed: "How would you like to know a very, very high official of a certain government was on our payroll?"[50]

Moreover, once they are briefed and understand an operation, committee members are in an awkward political position. They know about the covert action but cannot easily stop it if they disapprove. By custom, the CIA informs the White House of any dissent from the committees, and the lack of strong dissent is sure to be taken by the administration as tacit approval of the operation. Thus, the act of being briefed is more than receiving information; it is giving or withholding assent, even if the committees do not vote on a particular action once it is briefed to them.

The committees have more responsibility than they do authority. The operation may already be underway or will be by the time the briefing is over. If the administration is determined to proceed, it can fund the operation for a year from the Contingency Reserve.[51] Only in the next budget cycle do the committees have the opportunity to pass on the project as a line item in the budget.

The committees' power is the power to persuade. Presidents cannot lightly ignore their views, especially if those views are held by senior committee members reaching across party lines. The CIA needs to deal with the committees for its budget and for a range of intelligence issues; the president needs good relations with senior members for other business beyond intelligence. The committees have sought in several ways to enhance their power to persuade. Lest the president miss the point, committee members can write, or even visit, him. On a number of occasions the Senate committee has taken a formal vote to underscore its opposition to a particular proposal; more than once, apparently, its vote has induced a president to rescind approval of the operation.[52] As with Nicaragua, the committees can press the administration to refine its finding to make the operation more accountable.

The Messy Bargain

If an administration is still determined to proceed in the face of committee opposition, Congress has several other options, all of them messy and public. Members or their staffs can simply leak the operation to the press, which has happened rarely. Or the committees can take their case to the full house meeting in secret session. That, however, is likely to disclose the operation simply because too many people will then know of it. It also makes a travesty of the oversight process that was meant to build accountability by centralizing authority in Congress.

In extreme cases, however, when passions are high on both sides and the sense of frustration in Congress is deep, Congress has resorted to public legislation barring "covert" action. It did so with the Clark-Tunney Amendment on Angola and the Boland Amendment with regard to Nicaragua. In both cases,

Congress said, in effect, that it did not trust the administration, or its designated overseers of covert action, or both.

More than a decade ago, in designing new oversight arrangements for intelligence, it was apparent that covert action would be the most sensitive task. We tried to strike a delicate balance: Congress would have the power to persuade by having the ability to know; single points of oversight, constructed to be representative of the entire house, would enhance accountability by permitting a real sharing of information even about these most secret of governmental operations. At the same time, Congress would not have the right of prior approval; it would not have to vote up or down on every significant covert action. That did not then seem either wise or necessary, nor did it seem what either the executive or Congress desired.

Most of the time the process seems to have worked as it was intended. The congressional overseers have been informed of covert action and recorded their views; sometimes those views have prevailed. In others, they have said, in the words of one staff member, "Hey, do you know how risky that is?"[53] Hearing an affirmative response, they have let the program go ahead despite their doubts. Most of the time, in either case, the process has remained secret. The Reagan administration wanted to make use of covert action much more frequently than its predecessor, and the oversight committees, reflecting the mood of Congress and probably of the American people as well, assented to that expansion of covert action.

Indeed, the committees have been charged with becoming as much protectors of the intelligence community as overseers—the risk that runs through all relations between Congress and executive agencies from Agriculture to Defense. It was a risk we sought to minimize through rotating memberships. That charge, however, seldom has been leveled with regard to covert action. It is true that the committees have been instrumental in tripling the total budget of the intelligence community in a decade, to over $20 billion per year, most of that for large new technical collection systems. In a case or two, counterintelligence in the United States for example, the committees have been in front of administrations. They have done so both because they came to believe the administration was not doing enough and because they wanted to demonstrate that their attitude was not purely negative, that they could say yes as well as no.

Sometimes, however, the congressional overseers have been thrust into an unenviable position: either keep silent about an operation despite their misgivings, or take action that is almost certain to reveal that operation. In the one case, the power to persuade becomes instead an opportunity for the executive. In the other, the oversight process breaks down and, for better or worse, the option of covertness is foreclosed.

For instance, in first limiting, then cutting off, then resuming aid to the Contras, the Congress confronted an administration determined to continue to find ways to help them, an administration arguing that the United States had a commitment to the Contras. In that circumstance, Congress and the administration were bound to disagree over what the law required, all the more so since the 1984 wording *was* ambiguous, barring the CIA and any other entity "involved in intelligence" from giving direct or indirect support to military operations in Nicaragua. Was any administration official barred from doing anything to find other sources of such support? How could Congress enforce such a ban, much less do so privately? The confusion only increased in December 1985 when the intelligence committees approved some money for "communications" and "advice" to the Contras, subject to conditions negotiated with the committees. There then ensued an exchange of letters suggesting that even the two chairmen were uncertain—or disagreed over—what was permitted and what proscribed.[54]

There can be no full resolutions to these dilemmas, for they are rooted in the paradox of secret operations in a democracy. It still does not seem appropriate to make Congress approve every covert action in advance. There is a constitutional issue about whether that is "a legislative function," in former DCI Colby's words. More immediately, getting the intelligence committees to authorize and the Congress to appropriate specific budgets could take months. A partial remedy would be to require the intelligence committees to approve any withdrawal from the CIA Contingency Reserve. That would be uncomfortable for the committees in that it would put them more directly on the line in the eyes of their congressional colleagues, but it would at least spare them the discomfort of having to choose between silent opposition to an operation and public exposure of it.

So far, also, administrations have very seldom resorted to informing only the "Gang of Eight" when they feel secrecy is at a premium.[55] Had relations between Casey and the committees been better, the Reagan administration might have done so in the instance of Iranian arms sales. That would not necessarily have resulted in wiser policy, for it is conceivable that the Gang of Eight would have been seduced down the path from geostrategic interests to releasing hostages just as the president was. But the subsequent debate would then have been about the wisdom of the policy, not about whether Congress was deceived.

By the same token, it may now be time to consider a joint intelligence committee in place of the two separate ones in each house of Congress. That could diminish the risks of repeating the miscommunication between the houses that occurred over the mining of the Nicaraguan harbors, although it would not eliminate such tensions if the two houses were themselves as divided as they were over covert action in Nicaragua. Nor would a single committee reduce leaks from Congress, for those have been relatively few in any case. What a single committee would do is give the president less justification for excluding Congress as "too leaky." With luck, a single committee might even increase the chances of the kind of comity between executive branch officials and congressional overseers we hoped for a decade ago.

As in any process, much will depend on personalities. Reagan and Casey did not always want to avail themselves of congressional advice with regard to covert action, or they did not like what they heard. A Republican staffer described more colorfully the attitude of one recent CIA director of congressional affairs, a career Clandestine Service officer: He behaved like "Washington was a foreign country and he was the station chief in hostile terrain, mounting operations against the Congress."[56]

The fundamental conclusion to be drawn about overt "covert" actions like Nicaragua is the straightforward one: when covert operations are large and when both they and the larger foreign policies of which they are a part are fiercely contended by American political leaders, those covert operations cannot remain secret. In those cases, it is not that oversight has broken down but rather that in our democratic society no tidy, secret process can be sustained. For Senator Dave Durenberger, former chairman of the Senate Intelligence Committee: "For at least a generation, we're in for a series of smaller conflicts that shape our national security policy . . . in some way the American public is going to be involved in that without knowing how it's being involved."[57] Or as one Senate staff member said of the closed process: "No matter how much I liked that bottle, I don't think the genie can be put back in it."

If the United States is to have a Clandestine Service, especially one that engages in covert action, tension between accountability and operational necessity cannot be resolved. That is true within the executive branch; it is particularly true with regard to Congress. Covertness—secrecy—requires limiting the number of people informed of an operation. Accountability requires broadening the circle. It means broadening it to include people whose perspectives and political interests differ from those who manage covert operations—especially if the circle includes Congress. The process will be uncomfortable for both operators and overseers.

Covert operators will feel that their political masters, in both the executive and Congress, are always looking over their shoulders, that the daisy chain of authorization is so long that they cannot respond quickly to changing foreign circumstances. At the same time, overseers, especially in Congress, will feel that secrecy insulates them more than it hides covert operations from their foreign targets. Past cases provide grounds for such suspicion. The overseers will always feel they know less than they should.

Lessons, Not Processes

At first blush, none of these delicate dilemmas in relations between the executive and Congress seems to apply to the Iran-Contra affair. The January finding was explicit: Do not tell Congress. The congressional overseers did not find out about the Iran operation until the following autumn—not "fully and currently informed" by anyone's definition. Later on, it was the president himself who was not told, when the Iran and Contra operations crossed.

In another sense, however, the system "worked." In deciding to sell arms to Iran, the president pursued a line of policy opposed by his secretaries of state and defense both, about which he was afraid to inform the congressional intelligence committees, and which was liable to be revealed by Iranian factions as and when it suited them. It is hard to imagine any system providing more warning signals. When the opposition of most of the government's senior foreign policy officials means they have to be cut out of the policy, it is likely that the policy, and not they, are wrong. The president thus proceeded at his peril.

With regard to the diversion of money for the Contras, the lesson is not that the NSC staff should be eliminated or the national security adviser made subject to Senate confirmation. Presidents will always have need of a source of private advice and a means of brokering the actions of the many foreign policy agencies of government. Moreover, if presidents are determined to get something done, they will be able to find someone somewhere in the White House to do it. So, too, if the United States continues to have a Clandestine Service, presidents will be tempted to resort to covert action as a middle resort, not a last.

Rather, the lesson is a caution for presidents and those who advise them: Don't run covert operations from the White House. Two decades ago, it would have been unthinkable for an administration to do so; then, the reason was that presidents wanted to stay at arm's length from such things, even if they could not in a pinch plausibly deny them. Now, if covert actions are to be undertaken, they should be done by the agency of government constructed to do them—the Central Intelligence Agency, which has both the expertise and the accountability. That admonition, contained in Mr. Reagan's executive order, should be written into law as a requirement, albeit one difficult to enforce in a pinch.

Moreover, now as two decades ago, if the president's closest advisers become the operators, the president loses them as a source of detached judgment on the operations. The president's own circle become advocates, like Allen Dulles in the Bay of Pigs, not protectors of the president's stakes (even if he does not quite realize his need for protection). So it was with McFarlane and Poindexter; once committed, they had reason to overlook the warning signals thrown up by the process. Excluding Congress also excluded one more "political scrub," one more source of advice about what the range of American people would find acceptable. And the chances increased that someone like North, misguided, would interpret the president's interest after his own fashion.

In William Miller's reflections on the process from the Church Committee to the Iran-Contra misadventure: "If clear lines hadn't been drawn a decade ago, there would have been no hue and cry now."[58] The result of the Iran-Contra debacle, I hope, will be to draw those lines again, more sharply, as lessons for future administrations. If the process cannot provide guarantees against unwise policy, it can at least put administrations on notice. A few jail terms would underscore the lesson for White House staffers, one that the "plumbers" learned a decade ago. Faced with pressure to act, they might say to themselves, if not to their president: "Yes, Mr. President, I'll do it, but you realize I may have to go to jail."

NOTES

Preface

1. See *Covert Action in Chile, 1963–1973,* Staff Report of the Senate Select Committee to Study . . . Intelligence Activities, 94th Cong., 1st sess. (December 18, 1975) (hereinafter, *Covert Action in Chile*).

Introduction

1. At a press conference at the Capitol, July 19, 1975.
2. "Should the U.S. Fight Secret Wars?" *Harpers* (September 1984): 41.
3. Ibid., p. 37.
4. The Kissinger quote appeared widely in the press at the time. See Roger Morris, *Uncertain Greatness: Henry Kissinger and American Foreign Policy* (New York: Harper and Row, 1977), p. 241. For an attribution of the Stimson quote, see Anne Karalekas, "History of the Central Intelligence Agency," in *Supplementary Detailed Staff Reports on Foreign and Military Intelligence,* book 4 of *Final Report of the Senate Select Committee to Study . . . Intelligence Activities,* 94th Cong., 2d sess. (April 23, 1976) (hereinafter, "CIA History"), p. 1.

Chapter 1

1. *Foreign and Military Intelligence,* book 1 of *Final Report of the Senate Select Committee to Study . . . Intelligence Activities,* 94th Cong., 2d sess. (April 26, 1976), p. 477.
2. Ibid., p. 445.
3. This is my estimate. For roughly similar ones, see Loch Johnson, "Covert Action and American Foreign Policy: Decision Paths for the 'Quiet Option,' " paper presented to the American Political Science Association Annual Meeting, Washington, D.C. 1986; and "The CIA Report the President Doesn't Want You to Read: The Pike Papers," *Village Voice* (February 16 and 23, 1975).
4. This is my estimate. It roughly squares with one cited in the New York *Times* (July 7, 1986) and with that of John Prados in *Presidents' Secret Wars: CIA and Pentagon Covert Operations Since World War II* (New York: Morrow, 1986), p. 370.
5. This is my estimate, based on interviews and a variety of published sources. One, for instance, puts the 1983 CIA budget at $800 million. See Jeffrey T. Richelson, *The U.S. Intelligence Community* (Cambridge, Mass.: Ballinger, 1985), p. 21.

6. The Chilean examples in this section and the next are, unless otherwise noted, from *Covert Action in Chile*, Hearings before the Senate Select Committee . . . [on] Intelligence Activities, 94th Cong., 1st sess. (December 4 and 5, 1975).

7. See David Atlee Phillips, *The Night Watch* (New York: Atheneum, 1977), pp. 41 ff.

8. John Stockwell, *In Search of Enemies: A CIA Story* (New York: Norton, 1978), p. 194.

9. *Alleged Assassination Plots Involving Foreign Leaders: Interim Report of the Senate Select Committee to Study . . . Intelligence Activities*, 94th Cong., 1st sess. (November 20, 1975), p. 227 (hereinafter, *Assassination Report*).

10. Ibid., pp. 71 ff.

11. Loch Johnson, *A Season of Inquiry: The Senate Intelligence Investigation* (Lexington: University Press of Kentucky, 1985), p. 55.

12. Stockwell, *In Search of Enemies*, p. 10.

13. Richelson, *The U.S. Intelligence Community*, provides an exhaustive description of the U.S. intelligence services.

14. Johnson, *A Season of Inquiry*, p. 83.

15. Richelson, *The U.S. Intelligence Community*, p. 222.

16. The best history of the origins of the CIA was done for the first Senate Select Committee on Intelligence: Anne Karalekas, "CIA History." For a recent, extremely detailed history of the CIA, see John Ranelagh, *The Agency: The Rise and Decline of the CIA* (New York: Simon & Schuster, 1986).

17. Prados, *Presidents' Secret Wars*, p. 17.

18. Quoted in Walter Millis, ed., *The Forrestal Diaries* (New York: Viking Press, 1951), p. 387.

19. Reprinted in William M. Leary, ed., *The Central Intelligence Agency: History and Documents* (University: University of Alabama Press, 1984), pp. 131–33.

20. The phrase is John Bross's; interview, January 9, 1987.

21. Testimony before the Senate Select Committee on Intelligence, October 28, 1975, cited in "CIA History," p. 31.

22. Quoted in Frank Church, "Covert Action: Swampland of American Foreign Policy," *Bulletin of the Atomic Scientists* 32 (February 1976): 9.

23. "CIA History," p. 36.

24. Prados, *Presidents' Secret Wars*, p. 81.

25. Letter to author, February 25, 1987.

26. "CIA History," pp. 31–32.

27. Prados, *Presidents' Secret Wars*, p. 80.

28. As quoted in ibid., p. 33.

29. "CIA History," p. 38.

30. Ibid., p. 41.

Chapter 2

1. Cited in Kermit Roosevelt, *Countercoup: The Struggle for the Control of Iran* (New York: McGraw-Hill, 1979), p. 199. Roosevelt's account has not been independently documented, and therefore it should be taken as evocative, not gospel.

2. The most authoritative account of the Guatemalan intervention is Richard

H. Immerman, *The CIA in Guatemala: The Foreign Policy of Intervention* (Austin: University of Texas Press, 1982).

3. All these cost estimates are rough and would be so even if the accounting were not secret. One estimate would be for operating costs only; another would add CIA overhead for officers involved and the like. John Prados, in *Presidents' Secret Wars: CIA and Pentagon Covert Operations Since World War II* (New York: Morrow, 1986), puts the cost of Iran at $10–12 million, which, however, seems high by a factor of two at least (p. 97).

4. Eisenhower, diary entries, January 27 and June 11, 1949, cited in Immerman, *The CIA in Guatemala*, pp. 15–16.

5. Formally, "A Report to the National Security Council by the Secretaries of State and Defense and the Director for Mutual Security on Reexamination of United States Programs for National Security," January 19, 1953, cited in Immerman, *The CIA in Guatemala*, p. 11.

6. For a good summary of this period, see John Gillen and K. H. Silvert, "Ambiguities in Guatemala," *Foreign Affairs* 34, no. 3 (April 1956): 474–75.

7. Stephen Schlesinger and Stephen Kinzer, *Bitter Fruit: The Untold Story of the American Coup in Guatemala* (Garden City, N.Y.: Doubleday, 1982), pp. 58–59; Cole Blasier, *The Hovering Giant: U.S. Responses to Revolutionary Change in Latin America* (Pittsburgh: University of Pittsburgh Press, 1976), p. 155.

8. Report to the President, and Minutes of Cabinet meeting, March 5, 1954, both cited in Immerman, *The CIA in Guatemala*, p. 18.

9. New York *Times*, February 25, 1953.

10. See Richard Cottam, *Nationalism in Iran* (Pittsburgh: University of Pittsburgh Press, 1979), pp. 200 ff.

11. Ibid., p. 205.

12. Dean Acheson, *Present at the Creation* (New York: Norton, 1969), p. 504.

13. *Multinational Oil Corporations and U.S. Foreign Policy*, Hearings before the Senate Committee on Foreign Relations, 93rd Cong., 2d sess. (January 2, 1975), p. 58.

14. See Henry Grady, in *U.S. News and World Report* (October 19, 1951): 13–17.

15. Barry Rubin, *Paved with Good Intentions* (New York: Oxford University Press, 1980), pp. 95–96.

16. Stephen E. Ambrose, with Richard H. Immerman, *Ike's Spies: Eisenhower and the Intelligence Establishment* (New York: Doubleday, 1981), p. 218; Schlesinger and Kinzer, *Bitter Fruit*, p. 70.

17. The Corcoran interview is reported in Ambrose, *Ike's Spies*, pp. 92–93. Like all recollections several decades after the fact, it should be interpreted with caution.

18. Blasier, *The Hovering Giant*, p. 169.

19. Cottam, *Nationalism in Iran*, p. 211.

20. See ibid., p. 279; Rubin, *Paved with Good Intentions*, pp. 66 ff.

21. Rubin, *Paved with Good Intentions*, p. 76.

22. Henderson to Dulles, March 19, 1953, RG 84, box 2667, 350 Iran file, Washington National Records Center, as cited in Rubin, *Paved with Good Intentions*, p. 78.

23. Both letters are printed in the U.S. Department of State *Bulletin*, July 20, 1953, pp. 76–77.

24. E. Howard Hunt, "The Azalea Trail Guide to the CIA," *National Review*

(April 29, 1977); Allen Dulles, *The Craft of Intelligence* (New York: Harper & Row, 1963), p. 221.

25. M. Richard Shaw, "British Intelligence and Iran," *Counterspy* 6, no. 3 (May–June 1982): 119.

26. See Rubin, *Paved with Good Intentions*, p. 81.

27. Roosevelt, *Countercoup*, p. 8.

28. This sequence of events is also recounted in ibid., pp. 1–19.

29. The best account is Immerman, *The CIA in Guatemala*, pp. 118–22.

30. Acheson, *Present at the Creation*, p. 48.

31. Adolf A. Berle, "Memorandum: The Guatemala Problem in Central America," March 31, 1953, Berle diary, cited in Immerman, *The CIA in Guatemala*, pp. 130–31.

32. Interview cited in Ambrose, *Ike's Spies*, p. 225.

33. Schlesinger and Kinzer, in *Bitter Fruit*, fix the date as early August, but confirming evidence is not available. See Immerman, *The CIA in Guatemala*, p. 134.

34. By several accounts, including his own, Roosevelt was approached about running the PBSUCCESS task force. See, for example, Prados, *Presidents' Secret Wars*, p. 98. The timing makes that possible, but Roosevelt's background in the Middle East and in political operations makes it implausible.

35. New York *Times*, November 8, 1953.

36. Drew Pearson, *Diaries 1949–1959*, Tyler Abell, ed. (New York: Holt, Rinehart & Winston, 1974), p. 299.

37. See, for example, Schlesinger and Kinzer, *Bitter Fruit*, p. 132; or Immerman, *The CIA in Guatemala*, p. 136.

38. Thomas Powers, *The Man Who Kept Secrets: Richard Helms and the CIA* (New York: Knopf, 1979), p. 86.

39. "Memorandum for the President: The Situation in Guatemala as of 20 June," cited in Immerman, *The CIA in Guatemala*, p. 161 (original emphasis).

40. Blasier, *The Hovering Giant*, p. 172; William R. Corson, *The Armies of Ignorance: The Rise of the American Intelligence Empire* (New York: Dial Press, 1977), p. 356.

41. Interview with E. Howard Hunt, cited in Immerman, *The CIA in Guatemala*, p. 142.

42. See Ambrose, *Ike's Spies*, p. 226; and Schlesinger and Kinzer, *Bitter Fruit*, pp. 121–22, especially the interview with Fred Sherwood, the CIA agent who led the dissidents' air force.

43. "Memorandum for the President: The Situation in Guatemala as of 20 June," cited in Immerman, *The CIA in Guatemala*, p. 161.

44. David Wise and Thomas Ross, *The Invisible Government: The CIA and U.S. Intelligence* (New York: Random House, 1969), p. 191.

45. Dwight D. Eisenhower, *The White House Years: Mandate for Change 1953–56* (Garden City, NY: Doubleday & Co., 1963), p. 426.

46. Quoted in Immerman, *The CIA in Guatemala*, p. 264; Schlesinger and Kinzer, *Bitter Fruit*, p. 115.

47. E. Howard Hunt, *Undercover: Memoirs of an American Secret Agent* (New York: Berkley, 1974), pp. 97–99.

48. USIA, "Report on Actions Taken by the U.S. Information Agency in the Guatemalan Situation," August 2, 1954, cited in Immerman, *The CIA in Guatemala*, p. 144.

49. The documents were reprinted in a pamphlet prepared by the Arbenz government, *La democracia amenazada, el caso Guatemala*, cited in Blanche Wiesen Cook, *The Declassified Eisenhower: A Divided Legacy* (Garden City, NY: Doubleday & Co, 1981), p. 250; and U.S. embassy cable to State Department, February 12, 1954, cited in ibid; and New York *Times*, January 30, 1954.

50. State Department press release, January 30, 1954.

51. New York *Times*, February 8, 1954.

52. Ambrose, *Ike's Spies*, p. 205.

53. Rubin, *Paved with Good Intentions*, p. 82.

54. New York *Times*, August 4, 1953.

55. Henderson interview, cited in Ambrose, *Ike's Spies*, p. 209.

56. New York *Times*, August 19, 1953.

57. Corson, *The Armies of Ignorance*, pp. 352–53.

58. Cable to State Department, no. 522, December 18, 1953, quoted in Eisenhower, *Mandate for Change*, pp. 422–23.

59. Telephone call, May 19, 1954, cited in Immerman, *The CIA in Guatemala*, p. 160. The CIA conclusion is cited in *Hispanic American Review* 7 (August 1954): 12.

60. New York *Times*, May 20 and 26, 1953. The quote is from the U.S. Department of State *Bulletin*, June 7, 1954, p. 874.

61. David A. Phillips, *The Night Watch* (New York: Atheneum, 1977), p. 46.

62. See Immerman, *The CIA in Guatemala*, pp. 166–67.

63. Phillips, *The Night Watch*, p. 46.

64. Ibid., pp. 46–47; Immerman, *The CIA in Guatemala*, pp. 167–68.

65. This and the other quotes in this paragraph are from Eisenhower, *Mandate for Change*, p. 510.

66. Phillips, *The Night Watch*, p. 48.

67. See Corson, *The Armies of Ignorance*, p. 345.

68. Eisenhower, *Mandate for Change*, p. 164.

69. Richard and Gladys Harkness, "The Mysterious Doing of the CIA," *Saturday Evening Post* (November 6, 1954): 66–68.

70. Cottam, *Nationalism in Iran*, p. 227. Cottam had known of AJAX as a young CIA officer, so he had some reason to minimize the account.

71. Quoted in Immerman, *The CIA in Guatemala*, p. 178.

72. Eisenhower, *Mandate for Change*, pp. 425–26.

73. Bryce Wood, "Self-Plagiarism and Foreign Policy," *Latin American Research Review* 3 (Summer 1968): 184–91.

74. See, among several accounts, Prados, *Presidents' Secret Wars*, pp. 105–06.

75. New York *Times*, April 28, 1966. In a later interview, he qualified that admission somewhat, noting how hard it was to make sure that narrow limits would be observed in the middle of an operation. See Schlesinger and Kinzer, *Bitter Fruit*, p. 194.

76. This directive, formally "National Security Council Directive on Covert Operations," March 12, 1955, was declassified in 1977. The quote is from Prados, *Presidents' Secret Wars*, p. 112.

77. The directive, dated December 28, 1955, is reprinted in William M. Leary, ed., *The Central Intelligence Agency: History and Documents* (University: University of Alabama Press, 1984), pp. 146–47.

78. Cited in *Supplementary Detailed Staff Reports on Foreign and Military Intelli-*

gence, book 4 of *Final Report of the Senate Select Committee to Study . . . Intelligence Activities*, 94th Cong., 2d sess. (April 23, 1976) (hereinafter, "CIA History").

79. Memorandum, April 4, 1953, cited in Cook, *The Declassified Eisenhower*, p. 266.

80. Haggarty diaries 1954, May 20, 1954, cited in ibid.

81. Guillermo Toriello, *La batalla de Guatemala* (Mexico City: Ediciones Cuadernos Americanos, 1955), pp. 229 ff.

82. Blasier, *The Hovering Giant*, pp. 156–57.

83. Ambrose, *Ike's Spies*, p. 199.

84. Eisenhower, *Mandate for Change*, p. 162.

85. Ibid., pp. 422–23.

86. Quoted in U.S. Department of State, *American Foreign Policy, 1950–1955: Basic Documents*, vol. 1 (Washington, D.C.: Government Printing Office, 1957), p. 1310.

87. For a similar conclusion, see Ambrose, *Ike's Spies*, pp. 222–23.

88. Cottam, *Nationalism in Iran*, p. 219.

89. See Gary Sick, *All Fall Down* (New York: Random House, 1985).

90. Roosevelt, *Countercoup*, p. 209.

91. A CIA official quoted in Peter Wyden, *Bay of Pigs: The Untold Story* (New York: Simon & Schuster, 1979), pp. 20–22.

92. "Narrative of the Anti-Castro Cuban Operation ZAPATA," June 13, 1961, Taylor Report (I), published as *Operation Zapata: The "Ultrasensitive" Report and Testimony on the Bay of Pigs*, Classified Studies in Twentieth Century Diplomatic History, series editor Paul L. Kesaris (Frederick, Md.: Aletheia Books, 1981), p. 3.

Chapter 3

1. Quoted in Theodore Sorenson, *Kennedy* (New York: Harper & Row, 1965), p. 309.

2. Quoted in *History of an Aggression* (Havana: Venceremos, 1964), p. 402.

3. Kenneth P. O'Donnell and David F. Powers, with Joe McCarthy, *Johnny, We Hardly Knew Ye* (Boston: Little, Brown, 1970), p. 272.

4. The best brief account of the Bay of Pigs affair is a case prepared at the Kennedy School of Government, Harvard University: "Kennedy and the Bay of Pigs," KSG C14-80-279 (1983).

5. Peter Wyden, *Bay of Pigs: The Untold Story* (New York: Simon & Schuster, 1979), p. 19.

6. Maxwell D. Taylor, chairman, Cuban Study Group, "Narrative of the Anti-Castro Operation ZAPATA," June 13, 1961, partially declassified version released May 8, 1977 (part I of the Taylor Commission Report), published as *Operation Zapata: The "Ultrasensitive" Report and Testimony of the Board of Inquiry on the Bay of Pigs*, Classified Studies in Twentieth Century Diplomatic History, series editor Paul L. Kesaris (Frederick, Md.: Aletheia Books, 1981), pp. 3–4 (hereinafter *Operation Zapata*).

7. Quoted in Wyden, *Bay of Pigs*, p. 31.

8. See the interview with Richard M. Bissell, Jr., Columbia Oral History Research Office, 1967, pp. 29–30.

9. *Operation Zapata*, p. 6; Wyden, *Bay of Pigs*, p. 69.

10. See Bissell interview, pp. 30–31; and Arthur M. Schlesinger, Jr., *A Thousand Days: John F. Kennedy in the White House* (New York: Fawcett Premier, 1965), p. 220.

11. Schlesinger, *A Thousand Days*, pp. 197–98.

12. Ibid., pp. 213, 219; Wyden, *Bay of Pigs*, p. 69.

13. *Operation Zapata*, p. 9.

14. Ibid., p. 10.

15. Wyden, *Bay of Pigs*, p. 89n.

16. Ibid., p. 92.

17. Testimony before the House Foreign Affairs Subcommittee on Western Hemisphere Affairs, April 16, 1985, reprinted in *First Principles* 10, no. 4 (May–June 1985).

18. Schlesinger, *A Thousand Days*, p. 225.

19. Ibid., p. 227.

20. O'Donnell and Powers, *Johnny*, p. 271.

21. New York *Times*, January 10, 1961, cited in Wyden, *Bay of Pigs*, p. 46; *Time* (January 27, 1961): 26.

22. Taylor Report.

23. Ibid.

24. Bissell interiew, p. 25.

25. Schlesinger, *A Thousand Days*, p. 226.

26. Ibid., p. 239.

27. Ibid., pp. 239–40.

28. Wyden, *Bay of Pigs*, p. 123.

29. Schlesinger, *A Thousand Days*, p. 236.

30. Tom Wicker, *On Press* (New York: Viking, 1978), p. 238.

31. Schlesinger, *A Thousand Days*, p. 258.

32. Sorenson, *Kennedy*, p. 296.

33. Wyden, *Bay of Pigs*, p. 100.

34. Ibid., p. 158.

35. His cable to Rusk is excerpted in ibid., pp. 189–90.

36. O'Donnell and Powers, *Johnny*, p. 274.

37. Schlesinger, *A Thousand Days*, p. 266.

38. Quoted in Sorenson, *Kennedy*, p. 308.

39. This episode is recounted in Thomas Powers, *The Man Who Kept the Secrets: Richard Helms and the CIA* (New York: Knopf, 1979), pp. 233 ff. I was not the source for Powers's account, but it squares with my memory.

40. *Covert Action*, volume 7, Hearings before the Senate Select Committee to Study . . . Intelligence Activities, 94th Cong., 1st sess. (December 4–5, 1975) (hereinafter *Covert Action*).

41. See Powers, *The Man Who Kept the Secrets*, p. 223. See also the fascinating exchange between Korry and Senator Richard Schweiker in *Covert Action*, pp. 41–45. Schweiker said: "I think the most ridiculous argument I've heard in these hearings this year is to say because we voted for the Alliance for Progress, that this is a covert action trigger" (p. 45).

42. Powers, *The Man Who Kept Secrets*, p. 223.

43. *Covert Action*, p. 21.

44. CIA memorandum, "Policy Decisions Related to Our Covert Involvement

in the September 1970 Chilean Presidential Election," October 9, 1970, cited in *Alleged Assassination Plots Involving Foreign Leaders: Interim Report of the Senate Select Committee to Study . . . Intelligence Activities*, 94th Cong., 1st sess. (November 20, 1975), p. 230 (hereinafter, *Assassination Report*).

45. "Ambassador's Response to Request for Analysis of Military Option in Present Chilean Situation," memorandum, ibid., p. 230.

46. CIA memorandum, October 9, 1970, ibid., p. 230.

47. Ibid., apparently quoting the earlier authorization document.

48. Korry to Meyer and Kissinger, Situation Report, September 21, 1970, ibid., p. 231.

49. CIA memorandum, October 9, 1970, ibid., 231; and Korry to Meyer and Kissinger, ibid., p. 231.

50. Station to Headquarters, cable 424, September 23, 1970, ibid., p. 234.

51. Headquarters to Station, cable 075517, October 7, 1970, ibid., p. 232, apparently conveying a 40 Committee authorization.

52. Headquarters to Station, cable 236, September 21, 1970, ibid., p. 233.

53. Testimony, August 6, 1975, cited in ibid., p. 235.

54. For a brief account of early covert action in Nicaragua, see Jay Peterzell, *Reagan's Secret Wars* (Washington, D.C.: Center for National Security Studies, 1984).

55. For a discussion of these negotiations, see Roy Gutman, "America's Diplomatic Charade," *Foreign Affairs* (Fall 1984).

56. As reported in the Washington *Post*, March 10, 1982. The quotations are from NSC documents cited in that article. The calculation is mine, based on reporting in the Washington *Post*, October 19, 1986, and so should be regarded as no better than a ballpark number.

57. Peterzell, *Reagan's Secret Wars*, pp. 75–76.

58. See U.S. Senate, Select Committee on Intelligence, *Report, January 1, 1983 to December 31, 1984*, 98th Cong., 2d sess. (1985), pp. 4–5.

59. See ibid.; and New York *Times*, June 15, 1983.

60. For a colorful, if perhaps erratic, account of this process, see Edgar Chamorro, "Confessions of a 'Contra,' " *New Republic* (August 15, 1985).

61. New York *Times*, August 25, 1985.

62. See my "U.S. Strategy in Central America," *Survival* 28, no. 2 (March–April 1986): 128–39.

63. Quoted in the New York *Times*, August 27, 1985, and January 6, 1986, respectively.

64. Washington *Post*, April 6, 1986.

65. March 16, 1986, as published in the New York *Times*, March 17, 1986.

66. Powers, *The Man Who Kept the Secrets*, pp. 88–92.

67. William E. Colby and Peter Forbath, *Honorable Men: My Life in the CIA* (New York: Simon & Schuster, 1978), p. 421.

68. Powers, *The Man Who Kept the Secrets*, pp. 178–79.

69. See the Washington *Post*, October 24, 1984; and John Prados, *Presidents' Secret Wars: CIA and Pentagon Covert Operations Since World War II* (New York: Morrow, 1986), pp. 387–88.

Chapter 4

1. Peurifoy to the Secretary of State, cables, June 23 and 27, 1954, cited in Richard H. Immerman, *The CIA in Guatemala: The Foreign Policy of Intervention*

(Austin: University of Texas Press, 1982), p. 174.

2. Telephone conversation with Allen Dulles, June 28, 1954, cited in ibid., p. 174.

3. See Peurifoy to Secretary of State, June 29, 1954, cited in ibid., p. 32.

4. Dulles to American Embassy, Guatemala, June 29, 1954, cited in ibid., p. 176.

5. Telephone call to Peurifoy, June 1, 1954, cited in ibid., p. 176. Dulles's secretary transcribed the words as "put a couple of heads together."

6. See Peurifoy to Secretary of State, and American Embassy, Guatemala, to Department of State, both July 7, 1954, cited in ibid., p. 177.

7. Arthur M. Schlesinger, Jr., *A Thousand Days: John F. Kennedy in the White House* (New York: Fawcett Premier, 1965), p. 245.

8. Ibid.

9. E. Howard Hunt, *Give Us This Day* (New Rochelle, N.Y.: Arlington House, 1973), pp. 188–89.

10. Schlesinger, *A Thousand Days*, p. 247.

11. Arthur M. Schlesinger, *Robert Kennedy and His Times* (Boston: Houghton Mifflin, 1978), p. 444.

12. Schlesinger, *A Thousand Days*, p. 250.

13. Hans Tanner, *Counter-Revolutionary Agent* (London: G. T. Foulis, 1962), p. 85; Schlesinger, *A Thousand Days*, p. 251.

14. Hunt, *Give Us This Day*, p. 164.

15. Schlesinger, *A Thousand Days*, p. 252.

16. Quoted in Peter Wyden, *Bay of Pigs: The Untold Story* (New York: Simon & Schuster, 1979), p. 213.

17. Quoted in Tanner, *Counter-Revolutionary Agent*, p. 85.

18. *Covert Action*, volume 7, Hearings before the Senate Select Committee to Study . . . Intelligence Activities, 94th Cong., 1st sess. (December 4–5, 1975), p. 36 (hereinafter *Covert Action*).

19. Headquarters to Station, September 28, 1970, cable 380, cited in *Alleged Assassination Plots Involving Foreign Leaders: Interim Report of the Senate Select Committee to Study . . . Intelligence Activities*, 94th Cong., 1st sess. (November 20, 1975), p. 236 (hereinafter, *Assassination Report*).

20. Helms to Kissinger, November 18, 1970, memorandum, ibid., p. 235.

21. Cable 363, September 27, 1970, ibid., p. 238.

22. Cable 611, October 7, 1970, ibid., p. 234.

23. Cable 762, October 14, 1970, ibid.

24. Headquarters to Station, cable 882, ibid.

25. Respectively, cables 424, September 23, 1970; cable 441, October 1, 1970; and cable 477, October 7, 1970, all in ibid., p. 239.

26. Headquarters to Station, cable 612, October 7, 1970, ibid.

27. CIA, Report on Chilean Task Force Activities, November 8, 1970, ibid., p. 240.

28. Station to Headquarters, cable 483, October 8, 1970, ibid.

29. Quoted, respectively, from Task Force Log, October 13, 1970; Station to Headquarters, cable 504, October 19, 1970; and Station to Headquarters, cable 495, October 9, 1970, all in ibid., p. 241.

30. Headquarters to Station, cable 729, October 13, 1970, ibid.

31. Task Force Log, October 14, 1970, ibid., p. 242.

32. CIA memorandum of conversation: Kissinger, Karamessines, and Haig, October 15, 1970, ibid.

33. Station to Headquarters, cable 568, October 19, 1970, ibid., p. 243.
34. Headquarters to Station, cable 854, October 18, 1970, ibid., p. 244.
35. Station to Headquarters, cable 566, October 19, 1970, ibid.
36. Task Force Log, October 20, 1970, ibid.
37. Task Force Log, October 22, 1970, ibid., p. 245.
38. Cable 592, October 22, 1970, ibid., p. 245.
39. Cable 598, October 22, 1970, ibid., p. 246.
40. Cable 495, October 9, 1975, ibid.
41. Testimony, August 6, 1975, quoted in *Assassination Report*, p. 254.
42. David Phillips to Nathaniel Davis, cited in Nathaniel Davis, *The Last Two Years of Salvador Allende* (Ithaca, NY: Cornell University Press, 1985), p. 314 (hereinafter *The Last Two Years*).
43. Ibid., p. 315.
44. This account is pieced together from *Covert Action*, p. 38, and from interviews with Phillips, the deputy, and other CIA officers, in Davis, *The Last Two Years*, pp. 314–15.
45. *Covert Action*, p. 175.
46. Davis, *The Last Two Years*, pp. 311–13.
47. *Covert Action*, pp. 185–86.
48. Ibid., p. 185.
49. Davis, *The Last Two Years*, p. 311.
50. David Atlee Phillips, *The Night Watch* (New York: Atheneum, 1977), pp. 238, 274. The second cable is also mentioned in William E. Colby and Peter Forbath, *Honorable Men: My Life in the CIA* (New York: Simon & Schuster, 1978), p. 305.
51. See, for example, the New York *Times*, September 15, 1973.
52. This sequence is reported in Davis, *The Last Two Years*, p. 360. It generally squares with other accounts.
53. As quoted in *Assassination Report*, p. 254.
54. Colby and Forbath, *Honorable Men*, p. 305.
55. *Multinational Corporations and United States Foreign Policy*, Hearings before the Subcommittee on Multinational Corporations of the Senate Committee on Foreign Relations, 93rd Cong. (1973), part 1, p. 402.
56. This and other figures, unless otherwise noted, are from *Covert Action*, pp. 175 ff.
57. Davis, *The Last Two Years*, p. 309, n. 6.
58. *Covert Action*, p. 176.
59. Davis, *The Last Two Years*, p. 310.
60. Ibid., p. 328.
61. *Covert Action*, p. 177.
62. Davis, *The Last Two Years*, p. 329.
63. Interview with Robert R. Simmons, January 18, 1986.
64. U.S. Department of State, *Communist Interference in El Salvador: Documents Demonstrating Communist Support of the Salvadorean Insurgency* (Washington, February 21, 1981).
65. As quoted in Barry Rubin, "Reagan Administration Policymaking and Central America," in Robert S. Leiken, ed., *Central America: Anatomy of Conflict* (New York: Pergamon Press, 1984), p. 302.
66. Washington *Post*, April 3, 1983.

67. See the U.S. Senate, Select Committee on Intelligence, *Report*, January 1, 1983 to December 31, 1984, 98th Cong., 2d sess. (1985), pp. 4–5.

68. Officially the bans were attached to the fiscal 1983 appropriations bill (Public Law 97-377, Section 793) and the fiscal 1985 defense budget (Public Law 98-473, Section 8066).

69. The House-Senate conference report spoke of Nicaragua "providing military support (including arms, training, and logistics, command and control, and communications facilities) to groups seeking to overthrow the Government of El Salvador." See the Senate Intelligence Committee *Report*, pp. 6–7.

70. As quoted in the New York *Times*, October 3, 1985.

71. As quoted in ibid., August 24, 1986.

Chapter 5

1. John Marcum, "Lessons of Angola," *Foreign Affairs* 54, no. 3 (April 1976): 407.

2. Ibid., p. 412.

3. John Stockwell, *In Search of Enemies: A CIA Story* (New York: Norton, 1978), p. 67.

4. Ibid.

5. Marcum refers to the shipments as limited; see Marcum, "Lessons of Angola," p. 413.

6. Stockwell, *In Search of Enemies*, p. 67.

7. As cited in Marcum, "Lessons of Angola," p. 408.

8. See, for example, ibid., p. 414.

9. Stockwell, *In Search of Enemies*, p. 68; Marcum, "Lessons of Angola," p. 415.

10. As paraphrased in Stockwell, *In Search of Enemies*, p. 54.

11. As paraphrased in ibid., pp. 52–53 (original emphasis).

12. Quoted in Nathaniel Davis, "The Angola Decision of 1975: A Personal Memoir," *Foreign Affairs* 57, no. 1 (Fall 1978): 112–15.

13. As paraphrased in Stockwell, *In Search of Enemies*, p. 47.

14. Davis, "The Angola Decision," p. 112.

15. Report of the House Select Committee on Intelligence (the Pike Committee), as reprinted in the *Village Voice* (February 16, 1976).

16. Stockwell, *In Search of Enemies*, pp. 162, 206; and Henry Kissinger's testimony in *Angola Hearings*, Hearings before the Subcommittee on African Affairs of the Senate Foreign Relations Committee, 94th Cong., 2d sess. (January 29, 1976), p. 29.

17. See Marcum, "Lessons of Angola," p. 417.

18. These are Western intelligence estimates. See the New York *Times*, November 21 and December 21, 1975, January 17 and May 1, 1976. They may be low; see Jorge I. Dominguez, *Cuba: Order and Revolution* (Cambridge: Harvard University Press, 1978), who puts the peak at 20,000 (p. 354).

19. For accounts of this sequence, similar in most particulars, see Robin Hallett, "The South African Intervention in Angola, 1975–76," *African Affairs* 77, no. 308 (July 1978); and Arthur Jay Klinghoffer, *The Angola War: A Study in Soviet Policy in the Third World* (Boulder, Colo.: Westview Press, 1980), pp. 44 ff.

20. The South African Defense Force published its own account, detailed if somewhat cryptic. It was printed in the Rand *Daily Mail* and other South African papers on February 4, 1977.

21. Quoted in the London *Guardian*, January 13, 1976.

22. Quoted in the London *Observer*, November 30, 1975.

23. For Kissinger, see Marcum, "Lessons of Angola," p. 422; for Colby, interview, January 8, 1986.

24. Quoted in Hallett, "The South African Intervention," p. 364.

25. December 14, 1975, quoted in ibid., p. 363.

26. Ibid., p. 382.

27. Quoted in U.S. Department of State, *American Foreign Policy, 1950–1955, Basic Documents*, vol. 1 (Washington, D.C.: Government Printing Office, 1957), p. 1310.

28. This interview is quoted in Stephen E. Ambrose, with Richard H. Immerman, *Ike's Spies: Eisenhower and the Intelligence Establishment* (New York: Doubleday, 1981), p. 218.

29. See Thomas Powers, *The Man Who Kept the Secrets: Richard Helms and the CIA* (New York: Knopf, 1979), pp. 226–27.

30. *Covert Action*, volume 7, Hearings before the Senate Select Committee to Study . . . Intelligence Activities, 94th Cong., 1st sess. (December 4–5, 1975), p. 163 (hereinafter, *Covert Action*).

31. Ibid., pp. 160, 168.

32. Helms testimony, July 15, 1975, pp. 4–5, cited in *Alleged Assassination Plots Involving Foreign Leaders: Interim Report of the Senate Select Committee to Study . . . Intelligence Activities*, 94th Cong., 1st sess. (November 20, 1975), p. 228 (hereinafter, *Assassination Report*).

33. Claire Sterling, *The Terror Network: The Secret War of International Terrorism* (New York: Holt, Rinehart and Winston, 1981).

34. The fullest account of these plots is *Assassination Report*, pp. 71 ff.

35. Ibid., p. 71. According to the CIA, it had had nothing to do with the people mentioned in fifteen of the cases. In the other nine, it had been in contact with the people cited but not for the purpose of killing Castro.

36. I had the chance to review these assessments, all classified, in 1975. They are described in *Covert Action*, pp. 190–195, on which the following account is based.

37. See, for example, Connor Cruise O'Brien, "How Hot Was Chile?" *New Republic* (August 26, 1985): 37.

38. Ariel Dorfman, "The Challenge in Chile," *New York Times Magazine* (June 29, 1986): 26.

39. Press briefings in Washington, D.C., December 4, 1975.

40. David Atlee Phillips, *The Night Watch* (New York: Atheneum, 1977), p. 53.

41. Ambrose, *Ike's Spies*, pp. 233–34.

42. Phillips, *Night Watch*, p. 54.

Chapter 6

1. This account draws most heavily on the *Report of the President's Special Review Board*, known as the Tower Commission after its chairman, former Sen. John Tower, reprinted by Bantam and Times Books in 1987 (hereinafter *Tower Commission*).

2. *Tower Commission*, p. 38.

3. *Tower Commission*, p. 544.

4. Officially, this document was a revision of a Special National Intelligence Estimate, or SNIE, 34–84, *Iran: Prospects for Near-Term Instability*, May 20, 1985. See *Tower Commission*, p. 115.

5. As quoted in the New York *Times*, November 14, 1986.

6. The finding was printed in the Washington *Post*, January 9, 1987. See also *Tower Commission*, pp. 215–17. The president is quoted in the New York *Times*, August 13, 1987.

7. See the report by Attorney General Edwin Meese, reprinted in the New York *Times*, November 26, 1986.

8. Interview with Richard M. Bissell, Jr., Columbia Oral History Research Office, 1967, p. 25.

9. For accounts of both, see John Prados, *Presidents' Secret Wars: CIA and Pentagon Covert Operations Since World War II* (New York: Morrow, 1986), chaps. 8, 9.

10. *Time* (February 8, 1954).

11. Interview, January 9, 1986.

12. The best account of Washington's encounter with revolutionary Iran is Gary Sick, *All Fall Down* (New York: Random House, 1986). For mention of anti-Khomeini covert action, see the interview with Stansfield Turner, reported in the Baltimore *Sun*, May 12, 1983.

13. Interviews with CIA officials, November 1980, cited in Loch Johnson, "Covert Action and American Foreign Policy: Decision Paths for the 'Quiet Option,' " paper presented to the American Political Science Association Annual Meeting, Washington, D.C., 1986.

14. The observation is that of my colleague and astute Pentagon-watcher, Ernest May. See Richard E. Neustadt and Ernest May, *Thinking in Time: The Uses of History for Decision-Makers* (New York: Free Press, 1986), p. 218.

15. David Atlee Phillips, *The Night Watch* (New York: Atheneum, 1977), p. 49.

16. See, for instance, John Stockwell, *In Search of Enemies: A CIA Story* (New York: Norton, 1978), pp. 68–9.

17. As reported in numerous press accounts, for instance, the New York *Times*, July 7, 1986.

18. For a collection of that evidence, see Jeffrey T. Richelson, *Sword and Shield: Soviet Intelligence and Security Apparatus* (Cambridge, Mass.: Ballinger, 1986), esp. pp. 137 ff.

19. See Steven R. David, "Soviet Involvement in Third World Coups," *International Security* 11, no. 1 (Summer 1986): 3–36. Afghanistan in 1979 might be added to the list, but having to send in 100,000 troops hardly seems like a "success" and certainly not a covert one.

20. Reported in the *Far East Economic Review* (March 24, 1983): 18.

21. For the best account we have, see Raymond L. Garthoff, *Detente and Confrontation: American-Soviet Relations from Nixon to Reagan* (Washington, D.C.: Brookings Institution, 1985), pp. 887 ff.

22. Stephen Solarz, "When To Intervene," *Foreign Policy* 63 (Summer 1986): 20–29.

23. John Bross to author, January 8, 1986.

24. See the endowment report for 1985 and its listing of grants for 1986.

25. As reported by the New York *Times*, July 29, 1986.

26. As quoted in Jay Peterzell, *Reagan's Secret Wars* (Washington, D.C.: Center for National Security Studies, 1984), p. 9.

27. Interview with William Colby, January 9, 1987.

28. See the New York *Times*, September 25, 1975.

29. As quoted in ibid., September 26, 1975.

30. My checklist parallels that suggested in Solarz, "When To Intervene," although mine is more specific to covert action.

31. See, for instance, accounts of differing CIA and State assessments of Qaddafi's vulnerability. Washington *Post*, November 3, 1985. The intelligence committees also reportedly were worried that any plot would involve assassination.

32. See *The Observer* (London), April 6, 1986.

33. See *Covert Action*, volume 7, Hearings before the Senate Select Committee to Study . . . Intelligence Activities, 94th Cong., 1st sess. (December 4–5, 1975), p. 54.

Chapter 7

1. There was no shortage of press accounts. See, in particular, the detailed accounts in the New York *Times*, October 22, 1986, and the Miami *Herald*, October 28, 1986. This account also draws on the *Report of the President's Special Review Board*, known as the Tower Commission after its chairman former Senator John Tower, reprinted by Bantam and Times Books in 1987 (hereinafter *Tower Commission*); and on Congress's Iran-Contra investigation.

2. See the New York *Times*, October 9 and 24, 1986.

3. Quoted in ibid., October 11, 1986.

4. Estimated in ibid., August 25, 1985.

5. *Tower Commission*, pp. 57–61.

6. Washington *Post*, October 19, 1986.

7. As revealed in a U.S. General Accounting Office investigation, May 1986, cited in the Miami *Herald*, October 28, 1986.

8. Quoted in the New York *Times*, October 9, 1986.

9. *Tower Commission*, p. 476.

10. As quoted in the Boston *Globe*, August 11, 1985.

11. Testimony before the Congress Iran-Contra committee, quoted in the New York *Times*, July 16, 1987.

12. Shultz's testimony before the House Foreign Affairs Committee is excerpted in ibid., December 6, 1986; Weinberger's before the Iran-Contra committee, ibid., August 1, 1987.

13. The Poindexter message is reprinted in *Tower Commission*, pp. 60–61; North's testimony is quoted in the New York *Times*, July 11, 1987, and the Washington *Post*, July 9, 1987.

14. *Alleged Assassination Plots Involving Foreign Leaders: Interim Report of the Senate Select Committee to Study . . . Intelligence Activities*, 94th Cong., 1st sess. (November 20, 1975), p. 149 (hereinafter, *Assassination Report*).

15. See ibid., pp. 108 ff.
16. Ibid., pp. 99 ff.
17. Ibid., p. 95.
18. Oral History no. 86, taped by Hughes Cates, February 22, 1977, Richard B. Russell Library, University of Georgia, Athens, cited in Loch Johnson, "Covert Action and American Foreign Policy: Decision Paths for the 'Quiet Option,'" paper presented to the American Political Science Association Annual Meeting, Washington, D.C., 1986, p. 4.
19. Quoted in Anne Karalekas, "History of the Central Intelligence Agency," in *Supplementary Detailed Staff Reports on Foreign and Military Intelligence*, book 4 of *Final Report of the Senate Select Committee to Study . . . Intelligence Activities*, 94th Cong., 2d sess. (April 23, 1976), p. 54 (hereinafter, "CIA History").
20. Ibid., p. 55.
21. *Covert Action*, volume 7, Hearings before the Senate Select Committee to Study . . . Intelligence Activities, 94th Cong., 1st sess. (December 4–5, 1975), p. 189 (hereinafter *Covert Action*).
22. Ibid., p. 188.
23. Ibid.
24. Korry to Senator Frank Church, October 23, 1975, ibid., p. 125.
25. "CIA History," p. 72.
26. The numbers in this and the following paragraph are from *Covert Action*, p. 196.
27. Officially, Section 622 of the Foreign Assistance Act of 1974.
28. Quoted in Thomas Powers, *The Man Who Kept the Secrets: Richard Helms and the CIA* (New York: Knopf, 1979), p. 232.
29. Quoted in "The Two Oaths of Richard Helms," case C14-83-525, 1983, Kennedy School of Government, Harvard University.
30. William Colby and Peter Forbath, *Honorable Men: My Life in the CIA* (New York: Simon & Schuster, 1978), pp. 402–4.
31. Ibid., pp. 403–4.
32. Ibid., p. 436.
33. Ibid., p. 440.
34. Ibid., p. 444.
35. For an intriguing account of the Senate Select Committee, see Loch Johnson, *A Season of Inquiry: The Senate Intelligence Investigation* (Lexington: University Press of Kentucky, 1985).
36. The same could not be said of the Pike Committee, whose report found its way to the journalist Daniel Schorr after the House had voted down release. The Church Committee, however, was more often the victim than the perpetrator of leaks. See ibid., pp. 206–7.
37. For instance, Colby regards the outcome as "not unreasonable"; see Colby and Forbath, *Honorable Men*, p. 429.
38. See Stansfield Turner, *Secrecy and Democracy: The CIA in Transition* (Boston: Houghton Mifflin, 1985), p. 170.
39. Officially, Section 413 of the Intelligence Oversight Act of 1980.
40. Ronald Reagan, excerpts from speeches, as quoted in the Washington *Post*, October 25, 1985.
41. The order was printed in the New York *Times*, December 5, 1981.
42. William Miller, interview, January 16, 1986.
43. Turner, *Secrecy and Democracy*, p. 169.

44. Quoted in the Washington *Star*, November 12, 1975.

45. See reports in the New York *Times*: "Central Intelligence Agency: In the Feud with Congress, No Quarter is Given," April 13, 1984; "Democratic Candidates Assail Reagan on Salvador Aid Move," April 16, 1984; and "C.I.A. Now Asserts It Put Off Session with Senate Unit," April 17, 1984. See also the account in the Senate Select Committee on Intelligence, *Report*, pp. 4 ff.

46. Interviews with intelligence committee staff members, January 1987.

47. The letter was dated April 9; see the Washington *Post*, April 11, 1984.

48. Turner, *Secrecy and Democracy*, p. 168.

49. Interview, January 9, 1986.

50. As quoted in the New York *Times*, July 7, 1986.

51. Interview with the CIA officials, August 1986 and January 1987.

52. One reported instance was an operation in Suriname in early 1983; see the New York *Times*, June 15, 1983.

53. Interview, January 9, 1987.

54. *Tower Commission*, p. 56.

55. Interviews with CIA officials, January 1987.

56. Interview, January 18, 1987.

57. Durenberger is quoted in the New York *Times*, July 7, 1986; the staff quote is from my interviews, January 1987.

58. William Miller interview, January 16, 1987.

INDEX

Index

Index

Index

Index

Index

Index

Index

Index

Index

Index